Dissident Irish Republicanism

DISSIDENT IRISH REPUBLICANISM

Edited by
P. M. Currie and Max Taylor

continuum

2011

The Continuum International Publishing Group
80 Maiden Lane, New York, NY 10038
The Tower Building, 11 York Road, London SE1 7NX

www.continuumbooks.com

© 2011 P. M. Currie and Max Taylor

All rights reserved. No part of this book may be reproduced, stored in a retrieval system, or transmitted, in any form or by any means, electronic, mechanical, photocopying, recording, or otherwise, without the written permission of the publishers.

Library of Congress Cataloging-in-Publication Data
A catalog record for this book is available from the Library of Congress.
Taylor, Maxwell, 1945-
Dissident Irish republicanism / P M Currie, Max Taylor.
   p. cm.
  Includes bibliographical references and index.
  ISBN-13: 978-1-4411-2013-7 (hardcover : alk. paper)
  ISBN-10: 1-4411-2013-0 (hardcover : alk. paper)
  ISBN-13: 978-1-4411-5467-5 (pbk. : alk. paper)
  ISBN-10: 1-4411-5467-1 (pbk. : alk. paper) 1. Dissenters—Northern Ireland.
2. Northern Ireland—Politics and government—1994- I. Currie, P. M. II. Title.
  JN1572.A91T39 2011
  941.60824—dc22   2010048970

ISBN: 978-1-4411-2013-7 (HB)
            978-1-4411-5467-5 (PB)

Typeset by Pindar NZ, Auckland, New Zealand
Printed and bound in India

Contents

Chapter 1	Introduction *Max Taylor*	1
Chapter 2	Why do People Become Dissident Irish Republicans? *John Morrison*	17
Chapter 3	Who Are the Dissidents? An Introduction to the ICST Violent Dissident Republican Project *John Horgan and Paul Gill*	43
Chapter 4	Beyond the 'Micro Group': The Dissident Republican Challenge *Henry Patterson*	65
Chapter 5	An Enduring Tradition or the Last Gasp of Physical Force Republicanism? 'Dissident' Republican Violence in Northern Ireland *Jon Tonge*	97
Chapter 6	Radicalization and Internet Propaganda by Dissident Republican Groups in Northern Ireland since 2008 *John Nalton, Gilbert Ramsey and Max Taylor*	119
Chapter 7	'Not Like in the Past': Irish Republican Dissidents and the Ulster Loyalist Response *James W. McAuley*	143
Chapter 8	Conclusion *P. M. Currie*	167
Bibliography		179
Index		193

CHAPTER 1

Introduction

MAX TAYLOR
UNIVERSITY OF ST ANDREWS

L'homme, l'homme, l'homme armé,
L'homme armé
L'homme armé doibt on doubter, doibt on doubter . . .

The man, the man, the armed man,
The armed man
The armed man should be feared, should be feared . . .

The first three lines of this medieval French song capture the sense of terror felt then and now by communities faced by armed men.[1] The song is known to have existed in the fifteenth century, and contemporary scholarship suggests it may have a dual meaning – beware the armed men (soldiers) of the State, or those claiming to represent the State, but also beware the reciprocal of that, an armed citizenry[2] (which in medieval France might have been effectively the same thing). Armed citizenry, whether in the form of conscripted local militias, or in the form of a more distributed sense of armed individuals acting to a purpose, captures an important sense of what we might recognize in the contemporary world as terrorism, and as Burk notes, our modern day fears associated with terrorism echo those associated with the medieval '*l'homme armé*'.

Ireland has, over the past few centuries, had more reason than many European countries to fear '*l'homme armé*'. The violence associated with armed citizenry, whether armed by the State or by other forces, have been an inescapable quality of Irish community life. In more recent times, that violence has taken the form of sustained terrorist campaigns resulting in civilian casualties that have included all the communities of Ireland. Latterly, however, the pessimism of '*l'homme armé*' has been replaced by a more optimistic sense of peaceful change. A complex and faltering process towards peace that has lasted for 20 or more years has finally resulted in both loyalist and republican paramilitary organizations declaring a ceasefire, and engaging in power sharing initiatives. The 2006 St Andrews Agreement recognized and enabled that process to be expressed in political terms, through the creation of the Northern Ireland Assembly, devolution of power and the creation and filling of the Offices of First and Deputy First Ministers. Decommissioning of weapons seemed to offer at last the prospects of an Ireland no longer at the mercy of *'l'homme armé'*.

But perhaps it's in the nature of *'l'homme armé'* that as one expression of it reduces, another rises, and so it seems to be the case in Ireland at the moment. What might be termed the mainstream paramilitary groups (Provisional IRA, UDA, UVF) may have declared ceasefires, and may have either fully or partially decommissioned weapons; but rising to take on the mantle of *'l'homme armé'* are what have been termed 'dissident republican groups'. The series of papers in this book, which have their origins in a workshop held in the University of St Andrews by the Centre for the Study of Terrorism and Political Violence (CSTPV), explore what this rise in dissident activity is, and what it might mean for both Ireland and the UK.

Some Initial Contextual Comments on Dissident Republicans

As a number of contributors to this volume point out, the emergence of dissident groups, generally related to principled ideological disputes, is not in historical terms unusual in Irish politics. Brendan Behan allegedly quipped that the first item on the agenda of any republican group was 'the split'. However, it is worth noting that, in fact the principal republican terrorist group, the Provisional IRA, has been very resistant to disunity since its emergence in 1969, and indeed the broad republican paramilitary front remained strikingly coherent until the mid 1990s, when strong voices emerged dissenting from the 1994 ceasefire, and the subsequent stumbling steps towards a peace strategy. At least initially, even the emergence of the Continuity IRA in 1986 (around the ideologically and historically significant issue of abstention) failed to make much impact on broader republican unity. It is quite clear, however, that these dissenting voices became more evident and more significant towards the end of the 1990s and have continued to the present.

Events in Northern Ireland do not exist in isolation, and the broader UK context to political violence in which the Irish peace process developed is worth briefly exploring further. A number of authors in this volume emphasize the long timescale over which patient and detailed negotiations took place that eventually emerged in both the Good Friday Agreement, and subsequently the St Andrews Agreement. Indeed, the complex processes of discussion, negotiation and compromise between State and non-State actors that have characterized the changes brought about in Northern Ireland might be offered as a more general blueprint for conflict management and resolution. Yet alongside this detailed process of negotiation, the events of 9/11 occurred, which for many people has been heralded as a 'new' form of terrorism. The events of 9/11 precipitated the UK New Labour Government of the time into what has been described as a frenzy of activity that took a quite different shape from the response to Irish terrorism:

> New Labour's response to 9/11 contrasted with the way UK legislation and policy developed when faced with Northern Irish terrorism. Then, responses had been slower and more thoughtful, and there was much more careful working out of consequences (as illustrated in the patient and detailed negotiations associated with the implementation of the 1998 Belfast Agreement). The frenetic activity following 9/11 was thus something out of the ordinary. For example in the period immediately after the New York attacks, Blair held meetings with 54 foreign leaders and is thought to have travelled more than 40,000 miles on some 31 separate flights. Ironically, this was also the period when careful and detailed negotiations about the future of Northern Ireland were being conducted.[3]

UK experience of terrorism related to Northern Ireland had, of course, in the current wave of violence developed over a period of 30 or more years, and clearly defined patterns of behaviour had emerged (and perhaps even become institutionalized). Of critical significance in this regard, and in contrast to the situation faced by the UK government after 9/11 and radical Islamic terrorism, Irish terrorism tended on the whole to be very focused, very constrained and with limited goals. This is not to diminish its significance or the personal and property damage produced by it. However, in the main, the violence of Northern Irish terrorism tended to be graded, proportionate and 'knowable' in the sense that because it was enduring, there was always a context.

Furthermore, there was the capacity within government to either make direct contact in some sense with the terrorist organizations or to use informants to find out what lay behind the action – a means of contact and sometimes even negotiation might therefore be assumed.[4] This 'knowable' quality of terrorism in Northern Ireland was of particular importance, in that it gave policymakers a clearer sense of the broad historical context, likely outcomes and the options available to them, and also offered the opportunity, however deniably at arm's length or secret, of negotiation. No equivalent knowledge or route appeared to be available after 9/11 to contact al-Qaeda, and in any event, it seems that from the very beginning, contextual knowledge of al-Qaeda was lacking and the possibility of negotiation was not recognized as a viable option. Perhaps also of significance is that the response to 9/11 was largely driven by the US, with a distinctive and critical UK perspective being largely absent. In contrast, whatever role the US might have played in the negotiations leading to the reduction of terrorism in Ireland, it has to a large extent been a UK-dominated and structured process addressing UK and Irish interests rather than those of any other state.

However, what this also seems to point to is a disjunction or divergence in UK policy towards terrorism in general as exemplified on the one hand by the events of 9/11, and on the other Irish terrorism. There seems to almost be a sense in the years following 9/11 that the Irish experience of terrorism was regarded as *sui generis* – perhaps both different from other forms of terrorism – but also after the Good Friday Agreement, essentially a problem solved in principle. But there is a paradox here that contributors to this volume have pointed out: to observers even in 2001, the threat of future dissident violence in some form was clear. This can be illustrated by the short but prescient article published in 2001 in the *Irish Independent* by John A. Murphy, a distinguished Irish historian, and reproduced as Appendix 1 to this chapter. While pointing out the violence (at that time) associated with what even then was termed dissident groups, Murphy draws attention to the phrase 'it's not over yet'[5] on wall paintings located at the entrance to the Republican Plot in St Finbarr's Cemetery in Cork. As Murphy points out, the wall painting also has the 'Óglaigh na hÉireann' phrase and a large capital R. The front cover to this book illustrates a similar wall painting (again from Cork, but a different location) taken in August 2010 suggesting a continuity between, at least, 2001 and now of symbols, aspiration and, given the growing violence in Ireland, commitment.

Óglaigh na hÉireann is the official Irish language title for the Irish Defence Forces. But it has also been a term used by a number of republican paramilitary organizations and offshoots at various times[6] (a problem of naming Irish paramilitary groupings is their fluidity and multiple use of names). In the past it is a name that has been associated with an element of the Real IRA, and most recently it seems to be associated with a dissident faction of ex-Provisional IRA members in Belfast and South Armagh. It is one of the dissident groups that this volume is concerned with; others include the Continuity IRA and the Irish National Liberation Army (INLA). A brief synopsis of the current dissident groups is given in Appendix 2 to this Chapter.[7] All of these groups exist within a broader framework of community-level violence and intimidation that has continued despite the ceasefires and decommissioning of weapons, and in which the various dissident groups seem to be involved, and from which they draw.

Was the apparent disjunction in UK policy towards terrorism noted above appropriate and did it matter? And indeed, is Irish terrorism in general, and the dissident republican violence we are concerned with here, something unlike that which we currently experience from al-Qaeda, and is it in this sense *sui generis*? Certainly Irish terrorism has on the whole lacked a strong international character, in contrast to al-Qaeda, and its focus relates to a limited geographical nationalist aspiration. It is often asserted that Provisional IRA violence was controlled and did not seek the mass casualties that seems to characterize the current radical Islamic threat; there are, however, sufficient and extensive examples (the Omagh bombing being one notable example) to suggest this is untrue for both the Provisional IRA and the current dissident republican groups. On the other hand, Irish republican terrorism has shown itself to be at least at times ideologically driven in ways that might, for example, suggest parallels between al-Qaeda suicide bombings and the republican hunger strikes of the 1980s. A number of the contributors to this volume have also identified ideology as a critical factor behind the rise in dissident violence. Whatever other differences there may be between radical Islamic terrorism and Irish republicanism, the sense of underlying ideological commitment might seem to be a shared quality. Our knowledge of the relationship between ideology and violence is unclear, but at least in this respect, the parallels between Irish terrorism and al-Qaeda may be greater than initially might be imagined. A further point of similarity may lie in the unattainability of their respective alleged goals by means of violence. Although this book is a testament to the continued political violence in Ireland, such violence is not remotely at previous levels, and there can be no question that negotiation rather than violence yielded the benefits of peace. And that became possible when politics rather than violence became an element in the equation.

Did the disjunction between the way the UK government responded to 9/11 and its response to Irish terrorism matter? From the Irish perspective it seems the answer to that is likely to be no. The peace process was well developed by 9/11, and as contributors to this volume note, it had acquired such political momentum within both UK and Irish contexts that to derail that process was politically unthinkable. The other important factor was, of course, that there was no suggestion of any Irish involvement in 9/11; however, had there been, we may well have seen very different responses.

An alternative perspective on the rise of dissident republican violence (which does not necessarily contradict the discussion presented above) might be that such violence is perhaps an expected, even maybe necessary, feature of post–peace settlement conditions, as past activists adjust to both ideological compromises brought by peace, and to changing lifestyles; Tonge alludes to this in Chapter 5. Border, Darby and McEvoy-Levy identify a series of conditions that might be associated with why peace agreements fail, and why violence continues.[8] These are:

- The process or agreement was flawed
- Failure to carry supporters past the agreement
- Failure to implement the agreement
- Economic failure
- Security unrest
- Failure to deal with past violence
- Failure to inspire or pacify the next generation.

It would be a large undertaking in itself to explore in detail how these various conditions relate to contemporary dissident violence. But in some measure it might be argued that all (with perhaps the exception of the third – 'Failure to implement the agreement') seem relevant, although presumably when applied at an individual or even community level, the significance of the various conditions may well vary. The list offered by Border et al. might, however, in fact be extended by a further three conditions that seem particularly relevant to the current dissident republican content:

- Failure to address the ideological underpinnings of the original violence
- Failure to diminish local and community opportunities for violence
- Failure to control or counter significant dissident propaganda activity.

In different ways, all of these conditions are identified in the papers presented in this volume as having local relevance for the current situation in Northern Ireland, as critical variables that help to understand why dissident activity has continued after the broader peace agreements.

Looking Ahead

The workshop on which this volume is based was held in an effort to better understand the processes behind what is proving to be an increasingly deadly 'dissident' campaign. A series of questions were posed to contributors and participants, to focus discussion, and to help guide understanding:

1. Who are the dissident republicans and what distinguishes them from the rest of society?
2. What is the role of dissidents in Irish republicanism? Are current dissidents consistent with republicanism? Are there similarities with earlier dissident outbreaks?
3. What is the relationship between dissident activity and the Good Friday Agreement?
4. Do they have a strategy or political objectives?
5. Why are they still committed to physical violence?
6. How and why does someone become a dissident republican?
7. What would it take for them to disengage or move away from violence?

Perhaps not all of these questions can ever be satisfactorily answered; but they do represent a necessary research and political agenda if we are to better understand the particular Irish context to dissident violence, which in turn might reflect on the broader issue of violence following peace settlements.

The papers presented in this volume broadly fall into two categories: those concerned with essentially individual factors, and those concerned with political and ideological factors. In Chapter 2, Morrison addresses the issue of why people become dissident Irish republicans. Morrison highlights the significance of timing, context, influential individuals, regionalism and age as factors in the individual decisional process to engage in dissident activity, providing an important contextual and situational context to the individual's choice. Horgan and Gill in Chapter 3 extend that analysis exploring the demographics of those involved in dissident violence, and describe their work on cataloguing dissident activity. In contrast to Chapters 2 and 3, Patterson in Chapter 4 develops a much more politically focused analysis of the rise and qualities of dissident republicanism, suggesting that the dissidents are a product of the Northern Ireland experience of communal/sectarian logic. Tonge extends that analysis in Chapter 5 focusing on the ideological context. Nalton, Ramsey and Taylor in Chapter 6 focus on the propaganda context to dissident activity, and in particular the nature and extent of dissidents' use of internet media. They also draw out elements raised in previous chapters concerned with the development of counter-narratives. In Chapter 7, McAuley develops an account of the loyalist response to the dissidents, focusing on the significance of legitimacy for the various loyalist organizations within their own communities, and providing an explanation of their relative restraint in response to dissident provocation. Finally, in Chapter 8, Currie draws together the conclusions that might be drawn from the papers and in particular address the questions that were posed at the start of the workshop (and are detailed above).

One notable omission from the discussions presented by all authors is an emphasis on structural determinants of the dissident response. In part this may be because the necessary data to explore this is lacking (e.g. socio-economic details of dissident membership, etc.) although there is no evidence to suppose that those attracted to dissident involvement are not drawn from the same population as those who were involved in, for example, Provisional IRA activity. Morrison's emphasis on regionalism and localization also argues that this might be the case. The broadly positive economic climate in which dissident activity emerged also weakens this as a potential causative agent (to the extent that economic well-being has been evenly distributed). However, the rapid recent deterioration in the economic situation in Europe as a whole, and particularly in the Republic of Ireland and the UK might begin to influence and perhaps become a more evident causal factor for some. Weaknesses in youth employment may in particular represent a challenge. This must be a potent area for further future research.

That this book should have been produced at all is an acknowledgement that dissident republicanism has become a growing factor in Northern Irish politics. '*L'homme armé*' has indeed again returned to the streets of Northern Ireland, and all the indications are that as in the past, the scale, extent and significance of political violence will grow. Perhaps the final lines of the verse quoted at the beginning of this chapter also have significance:

> On a fait partout crier,
> Que chascun se viengne armer
> D'un haubregon de fer
>
> L'homme, l'homme, l'homme armé, l'homme armé,
> L'homme armé doibt on doubter.
>
> Everywhere it has been proclaimed
> That each man shall arm himself
> With a coat of iron mail.
>
> The man, the man, the armed man,
> The armed man should be feared.

APPENDIX 1

Bomb Proves It's Not Over Yet

John A. Murphy

Reprinted with the author's permission from *The Irish Independent*, 5 August 2001 (Annotated by M. Taylor and PM Currie).

These days, as funeral mourners approach St Finbarr's Cemetery, Cork's best-known necropolis, they will notice a prominent message printed on one of the gateway pillars, announcing that 'it's not over yet'. The bereaved may derive momentary comfort from what seems a reassuring sentiment about life beyond the grave until they take a closer look. Then they will see the 'Oglaigh na hEireann' phrase and a large capital R, and realise that this is a sinister proclamation from 'dissident' republicans about the continuation of 'the armed struggle'. The message is reminiscent of Gerry Adams' notorious reference to the Provos 'not having gone away, you know'. But why St Finbarr's Cemetery, you may ask? Because just inside the entrance lies the railed-off 'Republican' burial plot which holds the graves of Cork's revered Lords Mayor Tomas MacCurtain and Terence MacSwiney and of other patriots. The Republican plot is the mecca of numerous nationalist commemorations and it also contains memorial tablets to various IRA activists over the decades, including Provos[9] and Stickies[10] from the 1970s. When you claim a place in the pantheon, you hope to legitimise yourself in the republican apostolic succession. The Real IRA haven't got in here yet but they're staking their claim at the gateway.

The car bomb at Ealing[11] on Thursday night was a stark reminder that indeed, 'it's not over yet'. And, together with the significance of the messages at Cork's Republican plot, it should make us realize that, really, there is only one IRA, notwithstanding fluctuations in personnel or qualifying prefixes. All its variant forms lay illegal claim to the description 'Oglaigh na hEireann'. These last few years, we have been conditioned to credulously swallow the myth that there is a nice, peaceful IRA and a couple of nasty, violent IRAs. In truth, the main difference between the bombings at the Baltic Exchange

(1992) and Canary Wharf (1996),[12] on the one hand, and Ealing (2001) is that the terrorist faction responsible for the earlier atrocities has since moved on to a more successful ballot-box-cum-armed-ceasefire (more or less) strategy, whereas the perpetrators of Thursday night's outrage are showing themselves to be painfully slow learners. It is not as if the Provos at some stage experienced a sudden road-to-Damascus-type conversion in principle to peaceful means.

The average interested Southerner who wishes the North well must surely be baffled this weekend by the dismissive attitude of unionist and republican politicians to the Irish and British governments' proposals, published on Wednesday. Tony Blair, Bertie Ahern and their teams clearly tried their hardest in exhausting and exhaustive sessions at Weston Park,[13] and indeed elsewhere these last four years. Yet the ink was scarcely dry when the proposals were rejected out-of-hand by UUP Assembly back-benchers, and David Trimble himself grossly simplified the complex issues down to the single one of decommissioning. Moreover, as First Minister of 'all the people' his own claim Trimble failed to come out strongly enough against recent loyalist atrocities. The Sinn Féin reaction (at best, damning with faint praise from Gerry Adams) has been even more disappointing, given the consensus of balanced commentators that the proposals have a strong green flavour and that everything possible had been done to provide the IRA with the 'context' necessary to 'put their arms beyond use'. And the background to all this is one of psychological victory for nationalists ever since the Good Friday Agreement. Yet nothing will now satisfy Messrs Kelly, Maskey and Murphy,[14] apparently, but to draft the detailed policing recommendations themselves and draw up a programme for total demilitarization in South Armagh. The Sinn Féin Ard Chomhairle,[15] the mouthpiece of the republican leadership, dutifully calls for 'clarification' of the proposals, thus kicking indefinitely to touch. Meanwhile, governments, parties and media prayerfully and reverentially await the only call that really counts a statement from the IRA Army Council which will doubtless be interpreted for us by a breathlessly excited Charlie Bird.[16] What a ridiculing of parliamentary democracy in both jurisdictions!

On radio and TV programmes over the past week, Sinn Féiners have been rabbiting on about the Brits being responsible for excessive rainfall (I'm only half joking) and for reneging on the Good Friday Agreement. They never explain why the British would want to do that. I'm sure the real British priority is to divest themselves of the white man's burden as soon as possible. In any case, when Sinn Féin calls for the 'full implementation of the Agreement' they don't mention that the plain people of Ireland's understanding of 'full implementation' is the dissolution of all paramilitary groups, on ceasefire or otherwise.

Media interviewers continued to give Sinn Féin an easy ride. Even such normally incisive interlocutors as Fintan O'Toole or Jeremy Paxman fail to put the really basic questions such as: what possible justification can there be for the continuing existence of the IRA, or why don't Sinn Féin stand unequivocally on their own electoral seat, without recourse to armed fascist backing? When Gerry Kelly says that loyalist violence doesn't make IRA decommissioning any easier he is not asked how IRA retention of Semtex helps the situation in North Belfast. Meanwhile, this was the week when Gerry Adams uttered the most breathtakingly brazen piece of revisionism when he airily stated that, 'we have been through dreadful difficulties these last 30 years'. Nothing to do with the IRA terrorist campaign, of course! With Northern Ireland more polarised than ever this weekend, the big question for Southern politicians, particularly, perhaps Fianna Fáil, is whether Sinn Féin in their impressive electoral advance will get away with continuing to use the winning fascist formula of political mobilisation, vigilantism, some roughing up on the side, an IRA in the shadows and the cheap but effective incitement of anti-British sentiment. On the other hand, if the IRA has no intention of going out of business post-Weston Park, is it not high time for the Government to be mindful of its basic security obligations and consider applying the law of the land firmly to illegal organisations, and proceeding against their arms dumps in this jurisdiction? This is an inevitable and constitutionally required step which should be taken sooner rather than later.

John A. Murphy is Emeritus Professor of Irish History at University College Cork.

APPENDIX 2

Dissident Republican Groups

Óglaigh na hÉireann (translates as 'Soldiers of Ireland'; it is correctly abbreviated as ÓnaÉ rather than ONH)

Initially a small, fairly insignificant group formed from ex-PIRA and CIRA operatives. The group emerged around 2005 in the Belfast and Strabane area. A group operating under this title split from Continuity IRA in 2006 and more recently the name has been used by a faction of the Real IRA. In its current form, it is said to include some of the most experienced Provisional IRA operators. The IMC reported in November 2008 that the group '*continues to pose a serious threat, both as a paramilitary group capable of extreme violence and because of the criminal activities of its members.*' The group has been responsible for a series of increasingly violent attacks against the security forces, and seems to be capable of extending its range to a wide area.

Saor Uladh (SU) (translates as 'Free Ulster')

Small dissident republican grouping in Belfast, which includes former CIRA members. It takes its name from a short-lived paramilitary organization active in the Province in the 1950s. *Saor Uladh* was originally a mainly Tyrone-based offshoot from the post–World War II IRA founded by Liam Kelly who essentially initiated the abortive republican 'border campaign' of the 1960s. Contemporary *Saor Uladh* graffiti are reported to refer to a very small militant republican group based in Belfast though little is known of this secretive paramilitary group or if it even still actually exists.

Irish National Liberation Army (INLA)

Formed in 1975 as the paramilitary wing of the Irish Republican Socialist Party following the 1972 Official IRA ceasefire. It is thought to have been responsible for the deaths of some 150 people, but in recent years has been considered to be the least active of the dissident groups. In an announcement on 11 October 2009, the INLA stated its armed struggle was over and said its objective of a '32-County socialist republic' would be best achieved through exclusively peaceful means. In the past, the INLA regularly became involved in violent in-fighting, and also has a history of involvement in criminality.

Irish Republican Liberation Army (IRLA)

Centred around the Ardoyne area of Belfast, the IRLA appear to have splintered from CIRA dissidents in 2006. The 20th IMC report suggests the IRLA is 'essentially a group of criminals taking a republican banner in order to give supposed status to their activities'.

Continuity Irish Republican Army (CIRA)

Emerged as the military wing of the Republican Sinn Féin, which had been formed in 1986 by members of the provisional republican movement disillusioned by Sinn Féin's decision to take seats in Dáil Éireann. It is believed most of its members are concentrated in Counties Fermanagh and Armagh. After a period of inactivity, it reappeared in 1996 when it placed a large bomb which destroyed a hotel in County Fermanagh, and more recently has claimed responsibility for the murder of Stephen Carroll, a police officer, in March 2006.

Real Irish Republican Army (RIRA)

A more recent paramilitary group, having emerged in tandem with the 32 County Sovereignty Movement (32CSM) formed by members of the provisional republican movement opposed to the 1997 ceasefire and the Belfast Agreement of the following year. RIRA was founded by Michael McKevitt, an Irish Republican who was in charge of the Provisional IRA's armoury before he split over the IRA's new peace policy. McKevitt was arrested in March 2001, convicted in August 2003 and is currently serving a 20 year sentence in an Irish jail. There have been for some time two fairly distinct and autonomous factions of RIRA, each with its own leadership structures.

In Belfast especially, observers of political graffiti in republican working-class districts have noticed hitherto unknown terms such as 'O.n.H', IRLA and 'Saor Uladh' appearing from time to time. The O.n.H refers to Óglaigh na hÉireann (see above). However, although both the CIRA and RIRA and indeed the Provisional IRA refer to themselves as Óglaigh na hÉireann in official communications, it is widely believed that the O.n.H referred to in recent graffiti is an offshoot of the RIRA. The IRLA (Irish Republican Liberation Army) graffiti reportedly refers to a split from the Belfast CIRA (though not much is known of them except their alleged involvement in local punishment attacks on criminals and two civilian deaths reportedly due to an internal dispute).

RIRA was responsible for the Omagh bombing in August, 1998, which was probably the worst single atrocity in the history of the current period of violence in Northern Ireland. As a result of the general outcry against this bombing, RIRA declared a short ceasefire, launching a new campaign on 25 February 2000 with an attempted bombing of Shackleton army barracks in Ballykelly. This was followed by a wide range of attacks in Northern Ireland and Britain. On 22 January 2009, RIRA issued a renewed call to arms in a statement to the Irish News. The statement condemned the Northern Ireland Executive, and stated 'once again, Óglaigh na h'Éireann declares the right of the Irish people to the ownership of Ireland. We call on all volunteers loyal to the Irish Republic to unite to uphold the Republic and establish a permanent national parliament representative of all the people.'

Notes

1 Burk, K. 'The Hundred Years' War 1337–1453' (lecture, Gresham College, London, 9 February 2005), www.gresham.ac.uk/printtranscript.asp?EventId=299.
2 Lockwood, L. 'Aspects of the "L'Homme Arme" Tradition', *Proceedings of the Royal Musical Society* 100, 1, 97–122, 1973.
3. Taylor, M. 'New Labour, Defence and the "War on Terror"', in Daddow, O. and Gaskarth, J. (eds) *British Foreign Policy* (Basingstoke: Palgrave Macmillan, in press).
4. Powell, J. *Great Hatred, Little Room: Making Peace in Northern Ireland* (London: Bodley Head, 2008).
5. With the echoes of Gerry Adams response – 'They haven't gone away you know' – while Adams was addressing a demonstration in Belfast in

August 1995 when a member of the crowd called out to him to 'bring back the IRA'.
6. Reflecting the claims of most republican organizations to represent in some way the 'authentic' Irish State after the 1916 Easter Rising.
7. Provided by J. Nalton.
8. Border, T., Darby, J. and McEvoy-Levy, S. *Peace Building after Peace Accords: The Challenges of Violence, Truth and Youth* (Notre Dame, IN: University of Notre Dame Press, 2006).
9. 'Provos' refers to the Provisional IRA.
10. The term 'Stickies' was used to describe the Official IRA because they sold stick-on lillies to commemorate the 1916 Easter Rising. The Official IRA formed after the split in 1969 that led to formation of the Provisional IRA.
11. On 3 August 2001 a car bomb was detonated near Ealing Broadway Railway Station, London. Seven people were injured and there was extensive property damage. This attack was the work of the Real IRA, described at the time as a 'dissident republican group'. BBC News online, 3 August 2001, http://news.bbc.co.uk/2/hi/uk_news/1471284.stm.
12. The Provisional IRA planted bombs at the Baltic Exchange and Canary Wharf.
13. In July 2001 talks between the Irish and British government and the various Northern Ireland politicians (including Sinn Féin) were held at Weston Park, Shropshire, in an attempt to save the Good Friday Agreement. These talks were prompted by the resignation of David Trimble as the Northern Ireland First Minister on 1 July. He had refused to sit in government with republicans until the IRA began to decommission its weapons.
14. Prominent members of the leadership of Sinn Féin.
15. The National Executive.
16. Chief News Correspondent with RTÉ, the national Irish Broadcasting Station.

CHAPTER 2

Why do People Become Dissident Irish Republicans?

JOHN MORRISON
UNIVERSITY OF ST ANDREWS

A central tenet of the approach below is that our primary objective should be to understand those who engage in the behaviour. It is not our job to condemn, to condone or to find some objective 'truth'.[1]

Introduction

The Northern Irish peace process is internationally recognized as being a success. However, it is unmistakable that the republican threat is still prominent across Ireland, both in the north and the south, as well as in Great Britain. In contrast to the 'war' waged by the Provisional IRA the foremost current threat is that posed by small violent dissident groupings, with little or no public support. These dissidents are using a different variety and combination of tactics and strategies from those of their Provisional predecessors. In recent years there has been the explicit targeting of Catholic members of the Police Service of Northern Ireland (PSNI) and members of the British armed forces. However, alongside the threat to the security forces the dissidents are also targeting their former comrades in Sinn Féin and across 'mainstream' republicanism. The armed dissident groups which epitomize this current threat are the Real IRA, the Continuity IRA and Óglaigh na hÉireann. With the present and increasing danger posed by these groups it is more important than ever to achieve a greater understanding of the organizations involved as well as the motivations of their individual members. In particular, we need to understand why individual Irish republicans choose their organizational affiliation, and why they choose the violent dissident republican route as opposed to 'mainstream' or non-violent republicanism. This chapter aims to outline the reasons behind an individual's affiliation with a dissident republican organization.

Following the work of Rapoport and others the present author has focused on the processes by which the individual actors understand and portray their actions and those of their group.[2] The viewpoints represented throughout this chapter are based on a long series of interviews with both dissident and 'mainstream' republicans which took place between October 2007 and March 2009. This research was carried out as part of the author's doctoral studies. Both leadership and rank-and-file members of the mainstream and dissident groups were interviewed. The interviews included members of the armed as well as the political factions, with some interviewees being active in both. As the opening quote from Robert White suggests, the purpose of the chapter is not to condemn or condone any individual's choices, it is to take a step closer to understanding the reasoning behind people's dissident affiliation. This understanding should in no way be regarded as analogous to condoning or supporting the beliefs and actions of the organizations and/or its members, but rather as a crucial first step in enabling the threat to be countered.

Heterogeneity

In order to gain a comprehensive understanding of terrorist actors and their actions there must first of all be a clear respect for the heterogeneity of individuals who engage in terrorism[3] across groups, and even within individual movements and organizations.[4] This heterogeneity may be analysed and assessed in a variety of ways. However, for the purpose of analysing why individuals become dissident republicans it is posited that two of the most informative heterogeneities are those of timing of dissident affiliation and prior republican experience. An understanding of these as well as other factors will contribute to enhancing our understanding of what contributes to these critical choices.

With respect to the timing of dissident affiliation, one must consider whether or not an individual chooses their affiliation at the time of, or alternatively a significant time after, the relevant organizational split. Did the individual become a dissident at the group's inception or during a period of time afterwards? It is to be expected that the reasons for dissident affiliation at the time of a split will more likely be intrinsically linked to the cause of the intra-organizational conflict and split than for those who join the dissident organization during a period significantly detached from the separation of groups. This appreciation for timing, however, must only be considered as the foundation level to a multi-faceted understanding of dissident affiliation. The analysis must similarly assess the level of experience and organizational rank of the dissident prior to their decision to dissent. This analysis must distinguish between those with an extended history of experience and those newly affiliated with organized republicanism.[5] Within these considerations one must be aware of the role, if any, played by the actor within the local and/or national leadership and therefore the influence they may have had in, and the knowledge they may have had of, the decision making processes. Parallel to this must be an appreciation that at times in historically enduring movements, such as Irish republicanism, there are those outside the leadership who hold a significant influence in the movement and over members and leadership alike. This influence may come from the historical significance of their previous actions or a previously held leadership position. Therefore, with the assessment of the level of influence of individual members it is insufficient merely to divide the membership into the categories of 'leadership' and 'rank-and-file members.' These categories must be further scrutinized to acknowledge the different levels of experience and influence which may exist among the two categories. The heterogeneity does not, and the analysis must not, stop with timing, experience and rank. There must be a similar appreciation of the roles which age, regionalism and other factors can play in the decision making process. Within the following pages there will be a careful assessment of the roles which these factors can and have played, while still acknowledging that the factors assessed are far from an exhaustive list of influential variables.

Why do People Become Irish Dissident Republicans?

The current focus of the media, security and policy makers tends to be on those members of groups such as the Continuity and Real IRA but in our analysis of dissident republicanism we must not overlook the fact that the original republican dissidents of the Troubles are those who shifted their allegiance away from the Goulding leadership of the old IRA, a move which saw the birth of the dissident grouping of the Provisional IRA in 1969. This extended history of organizational dissidence and split, not just in the same conflict but within the same movement, presents the opportunity to analyse in a more reliable manner the relevant issues and themes which arise in an individual's decision to dissent and switch allegiance from 'mainstream' Irish republicanism. This opportunity is reflected throughout the present chapter as there is continuous reference, not just to the rationale of the post-1986 dissidents, but also to some of those original dissenters from the late 1960s and early 1970s. While they originated as dissident, the process that is modern-day Irish republican activism has gradually redefined that group as 'mainstream' republicans. During the interview process the themes involved in the development of the dissension of the original 'Provos', while not identical, display the same underlying factors as those of the modern-day dissidents.

Throughout this chapter there is continuous reference to individual reasoning for organizational exit which precedes joining or establishing an alternative republican group, and becoming a dissident republican. The form of exit outlined does not constitute an overall disagreement with the organizational aims but suggests a disparity with a specific attribute, or attributes, of the parent organization, whether this be a strategy, tactic, personality, goal or structure. Reflecting on the issues which can drive individuals and groups to organizational exit and the development of, or enrolment in, alternative groups not all individuals who have the same disagreements will react in the same manner. In order to take the significant action of leaving to develop a new autonomous group, individuals must view the conflict at the centre of their exit as significantly threatening to what they believe to be the organizational identity.[6] This is supported by Francie Mackey a leading member of the 32 County Sovereignty Movement (32CSM), the group widely believed to be the political wing of the Real IRA. In 1986, when Republican Sinn Féin and the Continuity IRA split away from the Provisional Republican Movement over the issue of elected representatives taking their seats in Dáil Éireann, Mackey disagreed with this decision. However, he did not regard it as an issue which warranted the formation of an independent group or his or others' exit from the organization.

> At a personal level I disagreed with going into Leinster House, but it wasn't a significant enough issue to create a major split in the Republican Movement.[7]

Converse to this are the views and actions of Ruairí Ó Bradaigh, Dáithí Ó Conaill and others who left the Provisionals to develop the new political and armed groups[8] of Republican Sinn Féin and the Continuity IRA.[9] They regarded the dropping of this section of the abstentionist policy, coupled with the removal of Éire Nua[10] a few years previously, as a denouncement of what it was to be regarded as 'true' Irish republicans.

> [O]ur attitude was that the people who did that [accept that elected Sinn Fein members could take their seats in the Dáil] had broken the constitution.[11]

This is supportive of the belief of Sani and Reicher that organizational exit is preceded by a change or action perceived to be threatening to what the dissidents regard to be their organizational identity.[12] It is similarly supported by the organizational theory posited by Hirschman who states that quality conscious members will exit when they believe there to be a significant drop in the quality of the 'product' produced or promoted by a group.[13] The exiting members of Republican Sinn Féin and the Continuity IRA can be regarded as defining their membership very much in terms of what they believed to be the core values of Irish republicanism, and central to this was the rejection of what they believed to be partitionist parliaments, Dáil Éireann, Stormont and Westminster. In the language of Hirschman, their continued membership was defined by an adherence to the 'quality of the product' produced by Sinn Féin and the IRA. Central to this adherence was an unremitting rejection of the three parliaments while continuing the armed struggle to achieve a united Ireland. However, when there was a significant drop in the quality of this policy, namely an electoral acceptance of Dáil Éireann, they could no longer recognize themselves as 'true Republicans' if they continued with the Provisionals, and therefore left to form their own group. Countering this, it can be proposed that those who remained with the Provisional Movement did not deem this to be a significant drop in the quality of the product or policies being adhered to and promoted by the Movement. On the contrary many believed this to be an improvement in quality and a change necessary to bring about the group's purposive goals.

While what has been detailed above can be regarded as an accurate reflection of what happened in 1986, it should not be regarded as painting the full picture of why people left the Provisionals. It only briefly details the ultimate rationale of the splitting of the group. This does not always equate to every individual's motivation for their own personal dissent, even if they do leave to join the same dissenting organization. It would be unwise to just focus on the reasoning of the leadership and those others intrinsically tied to and aware of the divisive issue. It is never the case that every individual member is aware of the full context of the disagreement. They can only come to their decision in light of the information that they have at any one time. Therefore, in order to gain a fair and accurate reflection of the overall spectrum of membership dissent, the reasoning of all levels of the rank-and-file membership is just as, if not more, important to understand. As with initial engagement into a terrorist group, a person's exit or dissidence can be regarded as the result of a gradual process. This can be true at both leadership and rank and file level. It can be argued that, in order to fully understand the origins of Republican Sinn Féin and the Continuity IRA, one must start by analysing the aftermath of the 1969/70 split, and the origins of the Real IRA have to be traced back to the aftermath of 1986. Similarly, in order to understand an individual's defection, often one must understand the process leading up to this dissent in the previous years. This was reflected in an interview with a leading 32CSM member, who was once imprisoned for her role in a Provisional IRA attack. While she did not leave the Provisional Movement until 1998, her discontent can be traced to the early 1990s.

> My real concern with the Provisional Movement started to come about in the [early] 1990s when I began to feel that the people at the top were more concerned with furthering their own agenda than they were with following the Republican agenda and that began to cause me problems.[14]

This supports the claim that a clear understanding is not achieved by focusing purely on the action of dissent or exit, but by first assessing the origins and process of this dissent. The process of exit and dissidence can be influenced by numerous factors, with some more pertinent than for others. These factors need not always be related to the stated factors of organizational split, or even any ideological, strategic or tactical differences with the parent organization. The diversity of factors is reflected in the subsequent sections which focus on the importance of timing, influential individuals, regionalism and age.

Timing and Context

As has been stated earlier, the reasons behind individuals joining or developing dissident organizations should not be regarded as being uniform in nature. Some of the key factors at play are those of context and timing. The individual reasons for dissidence can vary from time to time and across contexts. One of the most obvious issues of timing is whether dissidence takes place at a time of dissident organization inception, i.e. does it occur at the time of the split? If it does take place at this time, it can be assumed that the rationale for the dissidence of leadership members at least is likely to be intrinsically tied to the reasoning for organizational split. However, it must similarly be assumed for those rank-and-file members, who are not fully aware of the reasons for the split,[15] that their reasoning will not be as intrinsically tied to the rationale of schism. The assumption that dissidence at a leadership level is tied to the reasoning for the split does not mean that this reasoning is tied to the *official* reason for the divide. In an interview with a leading member from the Provisional IRA Executive[16] and Engineering Department of the mid to late 1990s, a man who was a founding leadership member of the Real IRA, the reasoning behind the 1997 split is detailed:

> The Army split on practical issues … prior to the split certain weapons were not being used, not allowed to be used. If weapons were there prior to the split, why couldn't we use them? We had new weapons coming from Libya that were never used, or even announced.[17]

This quote not only reveals some of the issues at the heart of the organizational split, but also the individual's own personal reason for dissidence. Within his role on the IRA Executive and within the Engineering Department, and through strong links with the Quartermaster General of the time, he would have been very well informed of the issues at the heart of the intra-organizational conflict as well as the operational capabilities of the IRA. This reasoning similarly displays a discrepancy between his cited 'practical issues' for the split and the official reasoning of acceptance of the Mitchell Principles.[18] While the two issues are not completely unrelated the dissident leadership was aware that in order to secure as much support as possible they would have to frame the origins of the new group in a more acceptable manner. With national and international support for the peace process, and a growing appreciation of the value of political solutions among a large section of the republican movement, if they had simply announced that they were splitting on the issue of use of new arms it would have proved near impossible to gain any level of credibility or support.[19] This is a view which was appreciated by the dissident leadership at the time.

> Representatives from the Army who wanted to split met with the political people (32 County Sovereignty Committee)[20] to decide how best to frame the split. We had to be seen to be splitting on an issue.[21]

While the reasoning for exit and dissidence at a leadership level may have originated to a large extent over the issue of use of arms, those less informed rank-and-file members who chose their affiliation on what they believed were the issues of split were not doing so on an entirely informed basis but with the information which had been issued to them by the their national or local leadership. Therefore, the reasoning for organizational affiliation, be it dissident or mainstream, is disparate due to levels of information available to the relevant actor. In some instances at times of split, potential members, especially those with no previous republican affiliation, may have little or no idea of the rationale of schism or the differentiation between the groups. This was quite common in the late 1960s and early 1970s when there was a large number of new recruits wishing to join the IRA. These potential recruits at times were not aware of the differences between the Officials and Provisionals, and, in some instances in the immediate aftermath of split, were not aware of the existence of any division at all. In such circumstances decisions are not made on the basis of differing organizational strategies, tactics or goals but of other issues less tied to the ethos and strategies of the group and more to do with the individual's opportunities for membership and the influence of others around them where they lived.

> At that particular time the Official IRA was at war as well with the British, so I mean they would be operating at one end of the street shooting machine guns at the army, and the Provisionals would be at the other end. I didn't really know, I was just too young . . . I didn't really understand it [the difference between the Officials and Provisionals] until I went into prison.[22]

This description by Joe Doherty of his early days as a young Provisional IRA member in West Belfast is similar to the experience of many other young recruits at the time. Their affiliation was not decided by their views on abstentionism, the National Liberation Front or socialism. The extended beliefs and ideology of the individual groups did not matter to them. They wanted to join the IRA to protect their communities in the short run. For a number of new recruits at that time, their initial involvement with the IRA was not even strongly linked to the aspiration for a united Ireland. The relevance of the context of their mobilization and choice of group was not linked to the inner workings and debates within the Irish Republican Movement, it was influenced by what they saw on the Falls Road, the Short Strand and in the Bogside. They were influenced by their peers and the influential individuals local to them. This is a description which is as true today across both Northern Ireland and the Republic of Ireland as it was in 1970. What follows is a description of some of these factors beyond the internal debates and ideologies which play a significant role in an individual's movement into dissident republicanism.

Influential Individuals

Throughout organizational involvement in the Republican Movement, and within other political and terrorist groups, decisions made by members are often significantly influenced by the viewpoint of another individual. This individual may be a peer, comrade, leadership member or relative.[23] These influential individuals can have either a negative or a positive influence. They need not even be members of the Republican Movement for their actions and viewpoints to play a role in the decision-making process. Throughout the research, every interviewee, without fail, detailed the significant role played by at least one influential individual in his or her decision-making processes. Nowhere was this more relevant than at the time of choice of group affiliation. It was found that the beliefs and actions of influential individuals can at times have more of an influence than policy or strategy.

As was detailed in the previous section, at the end of 1969 and throughout 1970 there were numerous new Republican recruits assessing whether to join the Officials or the Provisionals. To many of these recruits, the intricate ideological and strategic issues involved at the heart of what had first been an intra-organizational dispute but had now become an *inter*-organizational dispute held little or no significance. However, one of the factors, which time and again proved vital in their decision-making process, was that of the position and views of influential individuals. The group they eventually joined was often the one containing members to whom they could most relate on a personal level, or for whom they held the most respect. For some, the influential individual was a national or local leadership figure. However, the choice for others was similarly influenced by the rank-and-file members of each group. The period of time in the aftermath of the 1969/70 split was on occasion confusing for potential new recruits to the Republican Movement. They had to decide between membership of the Officials or Provisionals. This competition between groups, and confusion for recruits, caused a number of young members to switch allegiance after their initial recruitment. Often this was heavily influenced by their negative opinions of the individuals they encountered in their first group, or the positive influence of the members of the group they went on ultimately to join, and at times there was a combination of both.[24] One individual who switched initial allegiance was Martin McGuinness, who in late 1970 joined the Official IRA, initially unaware of the difference between the two groups, or even the existence of two separate IRAs.

> Both of us [McGuinness and a friend] decided that we would join what we believed to be the IRA at the time. Now at that time the IRA was going through its own turbulence in terms of the split and so forth. At that stage my knowledge of who was the IRA would have been like everyone else's, you would have thought there was only one IRA and this whole turbulence occurred because of different approaches and different ideas and suggestions about how things should go forward. For us we joined what we believed to be the IRA in Derry.[25]

However, after a period of initial engagement McGuinness realized that the group he had joined was not what he thought he had initially signed up for. His disillusionment stemmed from what he perceived to be the group's inaction and his dissatisfaction with the local membership he had encountered. However, coupled with this push factor of his negative opinion of the Official IRA membership was the pull factor of his respect for and friendship and familiarity with a number of prominent local Provisional IRA members.

Well I suppose it was mostly being unimpressed by the people that we met [in the Official IRA] after we effectively joined [which pushed us away] . . . In terms of then joining the Provisional IRA, I was familiar with some of the people who were associated with the Provisional IRA. In fact I realised that I was probably more familiar with some of the people who were in the Provisional IRA than I was with some of the characters I met in the Official Republican Movement. The Keenan family were a leading family in Derry city at the time and I had been a long time friend of Sean Keenan Junior, who is now sadly deceased, and also familiar with his father, and his father's role in the Citizen's Defence Group in Derry, and I was also familiar with the fact that he had spent a very long period in prison as a result of internment, in total from maybe fourteen to sixteen years.[26]

This example of McGuinness, a former leading member of the Provisional IRA and now Deputy First Minister of Northern Ireland, displays both the negative and positive influences that certain individuals can have on affiliation choice. While this illustrates the persuasive powers of influential individuals on young, less-informed new recruits, their impact continues right up to experienced and leadership levels. In each of the four major splits from 1969 to 1997 one of the most effective strategies employed to attract support and membership at the time of intra-organizational conflict and split was the use of well-respected influential individuals to legitimize the position taken by a specific group or sub-group. These influential voices were used in the preparation for the split, at a personal level as well as at significant membership meetings, General Army Conventions and Ard Fheiseanna. The success of such a strategy is acknowledged by all sides, as numerous members, fully aware of the dispute at the heart of the schism, were influenced by the position taken up by respected figures within the movement, people who they trusted. The effectiveness of these influential individuals is clearly illustrated by Mick Ryan, a former leading member of the IRA in the lead-up to the 1969/70 split and then a leading member of the Official IRA, in the decision-making process of a number of Republican members in the aftermath of the split between the Officials and the Provisionals.

Many people made up their mind on the basis of who was on particular sides, people they trusted and liked more . . . It was not clear cut hard political people deciding. It was human factors that were deciding why some people went with one side over another, and this is not in hindsight. The political orientation would have counted but to what degree with certain individuals is unclear.[27]

The employment of these influential voices was effectively utilized by the Provisionals at both a military and political level of involvement in the lead-up to and in the process of the 1986 split. Nowhere is this better illustrated than in the 1986 Ard Fheis where Sinn Féin delegates voted on whether or not to drop the abstentionist policy to the Dáil. The Adams leadership, which was proposing this change in electoral policy, was able to call upon the support of a variety of influential individuals from both the old and new guard at political and military levels. Similarly the Ó Bradaigh and Ó Conaill faction, who would later go on to form Republican Sinn Féin and the Continuity IRA, sought to legitimize their stance by gaining the support of the well-respected Republican leader General Commandant Tom Maguire. However, with respect to the use of influential individuals it is clear that the Adams leadership had the upper hand, and this legitimizing support from such a respected group of influential individuals proved vital in their maintenance of large levels of support. The chairman of this 1986 Ard Fheis, Seán MacManus, held an ideal position to view the effect which these individuals had.

> To have people of the calibre of John Joe McGirl get up, other people like Fergie Albert McGovern who would have been from Cavan would have been significant as well. People like Joe Cahill obviously as well, older republicans who had been through the mill, who had seen stuff and I'm sure there were hundreds if not thousands who had seen them as an inspiration, certainly hundreds of delegates who would have seen them as inspirational figures and they would have been to some degree swayed.[28]

The role played by influential individuals, while significant at the time of split remains important throughout all stages of involvement. These influential individuals are needed to retain support and membership, especially in the smaller dissident groupings. They not only exert their own positive influence on members and supporters, but at times they help to neutralize the negative influence which the leadership of Sinn Féin and 'mainstream' Republicans can have on their membership.

The negative impression of the current Sinn Féin leadership among certain individuals, groups and regions is manipulated so as to strengthen and gain membership and support. This is especially prevalent with reference to Sinn Féin's opinion of dissident Republicans. At times this is manipulated or exaggerated by dissidents in order to promote opposition to the mainstream Republicans among their members, supporters and potential recruits.

> They always have to find a term. I don't know what anyone else thinks but if he [Gerry Adams] calls me a dissident to me it's a badge of honour.[29]

The above quote is taken from an individual who in his own right could be classed as an influential individual in Republican West Belfast. He was prominent in the development of the Provisional IRA in the area in 1969. However, in the aftermath of the 1986 split he left the Provisionals to support the Continuity IRA and Republican Sinn Féin. This quote is relevant for two main reasons. The most obvious is his use of the critical opinion of Gerry Adams within certain populations to revise the negative connotations normally associated with a label such as 'dissident' and transfer a more positive 'badge of honour' onto the term. However, it is the legitimacy which he, as an influential individual, gives to the dissidents that is most interesting. It is assumed here that he uses similar sentiment when speaking to both potential and existing supporters and members of the dissident community. Without such legitimization provided by influential individuals it proves more challenging for people to associate themselves with the smaller dissident Republican groups.

Regionalism

The geographical location in which a person lives can have a significant impact on them joining a specific group. The influence of this regionalism can derive from the influential individuals living in the area, as well as the historical and modern day circumstances relating to the locale. These geographical areas may be as small as an apartment block or housing estate, or as large as a country or even continent, and therefore with respect to geographical influence on Irish republicanism one must look beyond whether a person is situated north or south of the border. Terrorist organizations can invariably find it easier to recruit in specific areas as opposed to others.[30] Within certain areas the organization's ideals are often entwined with local aspirations.[31] These ideals can be in reference to the purposive goals of a movement or a more specific goal with respect to the local area. A terrorist organization may have a specific role to play in a geographical region which supersedes the purposive goal of the organization in the eyes of local members. Such a role may be in regional defence or local policing. If the group is providing a specific public good for the local area and its residents, this may persuade individuals, not just to support the actions of the organization, but they may also be encouraged to join.

At a time of split, regionalism proves one of the most dominant rationales in the choice of whether to remain a member of the parent organization or join the newly established dissident group. This can be especially true for the ordinary rank-and-file members whose membership is not as closely tied to ideological and purposive elements. Members often tie their membership to that of local influential individuals. These may be family members, friends or the local leadership. If a member whom they trust and look up to is adamant on joining the dissidents or, alternatively, staying with the parent organization, this may have a significant influence on the choice made. Tied to this is the fact that if the vast majority of the membership within a designated geographical area are members of one specific organization, the cost of membership of their rivals rises dramatically. The most unmistakeable example of the influence of regionalism is in West Belfast where there have been clear divisions with respect to regional affiliations during and after the Republican splits. After the 1969/70 split, most of the Falls Road would have been Provisional dominated while areas very close by, such as Divis Street and Leeson Street, would have been under the control of the Official IRA, with a significant proportion of the residents there siding with those groups. This has earlier been illustrated by the Joe Doherty quote:

> ... they [the Official IRA] would be operating at one end of the street shooting machine guns at the army, and the Provisionals would be at the other end.[32]

With the split in the Official IRA in 1974, resulting in the formation of the INLA, regionalism further came into play.

Even at the time of the split in 74/75 all of the Divis Flats unit and 99% of na Fianna [the youth wing of the Irish Republican Movement] all went to join the INLA and it was the opposite in Leeson Street, 98/99% percent stayed and only one or two left.[33]

This dramatic division does not reflect a division of political views or beliefs. This reflects the power of regionalism and the influential individuals within these specific areas. Leeson Street and the Divis Street Flats are in particularly close proximity to each other, yet the division at this time of schism displays the power and influence of the allegiances of the local leadership and other influential individuals in the area. As is evidenced by the example of na Fianna, this influence can be particularly visible among young recruits, a finding which is described in more detail in a later section.

As with the previously detailed factors, the theme of regionalism is just as dominant today as it was in the 1970s. There are specific regions across the island of Ireland where certain groups, be they dissident or 'mainstream' Republicans, are dominant. One can look to areas such as the city of Limerick as a stronghold for the Continuity IRA. This is often worn as a 'badge of honour'. The local leadership of the area not only takes pride in the strength of their recruits on the ground, but also those from the area imprisoned for their role in dissident group activities.

> What we say is this there is youth in our organisation in Limerick. Limerick is very strong, Limerick is one of the strongest parts of Republican Sinn Fein in the south, even if you go to any part of the country. They are capable of doing anything . . . A lot of them would be political, most of them would be political. But within our youth are armed units, among the Continuity. Even now we had one of our members arrested lately, he is in Portlaoise [prison]. We had a lot of people in Portlaoise from Limerick. Going back years and years no matter what movement there was always a very militant element in it.[34]

This statement from a Republican Sinn Féin and Continuity IRA activist not only takes pride in the regional involvement in dissident Republican activity, both militant and political, but also in those prisoners from the area in jail in Portlaoise. The power of regionalism is similarly seen across the island of Ireland. Other small clusters similarly show the dominance of specific Republican groups in a region. The combination of regionalism and influential individuals often overpowers any political or ideological differentiation.

Age

Throughout this chapter there has been continued reference to the recruitment and affiliations of young Republicans. The importance of focusing on young recruits, especially young males, is supported by the findings of the most recent Independent Monitoring Commission (IMC) reports. In reference to dissident Republican groups it states that:

> The majority of recruits are inexperienced young males.[35]

This has been the result of a deliberate targeting of young males by the various dissident groups. One needs only look to the Republican Sinn Féin press conference in the aftermath of the Continuity IRA murder of PSNI officer Stephen Carroll in March of 2009. This press conference showed the young RSF press officer Richard Walsh positioned beside three young males from the Craigavon area outlining how he believed they had been unfairly treated by the PSNI. This can be seen as a deliberate attempt by the group to appeal in particular to young males, as that dissident group and their militant wing the Continuity IRA would be perceived among some people as being overly populated by old guard traditionalist Republicans, a reputation in need of alteration in order to maintain their survival.

The young modern-day recruits would have no clear memory of the Troubles, and in some cases would not even have been born. Therefore, the dissident leadership have the opportunity to glorify active involvement in militant republicanism. Their positioning of influence within specific areas provides them with the ability to influence, shape and form the beliefs of this youthful population, in some instances with no relevant alternative narrative clearly available to the young recruits and potential recruits. Active membership in a militant group can appeal to a young male's sense of adventure and rebellion. This sense of adventure is not reliant on an in-depth knowledge of the defining ideological issues relevant to a specific group, but on the framing of what active involvement will entail, the status among the peer group and a simplified justification based on the aspirations for a united Ireland.[36] This is once again resonant of the situation, particularly across Northern Ireland, during the early 1970s.

> At that stage there was three of us from the bottom of the Falls Road, Divis Street area and this guy approached us and asked if we wished to join the Republican Movement. Dream come true. 'Certainly, yes, incognito, cloak and dagger, a chance to do something.' In yourself you were a big lad, you were swore in, it was 'Ssssh don't say this, don't say that.'[37]

The above quote shows how easy it can be to appeal to a young male, in this case a 13-year-old boy, to join a violent Republican grouping. It was the status and adventure of membership and involvement which appealed to the young boys, rather than any particular desire to achieve the national or even local goals of the movement. While this case is an example of young male recruitment in 1970, this is also relevant today. The findings of the IMC report are backed up by the statement referred to earlier in relation to the Continuity IRA:

> What we say is this there is youth in our organisation in Limerick. Limerick is very strong.[38]

Taking all of this into consideration a strong ideology or purposive goals will not be sufficient to attract a significant number of new young recruits to any organization. The leadership must be able to put in place sufficient personal and social incentives to attract and retain recruits without which these dissident organizations will not last for any significant amount of time.[39]

Change of Organization

Traditionally, when looking at dissidents, one would focus on those who move from one group to another after a split between the two organizations. With respect to dissident Republicans, such splits have seen the former members of the Provisionals joining or setting up the Continuity and Real IRA, and former Official IRA activists developing and joining the INLA. However, this transfer of groups need not always be from the parent organization to their own dissident groupings. There are cases within the

Irish Republican context where individuals, or groups of individuals, have moved from one dissident organization to another. One such example is that of a large portion of the INLA and IRSP membership of Limerick and Clare moving over to the Continuity IRA and Republican Sinn Féin in 1998. If one assesses these groups on purely ideological and political grounds, then this movement, and especially the acceptance of these new members into CIRA and RSF, would seem counterintuitive. The leadership of the CIRA and especially RSF go to great lengths to frame themselves as the only 'true' Republican Movement, and dismiss and disparage the actions and beliefs of all others who had taken a different course at any time during the history of the Irish Republican Movement. They are publicly wary of those who have historically taken an 'extreme socialist' political standpoint or criticized and disposed of the abstentionist policy which they hold as the cornerstone of Irish republicanism. This standpoint would suggest an inherent distrust of all members past and present of the Irish Republican Socialist Movement or the Official Republican Movement. It was these individuals who they moved away from during the split of 1969/70 when they were part of the Provisional Movement denouncing the Goulding leadership of the Irish Republican Movement. However, when the case of the movement of Clare and Limerick INLA and IRSP members is looked at in more detail, it is clear that ideological and political beliefs and concerns played little or no part in the choice of organizational affiliation, or acceptance and recruitment into the movement. This departure took place in the aftermath of the 1998 INLA ceasefire, when it became clear to the dismay of these members that their organization, the INLA, was no longer going to continue with the armed Republican struggle. However, they still believed in the viability of an armed struggle in the pursuit of a united Ireland. At this stage they viewed the pursuit of this purposive goal to be more important than any political or ideological standpoint.

> There is an armed struggle and they [RSF and CIRA] hardly have deviated since 1921, they have the same policies, there is a lot to be said for it. The struggle is above everything else, there is nobody bigger than the struggle, not Leinster House, Stormont or Westminster or any of those places. The struggle for national reunification of the country, that would be a priority ... The Continuity or RSF was the only group I could see holding on to the Irish Republican end of things. The Provos had accepted, had a ceasefire and soon afterwards they decommissioned, we could see all this coming

on board. The Provos asked me to join them, but I wasn't going to join the Provos.[40]

The above quote from Patrick Kennelly outlines his, and his former INLA comrades', justification for joining Republican Sinn Féin. For this grouping, a collection of individuals with extensive experience in and knowledge of the armed Republican movement, political and ideological beliefs were surpassed by the imperative of continuing the armed struggle. This further supports the fundamental proposal of the present chapter. In order to understand why a person becomes a dissident Irish Republican, or a specific kind of dissident Republican, it is important to acknowledge that the reasons for dissidence are often independent of the political and ideological stance taken by a particular organization, and is more reliant on a rationale external to these beliefs.

Freelance Dissidents

While a number of dissidents will choose to change organizational affiliation, there are similarly those who have decided to continue their Republican activism in an independent or freelance manner. These individuals will at times offer their 'services' to a variety of armed dissident Republican groups for specific actions. The growing threat of freelance Republicans has been acknowledged as being very serious in nature.

> There are … now indications that former republican terrorists have as individuals provided services in some instances to dissident republican groups, which even if occasional can significantly add to the threat.[41]

These individuals are often recruited for their specific skills for an individual action by the local or national leadership of the dissident group. Similar to the case of those Republicans switching organizational allegiance from the INLA to the CIRA and RSF, the continuation of an armed Republican struggle outweighs any individual ideological or political belief structure. The freelance nature of their activism, and their organizationally independent Republican belief structure, leaves them open to assisting a variety of Republican groups in individual campaign or actions.

> I probably agree with most of what they [32CSM] say. I also agree with a lot of what Republican Sinn Fein say. I also agree with quite a lot of what the INLA would say, I would have a lot of common ground with a lot of different groups. But I wouldn't be comfortable lending my total allegiance to one group ... If it came to the bit, and it is not going to come to the bit, but if it came to the bit where I was needed to do something and I approved of it, I would certainly do it. But as it stands it is all different little groups and I believe that there is so little separating them all that they are not necessary.[42]

Dolours Price, the former Provisional IRA activist, outlines above the rationale by which she and others justify their organizationally independent Republican activism, and at times their association with the actions of specific dissident groupings. Her justification moves on to the hypothetical situation whereby she is requested to aid one of these groupings. She has outlined what is probably true for a number of independent dissident Republicans. They would be willing to take part in an action for a number of these groups if it were something of which they approved. Therefore, unlike the organizationally committed Republicans they can in a sense pick and choose the actions with which they wish to be associated, be they armed or political.

If the violent dissident Republican threat is to be successfully countered, then one must not only focus on the dissident groups but also on those freelance dissidents operating independently of organizational ties and leadership orders.

Conclusion and Policy Implications

The purpose of the present chapter has been to offer an understanding of the rationale behind an individual's decision to become a dissident Irish Republican. The language used and the studies referred to throughout have often originated in the political organizational literature. This is a section of political literature which has been developed from economic organizational theory and focuses on the characteristics of the group, its strategies, tactics and aims. Political organizational theory has been applied within the terrorism literature to help explain terrorist behaviour.[43] This approach provides a basis whereby one can move beyond the moral debates of whether these groups and their motivations are 'right or wrong' to focus on the rationale behind organizational and personal decisions made by members.

While these dissident Republican groupings often define themselves by their political and ideological belief system, this is not always reflected in the reasoning behind a person's decision to become a dissident or in their choice of dissident affiliation. An analysis of the interview data gathered during the author's research has pointed to the importance of the factors of *timing, context, influential individuals, regionalism* and *age*. While not an exhaustive list by any means, if one is to come close to an understanding of dissident group affiliation and selection, the importance of these issues must be acknowledged and appreciated. It is this understanding which must first be in place before any policy is developed to counter the current threat posed by these small but dangerous groups. The factor of *regionalism* would suggest that any strategy must not be developed solely at a national level but must also focus on individual areas, no matter how small, where there is a prevalence of dissident membership and activity. Policymakers and the security services must appreciate the heterogeneity of dissident affiliation and the different rationales and justifications for dissident activity. This regionally specific focus must not simply concentrate on the dissidents themselves but should also provide a safe environment where alternative peaceful voices can be heard. Often this alternative voice will not be respected if it comes from governmental politicians or 'mainstream' Republicans. Within each region there will be different *influential individuals* and groups who may be listened to and respected by potential members and supporters of, as well as those already affiliated with, the dissident groups. It is vital that the young people in these areas are not blinkered in their beliefs by the glorification of armed struggle, and the fictional adventure provided by armed Republican activism. They need to become aware of the significant steps which have been taken through a peaceful political process.

Without these young recruits, the dissident groups are not able to survive. Therefore, any attempt to counter the modern-day violent dissident threat must not only focus on the leadership and influential individuals within these organizations but must similarly attempt to deter the engagement of young males in particular from joining these groups. Arrests and judicial sentences alone will not succeed in doing this. The cornerstone of any initiative to counter the threat posed by the Real IRA, Continuity IRA and Óglaigh na hÉireann must be an understanding of these groups and the motivations of their members and supporters. It must be clear that the threat is not posed by dissident republicanism. There is nothing wrong with vocalizing one's Republican or nationalist viewpoints or an opposition to the policies and decisions of the Sinn Féin leadership. The problem is when those dissident Republican views and beliefs are expressed through violence and terrorism. Any attempt to address the threat must not focus on dispelling dissident republicanism, it must aim to counter *violent* dissident republicanism.

Notes

1. White, R. W. 'Issues in the Study of Political Violence: Understanding the Motives of Participants in Small Group Political Violence', *Terrorism and Political Violence* 12, 1 (Spring 2000), 95–108.
2. See Rapoport, D. C. Series Editor's preface in Bowyer Bell, J. *The IRA 1968–2000: Analysis of a Secret Army* (London: Frank Cass, 2000), p. viii.
3. For the purpose of this chapter any use of the word 'terrorism' refers to the use of violence or the threat of repeated violence by an individual or group intent on bringing about a social or political effect. The aim of this action is to bring about a state of fear in a wider audience than the direct physical victims of the initial act or threat of violence. A terrorist incident should be defined by the use of violence or the threat of violence to bring about social or political change, not by the specific motive of the perpetrators. Therefore, terrorism is a tactic which can be employed by any individual or group, whether they be state or non-state actors.
4. Horgan, J. *The Psychology of Terrorism* (London: Routledge, 2005), pp. 30–2 and 74–5.
5. Within this assessment it must be acknowledged that the length of time one has been a member is not always analogous to level of experience. This must include an assessment of the level of commitment and activity during the period of membership.
6. Sani, F. and Reicher, S. 'Identity, Argument and Schism: Two Longitudinal Studies of the Split in the Church of England over the Ordination of Women to the Priesthood', *Group Processes and Intergroup Relations* 2, 3 (1999), 279–300; see also Sani and Reicher, 'When Consensus Fails:

An Analysis of the Schism within the Italian Communist Party (1991)', *European Journal of Social Psychology* 28, 4 (1998), 623–45.
7. Interview with Francie Mackey, 25 June 2008.
8. The membership of Republican Sinn Féin and the Continuity IRA did not consider these as new groupings but as an unbroken continuation of the Irish republican movement which can trace their position and policies historically. They believed, and still espouse the position, that the Provisionals are the ones who had changed and therefore had moved away from what it is to be true Irish Republicans.
9. Republican Sinn Féin has never acknowledged, and at times denies, the official link between their group and the Continuity IRA. However, this linkage is widely confirmed by academics, policymakers and the security forces. White, R. W. *Ruairí Ó Brádaigh: The Life and Politics of an Irish Revolutionary* (Bloomington, IN: Indiana University Press, 2006).
10. With the formal structuring of the Provisionals in the early 1970s there had been the development of a social and economic programme for the movement, *Éire Nua* (New Ireland). This was approved as Sinn Féin and IRA policy in 1971. The central tenet of this programme had been the federalization of a united Ireland, divided into four federations, one for each province. In the 1980s the Adams leadership believed this to be, and sold it as, a 'sop' to the loyalists and unionists as they would more than likely have command of the Ulster federation and it was voted out of the constitution of the movement. See Feeney, B. *Sinn Féin: A Hundred Turbulent Years* (Dublin: O'Brien Press, 2002) pp. 320–1.
11. Interview with *Ruairí Ó Brádaigh*, 20 February 2008.
12. Sani and Reicher (1991); Sani and Reicher (1999).
13. Hirschman, A. O. *Exit, Voice and Loyalty: Responses to Decline in Firms, Organisations and State* (Cambridge, MA: Harvard University Press, 1970) p. 47.
14. Interview with 'Una', 14 May 2008.
15. At times of split there are rank-and-file members who are fully aware of the relevant issues, but this is not the case for all members.
16. For a detailed account of the organizational structures of the IRA, see Horgan, J. and Taylor, M. 'The Provisional Irish Republican Army: Command and Functional Structure', *Terrorism and Political Violence* 2, 1 (1997), 1–32.

17. Interview with 'Conor', 12 January 2009.
18. A set of principles put forward by Senator George Mitchell in addition to his report on decommissioning which required any paramilitary groups entering in to talks to commit to the use of exclusively peaceful means in the pursuit of their political objectives. Guelke, A. 'Political Violence and Paramilitaries' in Mitchell, P. and Wilford, R. (eds.) *Politics in Northern Ireland* (Oxford: Westview Press, 1999), pp. 29–53.
19. Across social and political movements whether they be violent or non-violent if the organization is to gain any degree of success it is vital that they have a significant degree of support. If they do not attain this the achievement of goals as well as the survival of the organization becomes increasingly difficult.
20. This was the original name for what is now known as the 32 County Sovereignty Movement.
21. Interview with 'Conor'.
22. Interview with Joe Doherty, 1 February 2008.
23. This list is not exhaustive.
24. This observation is in line with the description of 'push' and 'pull' factors outlined by John Horgan in detailing disengagement from terrorism. See Horgan, J. 'Disengaging from Terrorism', *Jane's Intelligence Review* 18, 12 (2006), 34–7.
25. Interview with Martin McGuinness, 23 June 2008.
26. Ibid.
27. Interview with Mick Ryan, 16 February 2009.
28. Interview with Sean McManus, 29 May 2008.
29. Interview with 'Alex', 23 January 2009.
30. Oots, K. L. *A Political Organisational Approach to Transnational Terrorism* (Wesport, CT: Green Wood Press, 1986) p. 54
31. Bowyer Bell, J. (1998). *The Dynamics of Armed Struggle* (London: Frank Cass, 1998), p. 250.
32. Interview with Joe Doherty.
33. Interview with 'Denis', 29 February 2008.
34. Interview with 'Frank', 11 March 2009.
35. Independent Monitoring Commission, Twenty-Second Report of the Independent Monitoring Commission, paragraph 2.7.
36. Crenshaw, M. 'Theories of Terrorism: Instrumental and Organisational Approaches', in Rapoport, D.C. (ed.) *Inside Terrorist Organizations*

(London: Frank Cass, 2001), p. 19; Crenshaw, M. 'An Organisational Approach to the Analysis of Political Terrorism', *Orbis* 29, 3 (1985), 465–89; Horgan (2006), p. 34; Horgan, J. *Walking Away From Terrorism: Accounts of Disengagement from Radical and Extremist Movements* (London: Routledge, 2009), p. 143; White, R. W. and Fraser, M. R. 'Personal and Collective Identities and Long-Term Social Movement Activism: Republican Sinn Féin', in Stryker, S., Owens, T. J. and White, R. W. (eds), *Self Identity and Social Movements* (Minneapolis, MN: University of Minnesota Press, 2000), p. 325; Irvin, C. L. *Militant Nationalism: Between Movement and Party in Ireland in the Basque Country* (Minneapolis, MN: University of Minnesota Press, 1999), p. 34.
37. Interview with 'Denis'.
38. Interview with 'Frank'.
39. Oots, K. L. 'Organisational Perspectives on the Formation and Disintegration of Terrorist Groups', *Terrorism* 12 (1989), 139–52.
40. Interview with Patrick Kennelly, 10 March 2009.
41. Independent Monitoring Commission, *Twenty-Second Report of the Independent Monitoring Commission*, paragraph 2.7.
42. Interview with Dolours Price, 21 April 2008.
43. See, for example, Crenshaw (1985), pp. 465–89; Oots (1989).

CHAPTER 3

Who Are the Dissidents? An Introduction to the ICST Violent Dissident Republican Project

JOHN HORGAN
INTERNATIONAL CENTER FOR THE STUDY OF TERRORISM
THE PENNSYLVANIA STATE UNIVERSITY

PAUL GILL
INTERNATIONAL CENTER FOR THE STUDY OF TERRORISM
THE PENNSYLVANIA STATE UNIVERSITY

Abstract

This chapter[1] introduces the Violent Dissident Republican (VDR) project currently underway at the International Center for the Study of Terrorism at the Pennsylvania State University (ICST). The project began in October 2009 and charts the rise in dissident Irish republican activity (both terrorism-related and more broadly subversive) since the development of the Northern Irish Peace Process. This chapter presents initial findings from the database and mainly focuses on demographic and related information of those who have engaged in both violent and non-violent dissident activity. We also present a preliminary examination of emerging patterns in dissident activity since the development of the Good Friday Agreement.

Introduction

The study of terrorism has long suffered a lack of data at the level of the individual terrorist. A failure to adequately redress this problem has sustained 'theoretical modeling that is often divorced from important policy questions', because the 'vast number of modelers ... have no conception of the empirical reality' to guide their research.[2] In addition, the dearth of primary-source individual-level data has contributed to the view that psychological and sociological perspectives on terrorism remain limited and underdeveloped. However, exciting developments in recent years have seen at least a partial reversal of that trend. Collectively they provide complementary sources to the range of incident-based data sets long available to researchers. Notable examples include Reinares' analysis of over 600 ETA activists,[3] Sageman's analysis of over 400 al-Qaeda members,[4] Magouirk et al.'s Global Transnational Terrorism (GTT) project on over 300 South East Asian militants[5] and, more recently, Merari's study of Palestinian suicide bombers and their organizers.[6]

Although it is too early to tell if such examples represents a long-term change, we should welcome their development, and support Magouirk et al.'s call for more 'comprehensive, freely available database[s] that the research community can utilize to guide and test theoretical models' (pp. 2–3). Such quantitative data sets provide the empirical basis for rigorous hypothesis testing about those who engage in terrorism – how, where, when they become involved in the first place, subsequently engage in terrorist activity, and ultimately disengage. This chapter presents preliminary findings from a similar data set in development at the ICST on members of Irish dissident republican groups and the events and activities associated with and organized by these groups.

The VDR Project

The study began mid-October 2009 and aims to understand the types of individuals participating in VDR activity and to provide a data-driven empirical research base that can inform efforts at the individual, team, group and community level for preventing, disrupting or hindering mobilization and recruitment to VDR groups, predict and control the extent and nature of VDR operations, as well as to facilitate disengagement for those already involved in and committed to VDR activity. The main questions associated with the project include:

1. How and why do dissident groups emerge?
2. How can the VDR phenomenon be characterized? Specifically, how many movements exist, where are they located, how are they structured, how are

they related to each other, what are their ideological and other signature features?
3. Who becomes involved in violent dissident republicanism? What are the socio-demographic backgrounds of recruits to VDR?
4. What does VDR activity look like and how has VDR activity developed and changed over time?

This chapter is primarily concerned with the latter two questions. We outline the two primary data-gathering components of the wider project to date, and offer a preliminary descriptive analysis. We are collecting data on (a) VDR activity and (b) VDR personnel. VDR activity was collated based on an investigation of open source media accounts – the result of this is an *event* database. VDR personnel were identified from these accounts and the result is documented in a *personnel* database. Of the activity documented in the event database, not all events are illegal in nature. Some may be characterized as subversive in nature, while others (though not violent) may be indicative of intent to engage in violence. Of the individuals identified in the personnel database, not all have been charged with, let alone convicted of, terrorist offences. The relationship between non-violent dissident activity and violent dissident activity represents an important analytic challenge. For the purposes of our analysis, therefore, the term 'dissident' is not interchangeable with 'terrorist'. When our database is eventually made available to the broader research community, VDR and 'regular' DR personnel will be anonymized, though, irrespective of this, the inclusion from open sources of individuals identified either/both in the event database and personnel database should not be viewed as, or interpreted as, indicative of involvement in terrorist activity. In the following sections, we make explicit the differences emerging between violent and non-violent dissidents and reflect upon the significance of these. As will become clear during the analysis, the individuals included in our personnel database are not all currently active members of dissident groups. Furthermore, our analysis considers as dissidents all those who have actively engaged in subversive and terrorist activity since the inception of the Good Friday Agreement in 1998 and onwards.

Database Structure

The VDR event database catalogues dissident republican activity. As of March 2010, the database catalogued 763 distinct violent and non-violent events. The database integrates information from four types of open sources (in order of relevance): (1) newspaper and media accounts, (2) republican literature/propaganda, (3) publicly available government publications and reports, (4) online terrorism event databases (e.g. the Global Terrorism Database [GTD] and the Oklahoma City National Memorial Institute for the Prevention of Terrorism [MIPT] Database). For each event, the database supplies 21 different pieces of information captured in as many fields. Four fields cover temporal aspects of the event, while five fields track geographical information. Organizations tied to the event and whether they claimed responsibility (in the event of violence) covers a further two fields. The event type (meeting, bombing, shooting, riot) and weapon used (if any) is also captured in the event database. In the case of a violent event, a further five fields capture information on fatalities, injuries and victimology. The final three fields tie individuals to events, provide a summary of the event and the sources from which we garnered data.

The VDR personnel database catalogues individual members of dissident organizations. It is important again to note that not all those included have engaged in illegal activities. Dissidents engaged in legal activities were included to provide a broader understanding of the dissident movement and whether there are discernible differences between those engaged in legal and illegal forms of dissident activity. As of March 2010, 500 dissident republicans were included. The personnel database uses the same data-gathering method as the event database, although there is far less reliance on online terrorism event databases. Published books such as Mooney and O'Toole's *Black Operations*[7] provided insightful information on particular individuals. For each individual, the database captures 23 different pieces of information stored in as many fields. The individual's name, alias, gender, date of birth and age encompass five basic pieces of information obtained. A further four fields cater for geographical variables (place of birth, known addresses, places of arrest and whether these locations are in the North or South of Ireland). The individual's occupation, socio-economic status, marital status, and whether he/she has children provide further biographical information. The database also captures information on the dissident organization(s) the individual is aligned with, the sub-grouping (unit, brigade, cumann) of the parent dissident organization the individual is associated with, republican groups the individual was previously associated with, their current status (active, imprisoned, deceased, etc.) and the position/role the individual played within the organization. A further three fields code information on network linkages with other dissidents across friendship, family and operational ties. A generic 'other information' field captures other interesting information about the individual that may be added to newly generated fields as the project develops. The final field documents the sources from which we obtained data.

Who are the Dissidents?

Personnel

Of the 500 individuals captured in our database of republican dissidents, seven separate organizations are represented. In total, 60.5 per cent of these individuals are or have been members of the traditionally militant wings of dissident Irish republicanism; the Irish National Liberation Army (INLA), the Continuity IRA (CIRA), and the Real IRA (RIRA). Another 39.2 per cent are members of the various political movements associated with dissident

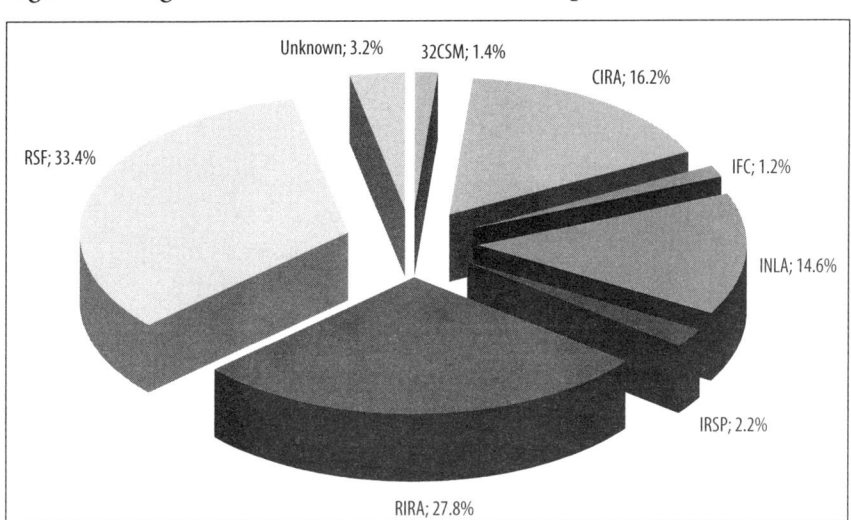

Figure 3.1 Organizational affiliation of dissident republicans

- Unknown; 3.2%
- 32CSM; 1.4%
- CIRA; 16.2%
- RSF; 33.4%
- IFC; 1.2%
- INLA; 14.6%
- IRSP; 2.2%
- RIRA; 27.8%

Irish republicanism: the 32 County Sovereign Movement (32CSM), the Irish Freedom Committee (IFC), Irish Republican Socialist Party (IRSP), and Republican Sinn Féin (RSF).

At present, the most represented militant group in our database is the Real IRA, whose members account for 27.8 per cent of our sum total and 47.4 per cent of actual violent militants in the data set. The Continuity IRA (16.2 per cent) is slightly more represented than the INLA (14.6 per cent) in the sum total. The most represented political group in our database is Republican Sinn Féin, whose members account for just over one-third (33.4 per cent) of the total data set and 87.4 per cent of the non-militant actors. This is probably due in no small part to Republican Sinn Féin's open communication networks that highlight their activities. These publications are quite visible and easily accessible both online and in print format. The other non-militant organizations barely registered on our database; the Irish Freedom Committee (1.2 per cent), 32 County Sovereign Committee (1.4 per cent), and the Irish Republican Socialist Party (2.2 per cent). This may be due to these groups being much smaller than Republican Sinn Féin or because they lack the same profile and/or coherent communication strategies that benefit data collection of the type carried out to date within this project.

The database includes the current status of 59.2 per cent of our individuals. The biggest single category here is those who are deceased which accounts for 27.7 per cent of the individuals on whose current status we have information. This reflects a number of things; those who die while engaged in militancy are promoted by the groups, and hence it makes data collection easier and a number of republican publications such as *Saoirse* contain obituaries from which we gathered data. Of those we have current status data, the next highest category is 'active' (26.7 per cent), followed by 'convicted' (15.2 per cent), imprisoned (14.5 per cent), charged (5.1 per cent), acquitted (4.1 per cent) and arrested (3.7 per cent). There is obviously some degree of overlap between these final categories. Further research will aggregate and update some categories such as 'convicted' and trace what occurred post-conviction.

Significant differences emerge when we cross-tabulate current status with the organizational affiliation of the individual. Nearly half (46.4 per cent) of our CIRA militants are currently imprisoned. This is compared to 14.7 per cent imprisoned for the Real IRA and the obviously smaller figure of 3.5 per cent for the INLA when we examine when most of their violence occurred. Of our INLA sample, 75.4 per cent are deceased. This figure is much smaller

Table 3.1 Current status of dissident republicans

	Frequency	%	Valid %
Acquitted	12	2.4	4.1
Active	79	15.8	26.7
Arrested	11	2.2	3.7
Charged	15	3.0	5.1
Charges dropped	6	1.2	2.0
Convicted	45	9.0	15.2
Deceased	82	16.4	27.7
Detained	3	0.6	1.0
Imprisoned	43	8.6	14.5
Total	296	59.2	100.0
Unknown	204	40.8	
Total	500	100.0	

Table 3.2 Current status by organizational affiliation

	CIRA (%)	INLA (%)	RIRA (%)	RSF (%)
Acquitted	10.7	1.8	3.2	2.7
Active	8.9	1.8	16.8	71.6
Arrested	3.6	1.8	8.4	0
Charged	8.9	0	9.5	0
Charges dropped	3.6	0	4.2	0
Convicted	12.5	15.8	27.4	0
Deceased	5.4	75.4	12.6	25.7
Detained	0	0	3.2	0
Imprisoned	46.4	3.5	14.7	0

for our INLA sample that has been active since 1998, and this is elaborated upon further in the next section. It is also not surprising to find the deceased INLA figure is greater than Republican Sinn Féin (25.7 per cent), Real IRA (12.6 per cent) and the CIRA (5.4 per cent). The vast majority (71.6 per cent) of our Republican Sinn Féin sample (on whom we have this particular data) are currently active. Given the mainly legal events that Republican Sinn Féin engage in, it is unsurprising to find that the majority of our sample here are known to be current activists; it is comparatively much higher than the three main militant groups whose members primarily come to prominence through high-profile arrests or convictions: RIRA (16.8 per cent), CIRA (8.9 per cent), INLA (1.8 per cent).

Focusing upon the region or last known address of the individuals illustrates some interesting findings. We have significant geographic data on 74.8 per cent of the individuals in the data set. Of these individuals, 54.5 per cent come from the Republic of Ireland compared to the 39 per cent from the six counties of Northern Ireland. Although we have no information on 25.2 per cent of the cases, there is no reason to believe that this is the cause of the significant difference between the two regions. Of individuals from the Republic, 37.1 per cent are from the Real IRA alone, while a further 32.5 per cent are from Republican Sinn Féin. The three main militant groups encompass the vast majority of individuals who come from Northern Ireland: RIRA (33.6 per cent), CIRA (25.2 per cent) and INLA (24.5 per cent). In other words, our preliminary data suggests that a highly significant amount of recruitment to the dissident movement (particularly RIRA and RSF) occurs within the southern 26 counties. Although a significant amount of these 'southern' dissidents engage in violent activity, the data suggests that dissidents from the south are far more likely to join non-violent dissident groups than their northern counterparts.

Of the total sample, 3.2 per cent also resided in or were born in Great Britain. This could imply one of two issues: such a low figure corresponds to anecdotal evidence on the Provisional IRA who preferred to embed

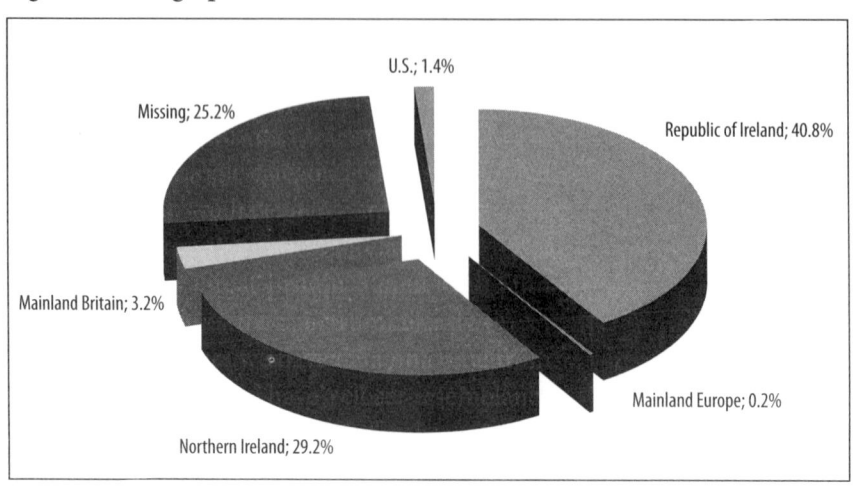

Figure 3.2 Geographical distribution of dissidents

- U.S.; 1.4%
- Missing; 25.2%
- Republic of Ireland; 40.8%
- Mainland Britain; 3.2%
- Mainland Europe; 0.2%
- Northern Ireland; 29.2%

individuals born on the island of Ireland within the British mainland rather than recruiting first or second generation Irish people who were brought up in England.[8] However, it could also imply that there is little motivation among the Irish diaspora in Britain to join the ranks of the dissidents. Further exploration of this issue will clarify which hypothesis can be supported.

Table 3.3 Geographical distribution by organizational affiliation

			CIRA	INLA	RIRA	RSF
Region	Republic of Ireland	Count	40	16	73	64
		% within organization	50.0	31.4	57.0	72.7
	Northern Ireland	Count	36	35	48	18
		% within organization	45.0	68.6	37.5	20.5
	Mainland Europe	Count	0	0	0	1
		% within organization	0	0	0	1.1
	Mainland Britain	Count	4	0	5	5
		% within organization	5.0	0	3.9	5.7
	US	Count	0	0	2	0
		% within organization	0	0	1.6	0
Total		Count	80	51	128	88

Table 3 illustrates a cross tabulation of the regions from which the individuals come from with the organizations they are associated with. As outlined above, the organizations we have significant amount of numbers to carry out adequate analysis are CIRA, INLA, RIRA and RSF. There are some interesting differences in their recruitment patterns. These four groups can be represented on a continuum of those groups who mainly recruit from the Republic or Ireland to those groups who predominantly recruit from Northern Ireland. The CIRA represents the middle ground of this continuum. If we collapse Northern Ireland and Great Britain into a single category, CIRA's personnel profile is split down the middle. In total, we have geographic data on 80 CIRA activists, 40 of which come from the Republic of Ireland, and 40 of which emanate from Northern Ireland or Great Britain. Republican Sinn Féin represents the Republic of Ireland side of the spectrum. Nearly three-quarters of the Republican Sinn Féin members we have data on come from the southern 26 counties. The Real IRA's personnel have a closer resemblance to the Continuity IRA's. Of the Real IRA militants in this database, 57 per cent come from the Republic, while 41.4 per cent are from Northern Ireland or mainland Britain. The INLA represents the other end of the continuum – 68.6 per cent of INLA members whom we have data on come from Northern Ireland, while the remaining are from the Republic. The INLA was also the only main group to have no recruits from mainland Britain.

Our data is rather sparse on the individuals' marital status. Currently, in over 90 per cent of the cases, we have no information. Of those remaining cases, just over 50 per cent are married, while a slightly smaller number are single. Our data is stronger, however, on whether these individuals have children. At least 17.2 per cent of that sample are reported to have children.

The Militants (1998–Present)

If we narrow this field of 500 dissident republicans to just those who have been actively involved with the militant groupings since 1998, interesting results emerge. We have data on 222 individuals who have been active, convicted and/or charged with various offences related to terrorism since 1998. Individuals affiliated with the Real (58.3 per cent) and Continuity (32.9 per cent) factions of the IRA dominate this subset of data. The rest comprise of members of the INLA (6.9 per cent), Republican Sinn Féin (1.4 per cent) and the Irish Republican Socialist Party (0.5 per cent). Just over half (51.2 per cent) of this sample are currently convicted and/or imprisoned, 11.5 per cent are active and a further 10.9 per cent are deceased.

We have data on the age of 209 individuals within this subset. Age ranges from 18 to 66 years. The average age at the time of first dissident activity that we could accurately account for was 35 years. This is a significantly older average than similar studies on other militant movements have illustrated. The average age of Florez-Morris' sample of Colombian militants was 20 years.[9] Sageman's work on global jihadists revealed an average age of 25.7 years.[10] Reinares' work on ETA shows that recruits over the age of 30 were rare. Of those recruited by ETA between 1970 and 1995, only 6.2 per cent were older than 30 years, and 84.3 per cent of recruits were between 18 and 26 years of age.[11] Similarly, 85 per cent of Fair's sample of Pakistani militants were between 12 and 25 years of age.[12] A parallel project underway at ICST is collecting information on former members of the Provisional IRA. Between May and July 2010, we collected information on 814 militants. They averaged 26.4 years of age. Those who joined in the 1970s average 25.5, in the 1980s 26.7 and in the 1990s 30.3 years. This suggests that the longer IRA militancy continued from the onset of the Troubles, the older the cohort of new recruits became.

While 91.8 per cent of our whole sample of dissidents was male, the figure for this subset of militants since 1998 is 97.3 per cent. While the numbers of female terrorists is increasing relatively and absolutely in a number of conflicts throughout the world such as Iraq and Afghanistan, women remain marginalized within the militant strands of dissident republicanism.

Table 3.4 represents the average age by organization, region, the type of activity the individual was charged with and employment type. There is very little to distinguish the average age between each of the militant organizations. There is also little to distinguish between the average ages according to gender and whether the individual is from Northern Ireland or the Republic. However, those from mainland Britain are markedly much older than both the sum average and each of the sub-sections captured in Table 3.4. Those who are unemployed and students are markedly much younger than the sum average and the other constituent sub-sections. One of the more interesting phenomenon is that those militants tasked with specifically violent acts (weapons/ammunition/IED possession) are on average six and a half years younger than those charged with non-violent or criminal behaviour (training, robbery, smuggling illicit goods, supplying safe houses, etc.). Although the average age of the militants is far older than in other organizations, it still holds true that the younger members are the ones ordered to engage in the actual violence itself. Those militants who have been active post-Good Friday Agreement and are now deceased, have relatively little impact upon the aggregate average age. They average 34.1 years of age at the time of their death.

In other words, when we look at the average age by organizational affiliation, role type, occupation, gender and birthplace, the only significant divergences from the aggregate average are INLA members, both role types, all occupation types except professionals, those who are deceased and those from Northern Ireland and Great Britain.

Just over half (52.7 per cent) of this subset hails from the Republic of Ireland, compared to 54.5 per cent of the whole database. This finding is important for a several reasons. First, it confirms that the general ranks of dissidents have always been swelled by Southerners. The patterns of dissident recruitment post-1998 (Good Friday Agreement) have not changed significantly. It also confirms that the seemingly large contingent from the

Table 3.4. Average age by category

	Average age (years)
Real IRA	35.5
Continuity IRA	34.5
INLA	34.1
Violent	32.6
Non-violent	39.2
Professional	34.4
Manual	37.1
Student	29.4
Unemployed	26.9
Republic of Ireland	35.3
Northern Ireland	33.8
Mainland Britain	42
Male	35
Female	34.4
Deceased	34.1

South is not biased by data collection on members from the wider dissident movement that do not necessarily engage in the violence itself (e.g. Republican Sinn Féin). That geographical recruitment patterns for both violent and non-violent republican activities are similar is of interest. The geographical recruitment patterns post-1998 hold constant for the Real and Continuity IRA. However, the INLA's pattern changes 180 degrees. The full database of INLA members reveals that 68.6 per cent come from Northern Ireland. This figure for the post-1998 subset dramatically falls to 33.3 per cent. Contemporary INLA dissidents, it seems, are far *more* likely to come from the Republic. This is a dramatic shift in recruitment patterns. It may also reflect a notion that the INLA was seen as a bigger threat within the Republic and more policing and security resources were allotted toward this organization to alleviate its threat.

We have data on 66 of the militants' employment status. Of this sample, 62.1 per cent come from what could be considered manual labour, semi-skilled or blue-collar work – mainly in construction, 15.2 per cent are professionals, a further 15.2 per cent are unemployed and 7.6 per cent are students. Although the data is sparse, there are some notable differences between the CIRA and RIRA. Of those CIRA militants that we have enough data on, 23.8 per cent are unemployed. This is compared to 10.3 per cent of RIRA militants. As one might expect from the aggregate data above, manual workers dominate both the CIRA and RIRA, although the RIRA does show notably higher figures than the CIRA (66.7 per cent versus 47.6 per cent). Both showed similar percentages of students and professionals among their cadre. This is very different than Sageman's findings on global jihadists. Of his sample, 43 per cent were professionals, while 33 per cent held semi-skilled occupations. There is a disparity, however, when we cross-tabulate employment status with the region the individual is from. Violent dissidents from the North (22 per cent) are more likely to be unemployed than those from the South (8.6 per cent). The same is also true for professionals but the difference is not as stark (18.5 per cent versus 14.3 per cent). The opposite is true for those in manual labour (65.7 per cent versus 55.6 per cent) and students (11.4 per cent versus 3.7 per cent) – both of which are more likely to be from the South.

The Militants (1998–Present) by Organization

Real IRA

Real IRA militants post-1998 average 35.5 years of age. Individuals have ranged from 19 to 66 years old. Geographically, 54 per cent hail from the Republic, 38.1 per cent from Northern Ireland and 3.2 per cent from Britain, while the location of 4.8 per cent remains unknown. Northern Irish RIRA militants are two years younger on average than their Southern counterparts (34 versus 36 years of age). At least 13.5 per cent of the sample have been married, divorced or engaged while a quarter of the sample have children. Of the sample, 96 per cent are male, although this figure is lower for those just from Northern Ireland (93.8 per cent). Females (31.3 years) were typically a number of years younger than their male counterparts (35.6 years).

Of those on whom we have employment details (n = 39), 66.7 per cent hold manual occupations, 15.4 per cent are professionals, 10.3 per cent are unemployed and 7.7 per cent are students. All of the students are from the Republic, while those who are unemployed are significantly more likely to come from Northern Ireland (21.4 per cent versus 4 per cent). Those from professional and manual professions are slightly more likely to come from the Republic (16 per cent versus 14.3 per cent, and 68 per cent versus 64.3 per cent). Women encompass one-third of the Professionals within the RIRA cadre. Professionals (32.2 years), and the unemployed (25 years) are both significantly younger on average than the aggregate ages elaborated upon in the above section.

Of those Real IRA militants captured in our post-1998 subset, significantly more of those currently convicted or imprisoned are from the Republic compared to the North (64.7 per cent versus 16.2 per cent). While 16.2 per cent of our Northern Irish RIRA dissidents are deceased, this figure is only 7.8 per cent for those from the Republic.

In terms of role types, of those we have data on, 69 per cent were engaged in violent activity. Militants engaged in non-violent activity are more likely to come from the Republic compared to Northern Ireland (29.6 per cent versus 21.1 per cent). All of the British RIRA militants engaged in non-violent activity. Non-violent militants average 39.6 years. Those with violent roles average a significantly younger 32.8 years of age.

Continuity IRA

Post-1998 Continuity IRA militants average an age of 34.5 years, with a range of 18–59 years. Geographically, 47.9 per cent hail from the Republic, 46.5 per cent are from Northern Ireland and a further 5.6 per cent are from Britain. Northern Irish CIRA militants are a significant four years younger on average than their Southern counterparts (32.1 versus 36.1 years of age). The mainland Britain-born CIRA militants average 40 years of age. Males make up 98.6 per cent of this post-GFA CIRA sample.

At least 9.9 per cent of the sample are married individuals while 21.1 per cent have children. Of those we have employment details on, 47.6 per cent are in manual occupations, 19 per cent are professionals, 23.8 per cent are unemployed and 9.5 per cent are students. The numbers of manual workers is remarkably smaller than in the RIRA while the numbers of unemployed is remarkably higher. Unlike the RIRA, those from professional professions are more likely to hail from the North (25 per cent versus 14.3 per cent). Professionals (37.8), manual workers (41.8) are both significantly older on average than the aggregate ages elaborated upon in the above section.

Of those Continuity IRA militants captured in our post-1998 subset, significantly more of those who are currently convicted or imprisoned are from the Republic compared to the North (61.5 per cent versus 27.3 per cent). While 9.1 per cent of our Northern Irish CIRA dissidents are deceased, this figure is only 3.8 per cent for those from the Republic.

Regarding the specific roles held by activists, of those we have data (n = 62) 82.3 per cent were engaged in violent activity. Again this is a far higher figure than the RIRA. Militants engaged in non-violent activity are more likely to come from the Republic compared to Northern Ireland (23.3 per cent versus 13.8 per cent). Non-violent militants average 38 years of age. Those with violent roles average a significantly younger 32.2 years of age.

INLA

We captured data on 15 INLA militants who have been active since 1998, all of whom are male. They average 34.1 years of age with a range of 22 to 55 years. Geographically, 66.6 per cent hail from the Republic while the rest are from Northern Ireland. While Northern RIRA and CIRA militants are significantly younger than their Southern comrades, the opposite is true for the INLA. INLA militants from the Republic average an age of 32.3 years compared to those from the North who average 37.8 years. At least 6.7 per cent of the sample comprises married individuals, while 26.7 per cent have children.

Events

Interesting results also abound for the event level data. In total, we have thus far coded 763 events of dissident republican activity, across eight separate republican groups. There is a good deal of overlap on the organizations included in both databases except Fianna Éireann and Óglaigh na Éireann were not captured in the personnel database while the Irish Freedom Council was not captured in this event database. This will be redressed in future work, and we explore particularly the extent of 'false flag' movements that in reality may well be convenient cover labels as opposed to genuine organizations. While Republican Sinn Féin members constituted one-third of our data set on activists, Republican Sinn Féin's activities only capture 12.6 per cent of our events. The most active group was the Real IRA (45.6 per cent), followed by CIRA (26.6 per cent), Republican Sinn Féin (12.6 per cent) and the INLA (11.5 per cent). Table 3.5 captures the differences between the databases in terms of organizational affiliation.

Table 3.5 Organizational affiliation/responsibility

	Individuals (%)	Events (%)
32 CSC	1.4	1.8
CIRA	16.7	26.6
INLA	15.1	11.5
IRSP	2.3	1
RIRA	28.7	45.6
RSF	34.5	12.6
Fianna Éireann	0	0.2
Óglaigh na hÉireann	0	0.8
Irish Freedom Council	1.2	0

Of the events for which we captured locational data (n = 648), two-thirds (66.1 per cent) occurred within Northern Ireland, 28.3 per cent in the Republic, and 4.1 per cent in Great Britain. Table 3.5 illustrates the vast difference in where dissident republicans come from, and their principal area of operations by region. While 54.5 per cent of dissident republicans hail from the Republic, only 28.3 per cent of their activities (violent and non-violent) occur in the Republic. While 39 per cent of dissident republicans come from Northern Ireland, two-thirds of their activities take place in Northern Ireland. Also, while virtually every county in Ireland has experienced some dissident activity, the main areas of operation are Antrim (21.4 per cent), Armagh (11.5 per cent), Dublin (9.6 per cent), Derry (9 per cent), Down (6 per cent) and Tyrone (4.8 per cent)

Table 3.6 Geographical distribution of dissidents and their activities

	Individuals (%)	Events (%)
Republic of Ireland	54.5	28.3
Northern Ireland	39	66.1
Mainland Europe	0.3	1.2
Mainland Britain	4.3	4.1
United States	1.9.	0.3

If we examine this issue further and compare area of operations across the main organizations, we find that the three main militant groups had strikingly similar levels of activity in Northern Ireland as a proportion of overall activity. A majority of CIRA activity (67.8 per cent) was in Northern Ireland, while the respective figures for the Real IRA and INLA are 63.8 per cent and 61.4 per cent. The INLA were slightly more likely to engage in activities in the Republic (36.8 per cent) compared to CIRA (28.7 per cent) and the RIRA (26.3 per cent). Interestingly, the Real IRA was nearly three times more active in mainland Britain (as a per cent of total events) than RIRA's nearest competitor, CIRA. 7.4 per cent of Real IRA activities occurred on the mainland. Republican Sinn Féin's primary activities occurred in the Republic (70.1 per cent).

Table 3.7. Geographical distribution of organizational activity

			Organization			
			CIRA	INLA	RIRA	RSF
Region	ROI	Count	41	21	64	47
		% within organization	28.7	36.8	26.3	70.1
	NI	Count	97	35	155	17
		% within organization	67.8	61.4	63.8	25.4
	Mainland Europe	Count	0	0	6	1
		% within organization	0	0	2.5	1.5
	Mainland Britain	Count	4	1	18	1
		% within organization	2.8	1.8	7.4	1.5
	U.S.	Count	1	0	0	1
		% within organization	0.7	0	0	1.5
Total		Count	143	57	243	67
		% within organization	100.0	100.0	100.0	100.0

Of the events on which we have sufficient data, 55.5 per cent are violent acts (bombings, shootings, possession of weapons and/or bomb-making equipment – the latter not 'violent' per se, but indicative of active preparation for violent acts). The remainder comprises a variety of conventional events (meetings, protests, etc.). There is a striking difference in the location of these two types of events. While 72.2 per cent of events that occurred in Northern Ireland were violent, 71.3 per cent of events in the Republic were non-violent. Again, the three main militant groups shared similar histories across their event data. Of INLA events, 62.3 per cent were violent, while the

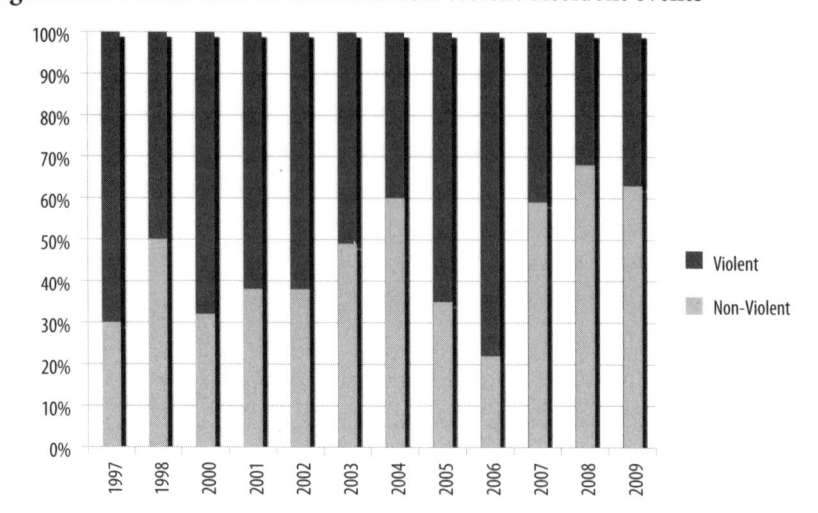

Figure 3.3. Annual ratio of violent to non-violent dissident events

respective figures for the RIRA and CIRA were 61 per cent and 60.3 per cent. The proportion of non-violent to violent events has fluctuated since 1998 (see Figure 3.3). After the signing of the Good Friday Agreement and the Omagh bombing in 1998, dissident violence decreased until 2000 when violence (as a percentage of total events) returned to 1998 levels before decreasing year on year until 2004. In the two years that followed, violent events rose to record levels of activity – the highest in fact since 1998. 2007 and 2008 witnessed steep declines of violent events (as a percentage of total) events before a slight rise in 2009. These results may be somewhat biased by the nature of the data collection. Recent non-violent activities are more likely to be captured through our data collection methods than non-violent activities that occurred ten or even five years ago.

Conclusions

The data presented here is preliminary and not indicative of final results. Our data collection efforts reveal approximately 20 new 'identities' per week from open source literature. At present, data collection is reliant on newspaper accounts. In several ways, this may well contribute to certain biases in the data in that there needs to be a significant effort to engage in more primary data collection of republican literature sources – for example, several well-known dissident republican (DR) figures do not appear in most open source newspaper searches (and therefore, at present, they remain absent from our database). Furthermore, the LexisNexis search engine tool does not incorporate Irish/English sources until several years after the split that created CIRA and RSF. Currently, efforts are underway to engage in a second data crawl through the non-public archives of the *Irish Times, Irish Independent* and *An Phoblacht/Republican News*. A search of the term 'dissident republican' via the OpenSource.gov archive in February 2010 revealed a further 1,500-plus data points which have yet to be incorporated into the data set. It would therefore be clear that there is substantial data yet to be analysed, interpreted and added to the databases.

The data collection to date on non-militant republicans mainly focused upon Real Sinn Féin literature that may account for their high numbers in the data set on the dissidents. Their activities constitute a much smaller number within our sample. To redress these issues, the next phase of our study will incorporate an increased focus on materials published by other non-militant dissident factions such as Éirígí, 32 County Sovereign Committee, Irish Freedom Committee and the Irish Republican Socialist Party. (Relevant materials are easily accessible, being published online at, for example: www.32csm.info; www.irishfreedom.net; www.irsm.org/irsp; and www.eirigi.org.)

Despite the preliminary findings, there are noticeable differences between and among dissident organizations in terms of activity, geographical distribution and recruitment patterns, age, employment status and role profiles. A major focus of the next phase of the study is to examine in extensive detail the data associated with each of these issues, but also a major effort will be undertaken to track changes in the 'current status' variable as it relates to individual DRs. At the moment, there is a data confidence bias towards those who are deceased. This is due to either newspaper coverage of militants dying in active service or through republican literature announcing the deaths of former and recently active members. Currently we have many categories that are likely to be aggregated upon further data collection (i.e. convicted, charged, imprisoned, etc.).

At present, there is no geographical data available for approximately one-quarter of our sample. Further data collection through court documents and local news sources is likely to reduce this figure significantly. There is also sparse data on marital, family and employment status. Looking ahead, we will begin to parse data across individuals for more optimal network analyses. The fluidity of membership between various dissident factions will be analyzed in detail, and, at present, there is virtually no reliable open-source information on Fianna Éireann and Óglaigh na hÉireann's membership.

Future publications from this project will, in particular, illustrate the networked nature of the various militant groupings and of select individuals that both migrate between different dissident factions as well as (in some cases) hold simultaneous membership in more than one faction. Data collection and coding is already underway to connect dissidents together through both pre-existing familial and friendship ties as well as through common activities captured in the event database. This will provide us with a broader understanding of how these militant groupings are connected together at the individual level and will effectively illustrate the fluidity of membership between the groupings.

In conclusion, this chapter presents a brief glimpse into the initial efforts at this developing project. As with all database work, there are serious gaps that at present prohibit the development of meaningful patterns to be drawn from the early stages of the work. However, the progress made thus far constitutes evidence that it is possible, not only to locate and record significant data from open sources, but that the development of a quantitative data set on terrorist activists and their supporters is no longer outside the realm of a short-term, focused research effort.

Notes

1. This research was made possible by a grant from the UK government to the Principal Investigator and first author, John Horgan. All opinions are those of the authors and do not necessarily reflect the views and policies of the sponsor. The authors thank Patrick McGowan and Susan Mira who assisted in the data collection. John Morrison and Jim Cusack provided input on several issues. Please direct all correspondence to the first author at: horganjohn@psu.edu
2. Magouirk, J., Atran, S. and Sageman, M. 'Connecting Terrorist Networks', *Studies in Conflict and Terrorism*, 31 (2008), 1–16.
3. Reinares, F. 'Who are the Terrorists? Analyzing Changes in Sociological

Profile among Members of ETA'. *Studies in Conflict and Terrorism*, 27, (2004), 465–88.
4. Sageman, M. *Understanding Terror Networks* (Philadelphia, PA: University of Pennsylvania Press, 2004); see also Sageman, M. *Leaderless Jihad* (Philadelphia, PA: University of Pennsylavania Press, 2009).
5. Magouirk, J., Atran, S. and Sageman, M. 'Connecting Terrorist Networks', *Studies in Conflict and Terrorism*, 31 (2008), 1–16.
6. Merari, A. *Driven to Death: Psychological and Social Aspects of Suicide Terrorism* (New York: Oxford University Press, 2010).
7. Mooney, J. and O'Toole, M. *Black Operations: The Secret War against the Real IRA* (Ashbourne: Maverick House, 2003).
8. Dillon, M. *The Enemy Within: The IRA's War against the British* (London: Transworld Publishers, 1994); McGladdery, G. *The Provisional IRA in England: The Bombing Campaign, 1973–1997* (Dublin: Irish Academic Press, 2006).
9. Florez-Morris, M. 'Joining Guerrilla Groups in Colombia: Individual Motivations and Processes for Entering a Violent Organization', *Studies in Conflict and Terrorism*, 30, 7 (2007), 615–34.
10. See note 2.
11. See note 3.
12. Fair, C. 'Who are Pakistan's Militants and their Families?' *Terrorism and Political Violence*, 20, 1 (2008), 49–65.

CHAPTER 4

Beyond the 'Micro Group': The Dissident Republican Challenge

HENRY PATTERSON
UNIVERSITY OF ULSTER, JORDANSTOWN

What's in a Name?

Part of the process of evaluating the threat from violent Irish republicanism is the interrogation of the terms in which the phenomenon is discussed. The term 'dissident' is one used by governments, the media and the republican mainstream. Some academic analysis has made the term problematic: Tonge and Murray prefer 'republican ultras' and Richard English favours 'dissenters': those republicans who sharply disagree with Provisional orthodoxy about the evolving peace process.[1] This uneasiness with the term 'dissident' reflects a recognition that it carries a negative charge by implicitly identifying the 'peace process', the Good Friday Agreement and the structures of government in Northern Ireland created by it as what those currently prepared to use violence are dissenting from. This is but a partial truth. Its dominance reflects the political and ideological resources that have been invested by the British, Irish and American states in bringing the Provisional IRA's 30-year campaign to an end. The period saw Ireland experience its 'Fukuyama moment' when one Irish historian could end his impressive overview of Ireland from 1798 to 1998 with an interrogatory conclusion, 'The End of Irish History?', in which he wrote:

> Militant republicanism has modified its traditional stand on the institutions of partition ... Gerry Adams becomes not so much the ideological heir of Liam Lynch, the republican military leader in the civil war, still less of Eamon de Valera, but rather of Michael Collins.[2]

The elision of those who were republicans but did not accept the trajectory of the Provisionals was widespread at the time despite the fact that the Provisionals had suffered their most serious defections in 1997 with the formation of the Real IRA. The heavy media coverage of the complex process of negotiations that led to the Agreement and then of the subsequent stuttering attempts to get power-sharing institutions established and consolidated inevitably meant that what would have appeared as arcane details of republican ideology and history were not a priority. The popular legitimization of the process through the dual referenda on the Agreement and the revulsion at the Omagh atrocity also ensured that violent republicanism was treated as an object of execration rather then something to be analysed and understood.

However, the radicalism of Sinn Féin's departures, not simply from what might be portrayed as republican metaphysics, but from much of what until very recently they defined as their own strategic project, meant that a reaction was inevitable. From the start, this challenged the mainstream's alleged manipulation of history and language. An early example was Marion Price, who, along with her sister, Dolours, and the current Sinn Féin junior minister, Gerry Kelly, was convicted for car-bombings in London in 1973. In an interview with a Spanish academic, she dismissed the use of the term 'micro group' used by mainstream republicans to refer to groups like the Real IRA (RIRA) on the grounds of their lack of a popular mandate: 'When Gerry Kelly went to London with me he'd no mandate, what's changed?' She also rejected the 'dissident' label referring to the recent murder of Joseph O'Connor, a leading member of the RIRA in Belfast, by the Provisionals:

> Volunteer Joe O'Connor was clear in his opposition to British rule; he did not dissent from republican principles or ideals . . . I know they like to term people like myself dissenters, but we haven't dissented from any republican principles, they are the people who have strayed from republicanism. I believe today the same things that I believed in the early 1970s when Gerry Adams was a comrade of mine. So he is the one that has changed, not me.[3]

The question of fealty to republican principles had been the central issue in the first significant split in the Provisionals when Ruairí Ó Bradaigh, Dáithí Ó Conaill, founding members of the Provisionals, left with their supporters over the decision to end abstentionism in elections for the Dáil. The very name of their organization, Republican Sinn Féin, was chosen to make the point that in embracing this important step into constitutional politics in the Republic the Provisionals were following a succession of reformist formations from Fianna Fáil to Official Sinn Féin that had forsaken the founding principles of allegiance to the 32 county republic declared by the first Dáil in 1919. Their newspaper *Saoirse* was, until this decade, the main critical republican voice and it maintains an acerbic and increasingly bitter focus on Sinn Féin's politics and strategy. Much of this takes the form of denunciations of those responsible for the 'revolution betrayed'. Its commemorations, perhaps because the Provisionals have continued largely to monopolize 'comrades' who died in the post-1969 campaign, focus on those involved in the War of Independence, Civil War and the 1956–62 campaign. But they are all used to make pointed comparisons with the present situation. Thus at a commemoration for Fearghal O'Hanlon, who with Sean South died in the IRA's attack on Brookeborough RUC station in Fermanagh in 1957, the main speaker compared O'Hanlon and his comrades to 'principled people prepared to give their all, in order to obtain a free and united Ireland' with 'the treachery embarked on by Gerry Adams and Martin McGuinness':

> Over the past year the Irish people have witnessed unbelievable events unfold, as counter-revolutionary forces took hold of the freedom struggle and treated the blood of hundreds of Irish Republican soldiers for a squalid little job in Stormont or Leinster House. Not one iota was delivered in terms of sovereignty.[4]

In the same issue the leader, 'Felon-Setting by Provos: Provos Part of the Brit War-machine', quoted a journalist specializing in security issues who had noted that a recent series of statement by Adams and other leading Sinn Féiners had used the term 'criminal' to describe the activities of 'dissidents'. The journalist had claimed these were important steps in Sinn Féin's support for the security apparatuses of the Northern Irish state. The leader's accusation of 'felon-setting' was a very familiar republican trope: the use of resonant phrases from iconic figures. The term was coined by the Fenian leader, Jeremiah O'Donovan Rossa, in 1858 about a local newspaper editor in West Cork who demanded the arrest of local Fenians who had been drilling and marching and were, he claimed, liable to prosecution under the Treason Felony Act of 1848.

After the murders of two soldiers and a member of the PSNI when Martin McGuinness denounced those responsible as 'traitors to Ireland' and called on those with information to give it to the PSNI, RSF issued a statement to the *Irish News*:

> The RUC/PSNI and the word Republican are a contradiction in terms. How dare these people tell Irish people to become informers to the same British armed forces of occupation who with the help of former Republicans are still occupying our country. We believe the time has come for those people to drop the name Sinn Fein and no longer claim to be the republican movement. No other republicans in our history have ever handed over weapons ... to the occupying forces ... We in Republican Sinn Fein, unlike the Provos, have no interest in Armani suits, expensive cars and holiday homes as a pay-off for accepting the rule of the enemy.[5]

However, both RSF and those who broke with the Provisionals a decade later, had more to their critique than arguments over republican principles. There has also developed a counter-narrative of the republican involvement in the peace process.

'Cheated Rather Than Defeated'?

The phrase that opens this section is taken from an assessment of the RIRA and CIRA by Anthony McIntyre. McIntyre had been a member of the Provisional IRA down to Sinn Féin's acceptance of the Good Friday Agreement but did not join any of the organizations who continued to justify armed struggle. In fact, he has stated on a number of occasions that he does not think armed struggle is justifiable in current circumstances, and also that he believes that the republican struggle has exhausted any possibility it ever possessed of achieving its objectives. Nevertheless, while arguing that none of the organizations involved in violence can succeed, the journalism by him and those who think like him have provided an eloquent, effective and influential demolition of mainstream republicanism's claims about the nature of the peace process and the possibilities of movement towards unity. According to him:

It seems that a large factor in the motivation of armed republicans is the feeling that they have been cheated rather than defeated. They take the view that the Sinn Fein leadership lied to them from the outset, the evidence for which is overwhelmingly in favour of the physical force school's claims.[6]

The most influential version of this thesis is contained in the journalist Ed Moloney's *A Secret History of the IRA*.[7] At the core of Moloney's thesis is the role of Adams and his closest allies in a 'secret peace process' setting out from the early 1980s to bring the armed struggle to an end through a process of 'broadening the battlefield' to build up Sinn Féin's electoral profile and constructing a pan-nationalist alliance with Fianna Fáil and the SDLP to pressurize the British government to act as persuaders for unity. This strategy was carried out behind the backs of the bulk of IRA volunteers and Sinn Féin members and involved obfuscation and lies. A key element was the containment of the IRA's armed struggle to those actions which would not jeopardize the overall strategic goal of working with constitutional nationalists and engaging with the British. Moloney emphasizes how a series of incidents in which key IRA active service units and personnel were wiped out by security force operations facilitated this process of the downgrading of the military campaign. He devotes a chapter to the wiping out of the cutting edge of the Provisional East Tyrone brigade at Loughgall in May 1987. By removing some of the IRA's most effective operatives Loughall dealt a death blow to IRA GHQ plans for a 'Tet Offensive' along the border. But Moloney also claims it left 'a huge black cloud' of suspicion about the identity and motives of those who may have betrayed the East Tyrone brigade: 'the speculation has never ceased about whether the traitor came from Tyrone or from elsewhere in the IRA and if so, how high up.'[8] Moloney's analysis has been criticized for an overly conspiracist view of how republicanism as a movement became involved in the peace process and for exaggerating the role of Adams as an arch-manipulator.[9] However, it is undoubtedly the case that his emphasis on the behind-the-scenes contacts with the British and Irish states and the degree to which the transformation of republicanism was instigated and orchestrated by a tightly knit elite around Adams has become a central theme in the discourse of republican opponents of the process. The issue of betrayal and the penetration of the organization by the intelligence agencies of the two states has also been taken up by Sinn Féin's republican critics, powered by revelations of high-level informers like Freddie Scappaticci and Denis Donaldson. The Moloney narrative is now a common currency for republican critics of Adams and the Provisionals. A leading member of RSF in Fermanagh, John Joe McCusker, used it in his speech to the O'Hanlon commemoration mentioned above:

> The Provo element had a well-advanced plan in place long before the 'split'; in actual fact the 'split' was an integral part of their plan . . .
>
> On the military side of the equation the Provo/Allied power house to drive the way forward was a small in-house Belfast based leadership, assisted in their endeavours by Freddie Scappattici [sic].
>
> The views of decent genuine people were sought out, within the ranks of the Provos . . . Those who were seen as against their way forward were cut adrift and marginalised. Some on the military side may have been singled out for special attention . . .
>
> It is highly unlikely that the truth will ever be known of the darker aspects to installing the so-called 'peace process'.[10]

Those who had remained in the Provisionals after 1986 were particularly virulent in their critique of the process, by which, between the Good Friday Agreement and the St Andrews Agreement, the leadership of Sinn Féin used the continued existence of the IRA as a bargaining chip to extract concessions from Blair and the Ulster Unionists which was then discarded. The most articulate and effective were former IRA volunteers who delivered a powerful and corrosive running commentary on what was portrayed as Sinn Féin attempting to dress up an effectively partitionist settlement as a transition to a 32-county democratic socialist republic. Much of this critique was on the blogosphere in two journals, *Fourthwrite* and *The Blanket*[11] and its most impressive figure was Anthony McIntyre.

Armed Struggle: Bound to Fail?

McIntyre's analysis, while powerful, is an unstable combination of an unreconstructed republican version of Irish history and the role of the British state and Unionism with a despairing view about the lack of any significant social force or objective conditions to make republican objectives achievable. Thus, of the prospects of those groups committed to armed struggle he supported the view of another influential critic of the republican mainstream, the former leading Tyrone Provisional, Tommy McKearney, that there was no popular support for a return of republican violence:

> An essential difference between the Provisionals and the recent crop hardly comes down to the prospect of success. The Real and Continuity IRAs will be as comprehensively defeated as the Provisionals. The difference lies in the size of the minorities willing to lend support to their campaign against both the British state and the democratically expressed will of the Irish people. The minority support for the Provisionals was considerably larger than anything so far mustered for today's rivals.
>
> Any armed republican confrontation with a government housing Sinn Fein is likely to run aground against a rock of popular sentiment. It would be akin to an armed assault on the government in Dublin firmly rooted in the people the insurgents need to win over. Northern Ireland will have its politically violent moments that explode in a blaze of publicity. But the hours, days, weeks and years will tick past as unobtrusively as they do peacefully.[12]

However, some dissenting republicans, while sharing the analysis of the Provisionals' degeneration, claim that McKearney and McIntyre are overly pessimistic. Thus, in a review of a collection of McIntyre's journalistic pieces Liam O'Ruairc commented:

> McIntyre's contention that republicanism is a spent force is debatable . . . While the book is the product of 'defeat, decommissioning and disbandment' it is much too early to say that it is the death of Irish republicanism. There is political space for Republicanism, even if it is reduced from what it once was. Viewed from a longer historical perspective, it is possible to make the case that it could grow if conditions are right.[13]

The emphasis in the Moloney narrative on deception and betrayal can in itself be used by those who currently support armed struggle. For, if the IRA was cheated and, as the Provisionals claim, that it was not defeated, some conclude that if the armed struggle had not been contained and shut down by the Adams leadership then it could have produced a settlement much more favourable to republican objectives. During the Provisionals' 'back-channel' contacts with British government representatives in the early 1990s the IRA had waged a bombing campaign on the British mainland including the massive Baltic Exchange and Nat West Tower attacks. Marian Price argues that the campaign was particularly effective and believes that more City bombs would have had a significant influence on the British government:

> I do believe that at the end of the day the British, they are staying here for whatever their reasons are, but I do believe that if push comes to shove, they protect the mainland . . . and they'll sacrifice anything to do that.[14]

This was the thinking behind the RIRA's English campaign in 2000/2001, which included attacks on Hammersmith Bridge, Ealing Broadway underground station, the MI6 headquarters and a car bomb outside the BBC Television Centre.[15]

A series of arrests and the trial and conviction of five RIRA members in 2003 effectively ended that campaign and the focus of violent republicanism since then has been largely on targets in Northern Ireland. Here, like the Provisional IRA from the late 1970s, its campaign was aimed at undermining and destabilizing any attempt to construct a consociational settlement, thus frustrating British attempts to portray the northern problem as a thing of the past. However, its capacity to achieve this was undermined by a split after the imprisonment of its key figures, Michael McKevitt, Liam Campbell and Seamus McGrane. The Independent Monitoring Commission (IMC), the body charged with monitoring paramilitary activity, claimed in 2008 that it was still divided into two factions.[16] Another significant restraint on the operational capacity of both the CIRA and RIRA was the continued existence of the Provisional IRA. As we shall see in the next section, the IRA's 'cessation' did not extend to those individuals and groups who challenged Sinn Féin's control of their core urban working-class constituency. The decommissioning of IRA weapons and the demobilization of the organization has increased the space within which the two main organizations can operate. Thus, it is no coincidence that within a year of the IRA's announcement of the end of its 'armed campaign', the IMC noted an escalation of RIRA activity, including attacks on the police, on Orange halls and incendiary attacks on six DIY stores and other businesses across Northern Ireland. This campaign intensified in 2007 with attacks on two off-duty Catholic police officers in Derry and Dungannon and the IMC has noted: 'dissident republican activity since the early summer of 2008 has been consistently more serious than at any time since we started to report in April 2004.'[17] The RIRA claimed that it had restructured and reorganized and was now a unified organization.[18] It describe its attacks as part of 'the tactical use of armed struggle', the implication being that it is well aware of the limits on what violence can achieve but hopes that by exacerbating the contradictions and limitations of the current dispensation at Stormont it can demonstrate that reform of the North can never stabilize the situation.

This period has also seen both organizations, but particularly the RIRA arrogate to themselves the role of meting out paramilitary justice to so-called anti-social elements. Once an activity of the Provisionals, the latter have now turned the issue over to the police and 'community restorative justice' schemes which are heavily staffed by former paramilitaries. However, one of the most potent legacies of the Provisionals' construction of what Kevin Bean has termed a 'state within a state' within nationalist working-class areas has come from their strategy for dealing with criminality through 'a contradictory mixture of revolutionary rhetoric, traditional communal punishment and direct action'.[19] The IRA presided over a system of harsh punishments and vigilantism on a range of issues from domestic violence and sexual abuse through to drug dealing and teenage drinking and rowdyism. The brave new world of 'peace process' Northern Ireland has not seen any of these problems disappear, and the persistence of a strong reflexive distrust of the police, despite its post-Patten makeover, has been increasingly exploited by the party's republican enemies. Recent IMC reports record a considerable number of 'dissident' shootings, assaults and threats against alleged drug dealers and other 'anti-social elements'.[20] This form of activity can be seen in part as a reaction to the transition to a new 'human rights compliant' system of policing and justice with which Sinn Féin has identified. However, it is also part of a wider challenge to the new dispensation in Northern Ireland whose most effective focus is on exploiting the decomposition of the Provisionals' most important power base: the so-called communities of resistance,[21] the nationalist working-class areas they hegemonized and policed.

A Culture of Insubordination

While McIntyre's critique of the utility of violence in the current situation will not be congenial to those engaged in or justifying the continuance of armed struggle, there is much in his dissection of the Provisionals' history since the 1980s that fortifies what can be termed a culture of insubordination, a culture which is fed by a mélange of individuals and groups that are bitterly dismissive of the Sinn Féin project. This culture of insubordination includes a range of activities from debates and discussion groups to marches and demonstrations against 'British occupation' along with street riots and anti-Orange Order manifestations. It has developed in a manner which has mirrored the twists and turns of the peace process and the deepening involvement of Sinn Féin in the governance and administration of Northern Ireland. A thread running through it has been a focus on Provisional involvement in policing their core bases of support. As mentioned above, before the ceasefires the IRA had played a central role in dealing with 'anti-social behaviour' and so-called touts (informers) and drug dealers. On ceasefire, such activities had to be reined in but did not disappear altogether. Instead their focus became more overtly politically directed. This was most brutally clear in the killings, abductions, beatings and interrogations of members of other republican groups committed to reinstalling armed struggle. McIntyre and Tommy Gorman, another leading former IRA man now turned bitter critic of Sinn Féin, had highlighted that it was the Provisionals who had shot Joe O'Connor dead in Ballymurphy in October 2000. For whistle-blowing, McIntyre and his family were visited and threatened by the leading Provisional enforcer in Belfast while their house was picketed by a group of 'enraged' locals.[22] Despite this the *Blanket* continued to carry stories of Provisional action against 'dissidents'. One concerned a West Belfast man, Brendan Shannon, who supported 'traditional republican values'. Shannon was a former Provisional prisoner and hunger striker who had resigned from Sinn Féin in 1995 over its alleged break with republican objectives:

> I was a member of the Sticks [Official IRA] at sixteen and I left them because they called a cease-fire and it was clear that they had got nothing. But I am not some rabid militarist. I supported the political strategy that the leadership promised would deliver. I did not leave the Provos because they gave up the war. I left them because they gave up republicanism.[23]

He was now under threat from the IRA for alleged membership of the Continuity IRA. Shannon spoke bitterly in an interview with McIntyre:

> Touts and drug dealers get a better deal in republican communities than republicans who oppose the present strategy ... if you are a dissident republican then you are scum.[24]

Shannon received rough treatment at the hands of the Provisionals. He was kidnapped and threatened with death if he got involved in any action against the security forces and later summoned to another meeting to be told that he was not to be seen in the company of any more than four dissidents or he would be killed. This was one of a number of such cases, which included the killing of the Armagh Real IRA member Gareth O'Connor who went missing in May 2003 and whose body was found in his car in Newry Canal in June 2005,[25] and Paul Quinn from Cullyhanna in south Armagh whose parents claimed that he was abducted and beaten to death by 'members of the Provisional movement' in October 2007.[26] The critics of Sinn Féin also focused on attempts by leading members of the party and the IRA to police anti-Orange protests during the Province's marching season. Here mainstream republicans faced a blowback from changes in strategy in the 1990s when after the IRA ceasefire republicans were encouraged to play a leading role in the development of nationalist residents groups in areas like the Garvaghy Road in Portadown and the Lower Ormeau in Belfast to contest the right of the Orange Order to parade contentious routes.[27] The rise of the residents' groups was part of a process described by Neil Southern: 'the political violence waged by republican groups during the Troubles has been strategically replaced with a form of culturally motivated "warfare".'[28] However, just as political violence left a bitter legacy, so did the strategy to shift away from it. Having mobilized communities in the 1990s, the Provisionals, with power in Stormont in their sights, moved to demonstrate their 'responsibility' by controlling the very militancy they had only recently encouraged. The result was clear during anti-Orange disturbances in Ardoyne in 2002 in which leading Sinn Féin figures along with IRA members from all over Belfast were drafted in to control local youths spoiling for a pitched battle with the 'Orangees'. A local resident was quoted in the *Blanket*:

> On the day of the march lots of 'RA' [IRA)] from all over the city were

drafted in to control the situation on the road. The people's blood was boiling at the idea of these Orangees walking up the road ... When the Orangemen were walking by, the 'RA' turned on us. Young people were beaten up the Crumlin Road ... They [PSNI] didn't have to draw their batons as Republicans did it for them.[29]

McIntyre portrayed the clash between IRA members and the young rioters of Ardoyne as a precursor of Sinn Féin's full-blooded endorsement of policing and justice structures: 'Nothing is more certain than that the pull of the RUC structure will prove irresistible to Sinn Féin, which will fall like an apple right into the rotten barrel it so long railed against.'[30]

Policing would be the issue that gave Sinn Féin's critics an energizing focus. It became the prism through which the different strands of anti-Provisional critique could fuse powerfully. The explosiveness of the issue was in part derived from the way Sinn Féin had attempted to manage the peace process both before and after the Good Friday Agreement. Managing the transition to 'unarmed struggle' involved an emphasis on the transitional nature of the 1998 Agreement with its allegedly inbuilt dynamic towards unity through a mixture of all-Ireland institutions and a 'greening' of the North based on a mixture of favourable demography and a policy of dividing and demoralizing unionism.[31] This strategy seemed irresistible down to 2005. In the North it had established an effective veto on political developments, in the process destroying the support base of its main Unionist interlocutor, David Trimble. Its role as the party that could deliver the IRA had given it centrality in negotiations with the two governments and the White House and this had brought major electoral benefits north and south. However, in 2005 the expansion of Sinn Féin ended as the fall-out from the Northern Bank robbery in late 2004 and the murder of Robert McCartney in January 2005 and concerns about republican criminality combined to damage the party's prospects. The resulting IRA announcement in July 2005 of 'an end to the armed campaign' followed by the decommissioning of its weapons meant that Sinn Féin had lost a prime source of political leverage at the same time as it faced the DUP as the dominant unionist party. The St Andrews Agreement concluded in the autumn of 2006 had a DUP–Sinn Féin concordat implicit within it.[32] But, although devolved institutions were restored in March 2007, this was only possible after Sinn Féin had accepted the DUP's *sine qua non* of acceptance of and support for the PSNI. In October 2006 Sinn Féin announced that it would begin a process of consultation with its members over the St Andrews proposals and a special Ard Fheis in January saw the leadership obtain 90 per cent support for a motion endorsing the policing and justice structures within Northern Ireland. Devolution since then has been singularly bereft of any substantive achievements in public policy. Rather the Sinn Féin–DUP duopoly has been dominated by the imposition of a series of communal vetoes, which unfortunately for republicans, have been on a series of issues of key symbolic importance: an Irish Language Act, the redevelopment of the Maze prison site as 'conflict resolution' centre, and the devolution of policing and justice. As a result it has appeared that unionism has been the dominant negative force.

This is the context in which long-standing criticisms of Sinn Féin by its republican critics have acquired a dangerous new potency.

New Political Fronts

One manifestation of this was the emergence of new organizations that sought to unify the disparate anti-Sinn Féin constituency and expand its potential recruitment base. As the Provisionals edged closer to full acceptance of the PSNI, a group of 'Concerned Republicans' organized a series of debates on the theme 'Policing: A Bridge too Far?' in republican heartlands in west Belfast, Derry and Toome. Sinn Féin participated in the debates but the majority of speakers were critics including the disaffected founding member of the Provisionals and former MLA, John Kelly, Tony Catney, another former Sinn Féin member from Belfast, Tony McPhillips of RSF and Francie Mackey of the 32 County Sovereignty Movement.[33] Catney was to emerge as a key figure in anti-Provisional mobilization in Belfast. A brother-in-law of Gerry Kelly, he had been a member of the Provisionals for 37 years when he resigned from Sinn Féin. He had served 16 years for murder and on his release had occupied a number of relatively senior positions in Sinn Féin including being the party's representative in Brussels in the mid 1990s and then its director of elections for Northern Ireland.[34] The 'Concerned Republicans' had challenged Sinn Féin in the Northern Irish Assembly elections in March with their three candidates averaging 2.3 per cent of the vote. In Derry's Foyle constituency Peggy O'Hara, the mother of the dead 1981 hunger striker, Patsy O'Hara, obtained 4.4 per cent of the vote.[35]

The 'Concerned Republicans' were encouraged by the Derry result,[36] and post-election they were part of a 'Republican Unity Initiative', which held a joint commemoration at the republican shrine at Bodenstown, between them, the 32CSM and the IRSP. This was aimed at 'the development of a radical Republican alternative to the failed politics of partition and the Good Friday Agreement'.[37] Out of this came a Republican Network for Unity, which focused on criticism of Sinn Féin's embrace of the 'RUC/PSNI' and mainstream republicanism's failure to challenge the 'British war machine' symbolized by the building of a large new MI5 headquarters in Belfast. RNU continued to bring the different anti-Sinn Féin forces together and at the Bodenstown commemoration in 2008 Marian Price declared that the debate as to where 'former republicans' had travelled to was, she declared, over with the Provisional leadership now part of the establishment.[38] The 32CSM had produced a document on republican unity which emphasized the importance of putting to one side past conflicts and ideological differences and forging a 'practical and pragmatic approach'.[39]

Tony Catney emerged as a leading member of RNU giving the main speech at their Easter Rising Commemoration in Derry in 2009.[40] In July 2009 there was three days of rioting in Ardoyne sparked by opposition to an Orange parade, during which shots were fired at the PSNI. Sinn Féin sources claimed that Catney and the RIRA had played a central role in organizing the rioting and he responded with an interview with a local newspaper in which he denied it declaring that 'Time is not right for a military campaign' and that 'the RIRA did not exist in Belfast apart from one person'.[41] The RNU's position on armed struggle was supportive in principle but publicly cautious. After the shootings of the soldiers and a policeman it issued a 'position for debate' in which it stated: 'We acknowledge the right of Irish people to resist British occupation using a wide range of tactics, including armed struggle'. But it then added 'a word of caution':

> Embarking on an armed campaign comes with many burdens and risks both to the volunteers involved and the community from which they come. Such a campaign requires a far-reaching strategy, material resources, logistics and an effective PR that communicates and gives guidance to the community. Those who conduct such a campaign also have a duty to monitor the mood of the people, assess conditions within the community and be able to organise to meet the need of the community.[42]

Such caution reflected the continuing fragmentation of the anti-Sinn Féin constituency and also the fact that RNU was clearly hoping by its activities to build up a critical mass by encouraging more defections from IRA volunteers who had, despite disillusion over policy shifts, remained with the mainstream. Such hopes would have been encouraged by the potent negative symbolic charge that Sinn Féin's embrace of policing and justice structures had given to the psyche of most Provisionals. The effects were compounded by a wider sense of disquiet with what appeared to be the decomposition of the mainstream movement's project.

This had emerged with particular intensity in the Republic where Sinn Féin had moved from electoral marginality in the early 1990s to a position where in the 2004 Dáil election it had five TDs, an MEP and 7 per cent of the national vote.[43] This upward electoral trajectory was on the back of Adams' and McGuinness' centrality in the politics of the peace process. But the political capital Sinn Féin had accumulated began to be depleted by a combination of the feeling amongst the southern electorate that the North had been 'solved' and the negative publicity surrounding the Northern Bank robbery and the murder of Robert McCartney. It was also the case that Adams' role as 'peacemaker' in the North did not insulate him from his less than sure grasp of the details of southern politics, particularly those to do with economic and social policy issues as was embarrassingly revealed during a television debate amongst the party leaders during the 2007 general election. Prior to the election, Sinn Féin had held out high expectations of a major breakthrough with Martin McGuinness that his party would be 'the story of the election' and did not demur from common media speculation that after it the party would be 'king makers' courted by Fianna Fáil to be partners in a coalition.[44] The party's strategy for Irish unity was increasingly based on the notion of it being in government north and south and so being able to energize and develop the 'all-Ireland' dimension of the Northern state. At a Sinn Féin conference in County Monaghan the party's general secretary, Declan Kearney, gave a presentation: 'Power in Ireland: The Road to Power' in which he predicted 'the party in government in the North, in government in the South, if that is our wish.'[45] In fact, the election result was a major blow to such pretensions: rather than double or even triple its number of seats, as some commentators had predicted, it actually lost one[46] and subsequently lost its European seat in Dublin to an unreconstructed Trotskyist.

The party's single-minded pursuit of electoral gains in order to achieve seats in a coalition government had, some of its militants believed, resulted in a forsaking of its radical vocation and this produced yet another set of defections. Éirígí (Rise Up), which emerged in Dublin in 2006, was based on a number of disaffected younger Sinn Féin activists. Although few in number – a founding member claimed it had six members initially – they did include a former Sinn Féin national organizer and the sister of Mary Lou McDonald, the party's MEP for Dublin and its rising star in the Republic. Éirígí's focus was on grass-roots activism and the development of 'revolutionary politics', which, it claimed, Sinn Féin had turned its back on in its single-minded desire to get into a coalition government with Fianna Fáil. Although in the 1980s, the Provisionals had gone through a leftist phase, the shift towards a pan-nationalist strategy and the concentration of its leadership on the peace process and seats in governmental had led its critics to detect a single-minded focus on governmental office and the forsaking of its earlier 'revolutionary project'.[47] This 'right turn', its critics claimed, was associated with an authoritarian internal culture and leadership cult around Gerry Adams which stifled internal debate. When Éirígí launched itself as a 'truly revolutionary party' at its inaugural Ard Fheis in Dublin in May 2007 its constitution proclaimed its 'socialist republican philosophy' and its web-based news sheet is headed with a quotation from the Irish socialist republican martyr James Connolly.[48] Although the socialist republican tradition has been a significant enough current within republicanism, an attempt to criticize Sinn Féin from a leftist anti-imperialist perspective might not have caused serious tremors in Connolly House (SF HQ in Belfast). However, what did concern Sinn Féin was Éirígí's expansion to the North and adoption of a strategy of tension in support of its 'Campaign for British Withdrawal'. In November 2008 it organized a protest against a homecoming parade of the Royal Irish Regiment in Belfast. Its threatened protest was sufficient to ensure that Sinn Féin, which had criticized the homecoming parade but not proposed opposition, was forced to organize a march of its own. Loyalist counter-demonstrations of support for the RIR raised the possibility of serious inter-communal conflict although a massive police presence prevented more than a few skirmishes. The speaker at the Éirígí rally was Brenda Downes, the widow of Sean Downes, who had been killed by a plastic bullet during a Sinn Féin rally in 1984. Also there was Alex McCrory, a former hunger striker.[49]

Éirígí also attracted some prominent former Provisionals outside Belfast notably the Lurgan republican Colin Duffy and Brendan MacCionnaith, the spokesman for the Garvaghy Road residents' group during the various confrontations at Drumcree. In August 2008 Duffy had been interviewed on local television about serious rioting in the Drumbeg estate, Lurgan, after vehicles were hijacked and set alight. On previous occasions hijackings, abandoned cars and bomb scares had been used by both the RIRA and CIRA to lure PSNI members into ambushes and the heavy police presence in Drumbeg was now blamed by Duffy for causing the violence.[50] Éirígí with its emphasis on popular mobilization against manifestations of British rule in Northern Ireland was a possible point of connection between violent republicanism and the sort of irruption of 'nationalist youth' that mainstream republicanism had once been happy to encourage and exploit. Although its web news-sheet does not contain a position on 'armed struggle' the organization's relation to violent republicanism was made clear in a keynote speech delivered by its chairperson in Belfast to a meeting in west Belfast the day after the CIRA's shooting of PSNI constable, Stephen Carroll, when he declared, 'Those who relied solely on constitutional politics within the British framework ninety years ago were doomed to failure. The same is true today.'[51]

Remembering the Past – Delegitimizing the Present

The commemoration of those who died in the struggle against British rule has been a central quality of the republican tradition: Patrick Pearse's concept of the political martyr – 'the laughing gesture of the young man . . . (who) is going into battle or climbing to a gibbet . . . an eternal gesture in Irish history.'[52] Provisional commemorative practices did not stop with the peace process and indeed it might be suggested that they attempted to sanctify current strategies by association with the memory of dead volunteers. A significant example was the launch of a DVD on the life of one of the Provisionals' most formidable members, Seamus McIlwaine. McIlwaine was the leading IRA figure in the Monaghan/south Fermanagh area in the late 1970s and mid '80s. According to *An Phoblacht*, 'by the time of his death (he was shot dead by the SAS in 1986) he had attained legendary status amongst the republican communities of border areas . . . where he led a relentless assault on the British military machine.'[53] In fact, according to Moloney at the time of his death, he was part of a group of dissenting militants centred on Jim Lynagh, also from Monaghan and the leading east Tyrone IRA man, Pádraig McKearney.

They had opposed the dropping of abstention and Adams' concept of armed struggle as 'armed propaganda', instead advocating a 'total war' along the border to make it ungovernable.[54] In 1987, despite Adams and McGuinness' attendance at his funeral and the Provisionals' erection of monuments to him at the site of his death and in Monaghan, McIlwaine's father, a veteran republican and a member of Monaghan County Council, became chairman of the Seamus McElwaine Cumman of Republican Sinn Féin.[55]

The film, *The Life and Death of an Irish Activist*, was launched at a time when disquiet in republican ranks over the policing issue was building up. It dwelt on McElwaine's military skills and his role in the mass escape from the Maze Prison in 1983 when, according to the leading Belfast Provisional, Brendan McFarlane, McElwaine guided a group of escapees in a long cross-country trek to the border. The SAS operation, in which McElwaine was killed, was narrated in detail by Sean Lynch, who had been seriously injured in the same incident. Lynch, who had been OC of the Provisionals in the Maze Prison from 1992–95, had become a leading member of Sinn Féin on the Fermanagh Council and was to join the county's District Policing Partnership in 2008.[56] However, in lauding past republican martyrs there was an inherent risk that the party's critics would pose the question of whether their sacrifice could be justified in terms of a result that fell far short of basic republican objectives. This was summed up in the withering riposte of Bobby Sands' sister, Bernadette Sands-McKevitt to the Good Friday Agreement:

> Bobby did not die for cross-border bodies with executive powers. He did not die for Nationalists to be equal British citizens within the Northern Ireland state. Bobby did not die for peace, he died for independence.[57]

The two-edged nature of commemoration was apparent in the case of McElwaine, who the film had glorified as a 'soldier of the Republic'. Inevitably, some republicans raised the issue of what the deaths of McElwaine and others like him had actually achieved. One such republican who featured in the film was Bernice Swift, a Sinn Féin councillor in Fermanagh who co-ordinated Fírinne, a group campaigning on the issue of victims of state violence. In October 2007 she was suspended from the party for criticizing the DPPs as 'meaningless talking shops'. She subsequently resigned and Sinn Féin in the county also lost another councillor and an MLA over the policing issue.[58] Swift and Fírinne have participated in a series of protests against local meetings of the Policing Board across Northern Ireland in which Éirígí, RNU and 32CSM have all participated.[59]

Cillian McGrattan has argued that the peace process and the Good Friday Agreement transformed republican politics but not in a progressive, accommodating sense:

> Rather it institutionalised an airbrushed historical narrative and a revisionist approach to the past that sought to legitimise republican violence.[60]

The politics of republican commemoration could be used to claim the imprimatur of fallen comrades for current policies. Sean Lynch undoubtedly possessed the credentials of someone who had barely survived his involvement in armed struggle but, as with other iconic figures like McGuinness and Gerry Kelly, the moral capital they had accumulated risked depletion if it was used too obviously to justify the exigencies of constitutional politics. Lynch might proclaim that the 'war is over' but his claim that it had obtained fundamental republican objectives relied on the assertion that 'The union is hollowed out as an increasingly confident nationalist community takes co-ownership of the Northern and all-Ireland institutions ... the North is being demilitarized and the police are coming under the account of the Irish people rather than the securocrats'.[61] At best, his was a realistic prognosis for a significant Sinn Féin role in the governance of the North. It left issues of British sovereignty largely untouched as the continuing role of MI5 and the British special forces demonstrated.

Éirígí was in the forefront of challenging the Provisionals' dominance of republican commemoration. The former hunger striker, Alex McCrory, was involved in Éirígí's campaign to challenge Sinn Féin's credentials on an issue of epochal significance – the 1981 hunger strike. They were able to exploit an impressive demolition of the Provisional narrative which depicted the death of Bobby Sands and his comrades as one of the greatest imperialist crimes, one perpetrated by perhaps the greatest hate-figure in their rogues gallery of British prime ministers, Margaret Thatcher. This was the book published in 2005 by Richard O'Rawe, the PRO for the hunger strikers, who now claimed that Thatcher, after the death of the first four strikers, had sent in a new and improved offer to settle the conflict. This he claimed was rejected by Gerry Adams and the Army Council, who wanted to continue the strike to ensure the election of a replacement for Bobby Sands in the Fermanagh and South

Tyrone by-election caused by his death. The remaining six deaths were unnecessary and the prisoners used as 'cannon fodder' to achieve the political ambitions of Adams, 'thus kick-starting the shift away from armed struggle towards constitutional politics.'[62] In 2008 Éirígí organized a series of hunger strike meetings throughout Northern Ireland and the Republic to coincide with the release of Steve McQueen's film, *Hunger*. Speakers included Tommy McKearney and the former prominent Belfast Provisional, Bernard Fox.[63] Commemorations have been and remain a central politico-cultural practice in reproducing the republican tradition and Provisionalism had hitherto easily dominated those that came out of the Troubles. But the challenge on the hunger strikes was not the only area of contest – the emergence of the degree to which the republican movement had been penetrated by the security forces was another embarrassing sub-current of present and future challenges.

Republicanism: Alive or Dying?

> There is no crisis. This is so because there is no longer any social phenomenon that we may term republican. The present pockets of the faithful exist here and there, for the most part taking cultural form. But as a social phenomenon of any political import republicanism has ceased to function.[64]

Given Anthony McIntyre's sharp critical analysis of the republican mainstream and his own important doctoral work on the origins of the Provisionals, considerable weight has to be given to his sceptical view of anti-Provisional republicanism. The IMC has also pointed out the history of factionalism within the RIRA and the amorphous nature of the anti-Sinn Féin constituency which, together with the lack of strategic coordination between RIRA and CIRA, leads them to conclude that 'they do not therefore present some coherent organization like PIRA ... much less do they have anything like the capacity to mount a consistent and substantial campaign.'[65] As we have seen, key spokesmen for dissenting groups like Éirígí and RNU have raised questions about whether at present the conditions exist for the prosecution of armed struggle. As Sean Lynch pointed out in his apologia for participation in the Policing Partnership, the position of Catholics within the Northern state has been transformed compared to what it was in the 1970s when the

Provisionals' campaign took off. 'The Orange State as I knew it is gone'.[66] Tommy McKearney makes a similar point in an evaluation of the political achievement of Gerry Adams:

> Although criticised by traditionalists for compromising on what was seen as bedrock principles, Adams's role in bringing an end to the IRA's armed campaign was welcomed by a majority of northern republicans. After a quarter century of pitiless struggle, there was a feeling in those communities that the war had run its course . . . the IRA campaign had not ended as on previous occasions, in dejection and defeat. The Peace Process did not remove partition or the union but the hard-pressed republican grassroots believed Sinn Fein's president had delivered a tolerable démarche.
> . . . Adams and his party have played a large part in undermining the old Orange state . . . The party's view has to be taken into account on all matters in the 6-Counties and in many instances the party exercises real influence over the direction of local affairs.[67]

The transformation of the position of Northern Catholics has been profound and wide-ranging from the equalization of economic conditions to political and cultural equality within a consociational framework. This means that the 'objective conditions' for an armed struggle like that of the Provisionals do not exist. However, violent republicanism, capable of being a continuous if sporadic challenge to the state, has shown a capacity to reproduce itself over the decades independently of changes in political and economic and social circumstances. Indeed, this was the case for a large part of the period from the end of the Irish Civil War to the outbreak of the Troubles.

This, in part, reflects the stubborn persistence of republican memory which is deeply rooted in the practice of commemoration. However, this has an uneven geographical basis with traditionalist sentiment being strongest in the border counties of Northern Ireland and the Republic and in such former bastions of republican intransigence as Kerry, Cork and Limerick. RSF's branches are heavily concentrated in the west and south-west of the Republic where anti-Treatyite support was strongest during the Irish Civil War.[68] In Northern Ireland, CIRA's most high-profile attack was its killing of a member of the PSNI in Craigavon, an area where it had been increasingly active since 2008, orchestrating public disorder and disrupting rail traffic with bombs and hoax devices.[69] Apart from the Craigavon/Lurgan its other main area was south-Fermanagh/Monaghan where it left substantial bombs near Newtownbutler in October 2008 and Rosslea in April 2009.[70] Both bombs failed to explode, but caused disruption as it took some time for them to be dealt with by the bomb squad.

The RIRA represents the most substantial challenge. Although the CIRA has a longer history, its possibilities of growth were tightly controlled by the determination of the Provisionals to stop RSF developing a military wing. The management of the transformation of the Provisionals by Adams and his allies was largely successful in keeping the vast majority of IRA volunteers loyal until 1997. The disaster of the Omagh bomb and the subsequent divisions in the RIRA ensured that its attractive power was extremely limited in comparison with what appeared to be the unstoppable upward political strategy of Adams and McGuinness in the 1998–2005 period. However, the standing down and effective disbandment of the IRA combined with the subsequent embrace of policing and the stalling and retreat of Sinn Féin in the Republic has changed radically the political context in which violent republicanism can operate. It has increased the leakage from PIRA to the RIRA.

However, it remains the case that the RIRA like CIRA relies disproportionately on support in the border counties of Northern Ireland and the Republic. It was in these areas where the perceived affront of partition was a physical reality that throughout the history of Northern Ireland there was a substantial constituency for physical force republicanism. In these border Catholic-majority areas the role of the IRA as community 'defenders' did not have the same salience as in Belfast and Derry. This has meant that border republicanism is likely to find the notion of ethnic parity of esteem at the centre of the Good Friday Agreement less appealing than republicans from nationalist working-class areas of Belfast where forcing the 'Orangees' to accept Sinn Féin's 'equality agenda', which aimed at parity of treatment for republicans and loyalists, might seem a communal victory even if it comes within the Union. These were the areas where it was possible to conceive, as in 1956, of an armed campaign to wrest control of territory from the state and where the guerrilla dimension of republicanism was a reality in a way it could never be in Ballymurphy and Andersonstown. The class basis of the IRA was also different as support and involvement went higher up the social ladder than in urban areas. The sons and daughters of farmers and the Catholic petty bourgeoisie provided a leadership stratum that was distinct.

It was easier for IRA men from the Republic to operate along the border than in Belfast and this in itself may have influenced the type of republican ideology that dominated. Such republicans came from rural and small town communities with little tradition of trade unionism and a predominant ideological conservatism, which meant that the social radicalism that appealed in Dublin and Belfast to at least a substantial minority of IRA volunteers was weak or non-existent. Border republicanism focused on territorial issues and the military means to end partition.

This border republican tradition was to be significantly strengthened during the post-1969 period. After 'Operation Motorman' had removed the 'no-go' areas in Belfast and Derry in 1973, the IRA's capacity to operate in urban areas was increasingly constrained. The border became a major strategic resource for the Provisionals, allowing relative ease of operation and retreat and providing a plentiful supply of easy targets among the locally recruited, part-time members of the UDR and RUC. The border counties were the base for some of the most proficient ASUs operating from late 1970s onwards, most notably those in south Armagh/Louth, south Fermanagh/Monaghan and Tyrone/Monaghan.[71] Theirs was the world of the 'soldiers' like Lynagh and McElaiwne, not of the incipient politicians and party apparatchiks of Sinn Féin who were often regarded with a mixture of contempt and suspicion. It was no accident that the first Chief of Staff of the RIRA, Kevin McKevitt, was from the border town of Dundalk[72] and that Seamus McGrane, his closest ally at the time of the 1997 split, was also from County Louth.[73]

A number of those arrested for involvement in RIRA activity have come from parts of Northern Ireland and the Republic close to the border. The dominant figure in Fermanagh is John James Connolly from Newtownbutler, who was sentenced to 14 years in 2002 for possession of a Mark 15 'Barrack Buster' mortar bomb. Released in November 2007, his supporters in 32CSM claimed he was subject to constant harassment from the 'RUC/PSNI'.[74] Connolly was one of six republicans listed in a leaked government document which claimed they were key figures in the RIRA. The others included Don Mullan, a former Provisional active in the Dungannon area of East Tyrone, and Kevin Barry Murphy, also a former east Tyrone Provisional. Mullan, Murphy and Brendan O'Connor from Pomeroy had all been acquitted of RIRA membership in 2004, when they alleged at their trial that O'Connor had informed on them to the PSNI.[75]

Fermanagh and east Tyrone have been joined more recently by the former

Provisional stronghold of south Armagh as areas of increasing support for the dissidents. The murder of Gareth O'Connor and Paul Quinn were stark examples of the continuing dominance of PIRA down to the middle of the decade. However, since then there have been signs of growing dissent. Initially this was associated with the open challenge of Quinn's parents and their supporters to local Sinn Féin representatives, particularly the MP, MLA and Stormont minister, Conor Murphy, to condemn the killing and admit that it was done by the Provisionals. Subsequently, it has expanded into the vandalization of Murphy's home and car and eventually to the use of IEDs in Jonesborough in September 2008 and Forkhill in August 2009. Later that month armed and masked RIRA members mounted a roadblock in Meigh to hand out leaflets threatening anyone who gave information to the PSNI, the Garda or Sinn Féin.[76] A report in the *Sunday Times* claimed that there had been significant defections in south Armagh including experienced snipers and the bomb-makers who were involved in the IRA's attacks on the City of London in the 1990s.[77]

The recent growth of violent republicanism is thus heavily reliant on its membership in border areas and part of the scepticism about its possibilities on the part of commentators like McIntyre and McKearney is its continuing weakness in the urban heartlands of Provisionalism, particularly Belfast. However, we have already seen some evidence of increasing activity even in former Provisional strongholds like Ardoyne and Ballymurphy. It is also necessary to consider the analysis of those who have argued that the peace process has not dissipated the strong ethno-sectarian feelings that are particularly concentrated in urban interface areas around issues of space and territory. These are examples of what Robert Rothstein has called 'the conflict syndrome' – 'a set of attitudes, assumptions and beliefs that become embedded over decades of bitter conflict and are difficult to unlearn even if some kind of peace agreement... has been signed.'[78] It is no coincidence that republican violence in Belfast has a symbiotic relation to the mobilization of Catholic grievances over a number of contested Orange parades in north and west Belfast. Sectarian feeling in these interface areas has the potential to generate street level conflict and violence and provides a pool of potential recruits from young working-class Catholics. This group is also open to the claim that Sinn Féin has merely shifted from justifying the harsh justice of IRA punishment squads to defending 'RUC-PSNI' harassment. The significant anti-PSNI rioting in Mayobridge, County Down, in February 2009, was reported with some relish by *Saoirse*.[79] In April, after serious rioting in Belfast and Lurgan in response to arrests following the shootings of British soldiers and the policeman, *Saoirse* praised 'the remarkable courage of local youths in resisting British forces of occupation'.[80] The IMC has noted similar exploitation of sectarianism in republican involvement in the intimidation of Protestant families in Ballymena and the widespread vandalization of Orange halls.[81]

Conclusion

As the first anniversary of the republican killings of two soldiers and a policeman approached, the Republic's Minister of Justice, Dermot Ahern, warned that the Real IRA and the Continuity IRA posed as serious a threat as any paramilitary organization during the Troubles.[82] This seems to have reflected the government's efforts to persuade politicians in Northern Ireland that the security threat was so severe that there was no justification for further delay in the devolution of policing and justice powers to Belfast. This chapter has argued that, while the threat does not and will not approach that represented by the Provisional IRA in the 1970s and 1980s, it is not a passing hiccup in the peace process. It will be more like the nagging but only occasionally chronic IRA challenge that faced both states between 1923 and the 1950s. The devolution of policing and justice powers in April 2010 will not have the positive effects on stemming support for the republican ultras that both Sinn Féin and the NIO have claimed. In the cynical words of a local journalist about the forthcoming appointment of the Alliance Party's leader as the new Justice Minister: 'Will the dissidents really disappear . . . at the thought of David Ford getting on their case? Unlikely you might think.'[83] Those who support violence are indifferent to whether the policing and justice powers are wielded by a British direct rule minister or what they will depict as a local agent of 'imperialist' rule.

The possibility that the intra-executive wrangles that have paralyzed decision-making in other areas could now extend into the area of security policy must be a matter of concern, although the Chief Constable's operational independence together with the fact that M15, which is playing a key role in gathering intelligence on the RIRA and CIRA, is not answerable to a local minister may mitigate this danger. There is some evidence that both CIRA and RIRA have been able to exploit the running down of the British Army's presence in border areas and that the PSNI has not fully adjusted to the serious level of threat that is now posed in these areas. The extent of the problem was revealed after the successful car-bomb attack on Newry Courthouse in February 2010 when the PSNI were criticized for delay in response and follow-up. This led one Sinn Féin member of the Policing Board to suggest the need for the formation of a special unit of 'specially trained officers' to deal with the terrorist threat, leading to its republican critics alleging that it was in favour of what it used to denounce as 'state death squads'.[84]

The dissidents should be seen, not as an anachronistic threat to the peace process but as a product of its essentially communal/sectarian logic. The conflict is now being managed by the empowerment of two militantly ethno-nationalist blocs. The leadership of neither has resiled from their fundamentally antagonistic understandings of Northern Ireland's past and its future direction. Thus the leading Belfast republican, Bobby Storey, proclaims that Sinn Féin in government is gradually dismantling 'the Protestant state' and creating the conditions for a united Ireland.[85] Whether these claims have any basis in reality is not the point. What they demonstrate is that mainstream republicans will continue to foreground the 'transitional nature' of the present settlement and the centrality of nationalist and sectarian issues. For the majority of the North's Catholic population, rhetorical indulgence of thirty-two county aspirations is sufficient provided they are satisfied of 'parity of esteem' within the Northern Ireland state. However, a significant minority remains which is determined to use Sinn Féin's proclaimed objectives to provide justification for the continuation of violence. In working-class areas of Belfast and Derry they can rely on a large reservoir of disaffection and militant anti-Orangeism, particularly but not solely among young males. With the region facing prospective cuts of dimensions not experienced since 1945, there is little prospect of the threat diminishing in the foreseeable future.

Notes

1. Murray, G. and Tonge, J. *Sinn Fein and the SDLP: From Alienation to Participation* (London: Hurst 2004), p. 219; English, R. *Armed Struggle: The History of the IRA* (London: Macmillan, 2003), p. 313.
2. Jackson, A. *Ireland: 1798–1998* (Oxford: Blackwell, 1999), p. 417.

3. Alonso, R. *The IRA and Armed Struggle* (London: Routledge, 2006), p. 129.
4. 'Fearghal Ó hAnluain remembered in Monaghan', *Saoirse*, February 2009, p. 7.
5. 'Provos call on nationalists to inform', *Saoirse*, March 2009, p. 2.
6. McIntyre, A. 'Be honest Mr Adams: You no longer have a strategy for a United Ireland', *Parliamentary Brief*, April 2009.
7. Moloney, E. *A Secret History of the IRA* (Harmondsworth: Penguin 2002), p. 305.
8. Ibid.
9. Frampton, M. *The Long March: The Political Strategy of Sinn Fein, 1981–2007* (London: Palgrave Macmillan, 2009), pp. 62–3.
10. *Saoirse*, February 2009.
11. Neither exists any more but selections are to be found in McIntyre's website: *The Pensive Quill*.
12. McIntyre (2009).
13. O'Ruairc, L. 'Speaking Truth to Power', *Sovereign Nation*, May–June 2009.
14. McGladdery, G. *The Provisional IRA in England: The Bombing Campaign 1973–1997* (Dublin: Irish Academic Press, 2006), p. 223.
15. Ibid., p. 219.
16. International Monitoring Commission, *Twentieth Report of the Independent Monitoring Commission*, 10 November 2008.
17. International Monitoring Commission, *Twenty-Second Report of the Independent Monitoring Commission*, 4 November 2009.
18. 'IRA Easter Statement', *Sovereign Nation*, May–June 2009.
19. Bean, K. *The New Politics of Sinn Féin* (Liverpool: Liverpool University Press, 2007), p. 111.
20. Independent Monitoring Commission, *Twenty-First Report of the Independent Monitoring Commission*, 7 May 2009.
21. Bean, *New Politics of Sinn Fein*, pp. 94–8.
22. Bean, *New Politics of Sinn Fein*, p. 112.
23. 'Living in Fear', *The Blanket*, 15 September 2003, reprinted in McIntyre, A. *Good Friday: The Death of Irish Republicanism* (New York: Ausubo Press, 2008), p. 139.
24. McIntyre, A. 'Hammering Dissent', *The Blanket*, 5 January 2003.
25. Diarmaid McDermott, 'Man on Real IRA charge subject to murder

probe', *Irish Independent*, 14 January 2004; 'Adams silent on IRA murder claims', *BBC News Channel*, 14 June 2005.
26. 'Family blames IRA for murder', *News Letter*, 22 October 2007.
27. Kaufmann, E. P. *The Orange Order: a Contemporary Northern Irish History* (Oxford: Oxford University Press, 2007), pp. 236–86.
28. Southern, N. 'Territoriality, Alienation and Loyalist Decommissioning: The Case of the Shankill in Protestant West Belfast', *Terrorism and Political Violence*, 20, 1 (2008), 66–86.
29. 'Out of the Ashes of Armed Struggle Arose the Stormonistas and they fought . . . Ardoyne youth', *The Blanket*, 5 September 2002, in McIntyre, *Good Friday: The Death of Irish Republicanism*, p. 125.
30. Ibid.
31. Frampton, *The Long March*, p. 185.
32. Bew, P. *The Making and the Remaking of the Good Friday Agreement* (Dublin: Liffey Press, 2007).
33. Frampton, M. 'After Truce and Treaty: The Return of Militant Republicanism', paper delivered at a seminar organized by the US Institute of Peace, London, November 2009.
34. Information from McIntyre, A. 'Felon Setting', *The Pensive Quill*, 25 July 2009, and Breen, S. 'Provos Move to Smash Dissent', *Sunday Tribune*, 3 December 2006.
35. Frampton, 'After Truce and Treaty'.
36. Video on 'Republican Unity Meeting, Derry', 13 May 2007, www.youtube.com/watch?v=9b69csAZWSA (accessed 26 January 2010).
37. 'Republican Unity Bodenstown Commemoration – Small but Significant Step Taken', *Sovereign Nation*, July–August 2007, quoted in Frampton, 'After Truce and Treaty'.
38. Ibid.
39. Marian Price, 'Republican Unity Meeting, Derry.'
40. 'Thread: Tony Catney speech at easter comm. Derry 2009', http:www.irishrepublican,net/forum/showthread.php?30731-Tony-Catney-speech-at-easter-comm-Derry-2009 (accessed 17 December 2010).
41. Ciaran Barnes, 'Killer – I'm no terror boss', *Sunday Life*, 19 July 2009.
42. Republican Network for Unity. 'Armed Struggle: a RNU position for debate', RNU Response Document. www.republicannework.ie/readArticle.aspx?ID=23 (accessed 26 January 2010).

43. Patterson, H. *Ireland since 1939: the Persistence of Conflict* (London: Penguin, 2007), p. 308.
44. Frampton, *The Long March*, p. 181.
45. Jim Gibney, 'Conference: Spirit of McElwaine evident among delegates', *An Phoblacht*, 15 June 2006.
46. Frampton, ibid.
47. Bean, K. *The New Politics of Sinn Féin*.
48. 'Éirígí: for a Socialist Republic', Éirígí website, www.eirigi.org (accessed 26 January 2010).
49. 'Éirígí oppose RIR parade 2/3', 14 December 2008, www.youtube.com/watch?v=L7gT1bnB-ZQ (accessed 26 January 2010).
50. 'Rioting Returns', *Lurgan Mail*, 28 August 2008.
51. 'Éirígí's Rab Jackson addresses Belfast supporters', 13 March 2009, www.youtube.com/watch?v=qU5RdCSmUlg (accessed 26 January 2010).
52. See Boyce, D. G. '"A Gallous Story and a Dirty Deed": Political Martyrdom in Ireland since 1867' in Alexander, Y. and O'Day, A. *Ireland's Terrorist Dilemma* (Dordrecht, Boston and Lancaster: Martinus Nijhoff, 1986), p. 7.
53. Mac Domhnaill, Brian. 'Remembering McElwaine', *An Phoblacht*, 25 May 2006.
54. Moloney, *Secret History*, pp. 312–15.
55. *Saoirse*, September 2000.
56. 'I Fought the War but the War is Over says Lynch', interview with Sean Lynch, *Impartial Reporter*, 3 April 2009; 'Fury as IRA Leader Joins the Policing Board', *News Letter*, 27 March 2008.
57. 'Bobby Sands MP (1954–1981)', h2g2, 3 September 2009, www.bbc.co.uk/dna/h2g2/A51822849 (accessed 26 January 2010).
58. Frampton, 'After Truce and Treaty'.
59. 'Fírinne Protest Against Section 44', 22 January 2010, an account of a Fírinne protest outside Killyhevlin Hotel, Enniskillen, www.eirigi.org/latest/latest220110.html (accessed 26 January 2010).
60. McGrattan, C. *Northern Ireland 1968–2008: The Politics of Entrenchment* (London: Palgrave Macmillan, 2010) p. 160.
61. 'I fought the war but the war is over' (see note 56).
62. O'Rawe quoted in Angelique Chrisafis, 'Hunger strike claims rile H Block veterans', *The Guardian*, 4 March 2005.
63. 'Éirígí organises series of Hunger Strike Meetings', Éirígí, 8 November

2008, http://www.eirigi.org/latest/latest081108.html (accessed 27 January 2010).
64. McIntyre, A. 'Republicanism: Alive or Dying?' *The Pensive Quill*, 1 January 2008.
65. *Twenty-First Report of the Independent Monitoring Commission*, 2009.
66. *Impartial Reporter*, 3 April 2009.
67. McKearney, Tommy. *The End of the Adams Era*, quoted in *The Pensive Quill*, 11 January 2010.
68. Based on information taken from *Saoirse*, February 2009, which showed five branches in Cork, Kerry and Limerick but only one in Dublin and none in Belfast or any of the six counties of Northern Ireland.
69. *Twenty-First Report of the Independent Monitoring Commission*, 2009.
70. *Twenty-First* and *Twenty-Second Report of the Independent Monitoring Commission*, 2009.
71. 'Background to the Border security problem', 16 May 1974, National Archives, FCO 87/37, in Patterson, H. 'Sectarianism Revisited: The Provisional IRA campaign in a border region of Northern Ireland', *Terrorism and Political Violence*, 22, 3 (July 2010), 337–56.
72. Dudley Edwards, R. *Aftermath: The Omagh Bomb and the Families' Pursuit of Justice* (London: Harvill Secker, 2009), p. 30.
73. Moloney, *A Secret History*, p. 472.
74. 'Unwanted media harassment of former Fermanagh Republican POW', *32CSM Fermanagh*, 27 July 2009, http://32csmfermanagh.blogspot.com/2009/07/unwanted-media-harrasment-of-former.html (accessed 13 December 2010).
75. Clarke, L, 'IRA blamed for murder of "informer"' *Sunday Times*, 19 June 2005.
76. *Twenty-First* and *Twenty-Second Report of the Independent Monitoring Commission*, 2009.
77. 'Radical Provo brigade splits', *Sunday Times*, 17 January 2010.
78. Quoted in Southern, 'Territoriality, Alienation and Loyalist Decommissioning', p. 74
79. 'RSF salutes Mayobridge', *Saoirse*, February 2009, http:www.rsf.ie/saoirse/current/feb09.pdf (accessed 17 December 2010)
80. 'British occupation forces killed in Six County attacks', *Saoirse*, April 2009.

81. *Twenty-Second Report of the Independent Monitoring Commission*, 2009.
82. Tom Brady, 'Dissidents the biggest threat to security since the Troubles – Ahern', *Irish Independent*, 15 April, 2010.
83. Alan Murray, 'Intelligence failings hand initiatives to the dissidents', *Belfast Telegraph*, 24 February 2010.
84. Adrian Rutherford and Deborah McAleese, 'Sinn Fein's Dáithí McKay calls for specialist police units to deal with dissident threat', *Belfast Telegraph*, 10 March 2010.
85. 'Who is behind these groups?' Bobby Storey interview in *Gara* (Basque nationalist paper), 22 July 2010.

CHAPTER 5

An Enduring Tradition or the Last Gasp of Physical Force Republicanism? 'Dissident' Republican Violence in Northern Ireland

JON TONGE
UNIVERSITY OF LIVERPOOL

Introduction: The Perpetuation of Violence

The activities of 'dissident' armed Irish republican groups have qualified claims that the 1998 Good Friday Agreement and subsequent consociational power sharing between former enemies in Northern Ireland brought closure to an enduring problem. Sporadic in nature, the armed campaign of 'dissident' IRAs is nowhere near the level maintained by their Provisional IRA (PIRA) predecessor and cannot derail an ongoing political process. Nonetheless, the continued existence of these 'spoiler groups', predominantly the Real IRA (RIRA) and Continuity IRA (CIRA), indicates that assumptions that violence would disappear entirely were overly optimistic. Having targeted British soldiers and police officers, 'dissidents' remain committed to maintaining some form of armed campaign against British rule in Northern Ireland, regardless of their political isolation, their lack of 'military' utility and amid the onset of power sharing between Protestant British Unionists and Irish Catholic Nationalists. In the 12 years since the Good Friday Agreement, 'dissident' republicans killed 38 people. Between 2003 and 2009, 'dissidents' were responsible for 288 shootings and assaults.[1] During the same period, there were 413 bombing incidents in Northern Ireland.[2] By the end of the first decade following the Good Friday Agreement, 57 dissident republican prisoners were in jail in Northern Ireland for their actions with a larger number imprisoned in the Irish Republic.[3] Additionally, 447 persons were arrested under anti-terrorism legislation by the Police Service of Northern

Ireland between 2003 and 2009, with over 28,000 stop-and-search operations carried out under the same laws by the Police Service of Northern Ireland in 2009 alone.[4]

Grandiose 'end of Irish history' claims were to be expected from those politicians and their advisors with vested electoral interests in claiming to have solved an age-old problem.[5] Yet academics could also be accused of naivety in perceiving the Good Friday Agreement as the end of the story. There existed cautious scholarly assessments, but these were in a small minority. As Ruane argued, '[C]ultural learning under conditions of conflict is Janus-faced: if the ability to contain conflict and to make peace is learned, so too is the ability to make war'.[6] Hayes and McAllister noted the possibility that those socialized and conditioned by violence might continue its exercise, while Bric and Coakley were early contenders that 'dissident' republicans already pose a serious threat to peace and stability'.[7] An early account of the historical determinism which underscores 'dissident' republican thinking, based on the inevitability of armed conflict while the British government claims sovereignty over Northern Ireland, suggested that violent Irish republicanism might not entirely disappear.[8]

Aside from the commonality of 'spoiler' groups emerging in other peace processes, assumptions of endgame in Ireland overlooked the historical tendencies towards splits within republican armed groups.[9] Moreover, such assumptions took little account of the manner in which the sheer scale of change and compromise by those who came to be seen as 'mainstream' republicans, i.e. the PIRA and Sinn Féin, was likely to provoke dissent and accusations of 'sell-out'. This chapter examines how the extent of compromise and reliance upon violence as a tool was more likely than not to produce new republican armed groups. The piece contends that, given that these groups (to varying degrees) mark their republicanism's historical antecedents as pre-dating that of the PIRA and Sinn Féin, the term 'republican dissidents' is inadequate and reductionist, a partial account of republicanism which suggests that it is merely what PIRA did and Sinn Féin now does. A more realistic appraisal of Irish republicanism is one which incorporates numerous forms, epitomized in Laffan's assertion that numerous republican parties under the name Sinn Féin have existed since Ireland was divided in 1920, all eventually tempted by the lure of constitutional politics and leaving behind a rump of militants.[10] The emergence of Irish republican 'dissidents' reflects the latest tensions between, firstly principle and tactic and secondly, the utility of 'armed struggle'. This chapter examines these tensions and discusses the heterogeneity of contemporary republican armed groups before assessing their current strengths and weaknesses.

Contextualizing the Emergence of 'Dissident' Republicanism

The emergence of 'dissident' Irish republican armed groups might be seen as unsurprising when international and local contexts are considered. Ultra groups are very common features of peace processes, developing in response to perceived compromises, or unacceptable supposed negotiating capitulations, by the military and political leaderships of armed groups. Within Ireland, the tendency for hitherto hard-line republicans to move from violence towards constitutional politics, leaving a rump of ultras outside political institutions has been a feature of the polity since the partition of Ireland. The extent and rapidity of change within mainstream republicanism undertaken since 1986 made likely the further splits which have duly transpired.

The catalogue of mainstream republican change is indeed startling. It began with recognition by Sinn Féin and the PIRA of Dáil Éireann, the Irish Parliament, in 1986, an institution previously dismissed as illegitimate and partitionist, given that it presided over only 26 counties (the Irish Republic) on the island of Ireland, rather than over the 32 county Irish state demanded by republicans. Eight years later, a PIRA ceasefire was declared, one which, following brief fracture in 1996–97, extended into the disbandment of the organization in 2005. The earlier insistence by republicans that the PIRA would not get rid of its weapons was replaced by full decommissioning of its arsenal. These moves were undertaken despite the absence of an undertaking from the British government to withdraw from Northern Ireland, previously a non-negotiable demand of the PIRA and Sinn Féin. In 1998, Sinn Féin supported the Good Friday Agreement, a deal which makes clear that Northern Ireland will remain part of the United Kingdom for so long as the majority of its citizens so choose. Previously, Sinn Féin had contemptuously dismissed this as a 'Unionist Veto', arguing that only the wishes of the electorate mattered, not merely those of the population with the 'artificial statelet' of Northern Ireland. Following the Good Friday Agreement, Sinn Féin entered a Northern Ireland Assembly and Executive at Stormont, despite having previously refused to recognize the political entity of Northern Ireland, let alone its political institutions. The Irish identity and political aspirations of nationalists in Northern Ireland were recognized by the establishment of an Irish dimension, via a North–South Ministerial Council and modest cross-border bodies. Republicans had previously dismissed an Irish dimension as a 'sickening English term'.[11] In 2007, Sinn Féin declared support for the Police Service of Northern Ireland (PSNI), the successor to the Royal Ulster Constabulary (RUC), which lost nearly 300 officers due to PIRA actions. This backing for the police allowed devolved power-sharing government to be restored, under an Executive headed by the Democratic Unionist Party and Sinn Féin.

According to 'dissident' republicans, republicanism cannot be based upon repudiation of all that was previously held as essential to the integrity of the ideology. For mainstream republicans, the changes chronicled above represent merely revised tactics, not the abandonment of republican principles or end goals. Academic explanations of these changes can be divided into three broad categories, which are not mutually exclusive. The *lack* of fidelity to traditional republican politics and the absence of deep-rooted commitment to the supposed cornerstone of Irish republicanism, the 1916 Easter Rising against British rule and proclamation of an Irish Republic, eased the changes within Sinn Féin and the PIRA brought about by their leaderships.[12] Under this interpretation, republicans in Northern Ireland were mainly creatures of their time, joining the IRA predominantly to hit back at perceived oppressors, the RUC and British Army, while some were motivated due to sectarian antipathy towards local Protestants. These local and temporal motivations outweighed vaguer concepts of support for an indivisible Irish Republic, supposedly the primary concern of the modern day 'dissidents'. Given the removal of those security forces, the rationale behind 'armed struggle' diminished.

The second category of explanation for republican diversion into constitutional policies lies in the failure of tactics. English and Patterson highlight how the contradictions of the 'armalite and ballot box' strategy soon became apparent.[13] PIRA violence provided a ceiling to Sinn Féin's electoral growth, given the latter's support for the former. One of these two elements needed to be removed and it was more logical and convenient to end the 'armed struggle'. McGladdery and Moloney emphasize the inadequacies of that struggle in delivering results, emphasizing the importance of the failure of the English bombing campaign and the demise of the arms supply line from Libya respectively.[14] Smith's account gives greater credibility to the IRA's campaign, but emphasizes the need of republicans to 'cash in' those military chips by the mid 1990s.[15]

A third broad explanation of republican change is rooted in the changed structural conditions experienced by republicans.[16] At the outset of the PIRA campaign, Irish nationalists saw themselves as second-class citizens suffering actual and relative (to the Unionist population) deprivation. By the time of the conclusion of PIRA's campaign, nationalists were treated far better and had largely de-ghettoized. This change came amid determined amelioration of their economic plight by the British government, as part of its strategy to diminish the conflict. Bean's argument is supported by republicans who remained loyal to the direction taken by the leadership of Sinn Féin *and* among those who defected. Among the former, one former IRA life sentence prisoner, Michael Culbert, expressed the new reality:

> When I was coming home on weekend leave from the prison [in the early 1990s] I couldn't believe what I was seeing in our communities. Things had changed and changed for the better. We couldn't claim that we lived in a ghetto anymore. I knew then that the war was over.[17]
> (Interview, 6 August 2008)

Among those later to associate with 'dissident' republicanism while denying any particular new allegiance, Tony Catney, former Director of Elections for Sinn Féin, described how that party's growth

> coincided with the rise of a monied class, which had previously felt that its interests were best served by remaining politically anonymous, now wanting to assert itself in any new political dispensation. This view I will describe as 'new Catholic money'. Largely apolitical but nationalistic in its aspirations this section of the electorate found much that was attractive in Sinn Fein's demand for parity of esteem and equality of opportunity'.[18]

Yet Catney indicated that his unease on the implications of this new support, fearing that the imperative of electoral advancement within this new repository of support would eclipse Sinn Féin's original ideals. He cautioned:

> [D]espite the unchecked electoral growth [of Sinn Féin] republicans are well advised to think cautiously where it may all lead. Riding the two

horses of working class resistance and Catholic new money – unnatural bedfellows – carries with it an inherent contradiction. That contradiction may be masked in a state of political flux but it carries the potential to arrest progress once the political dust has settled. Therein lies the danger.[19]

For Catney and other post-1998 'dissidents', Sinn Féin's accommodation with the emergent Catholic middle class had diluted republicanism and removed its challenges to the existence of Northern Ireland, in favour of an equality agenda pursued through state institutions. The culmination of working, rather than removing, the state lay in Sinn Féin's 2007 decision to support the PSNI. This decision provoked some dissent even among those hitherto supportive of the changes wrought by the peace process. There was seemingly a 'growing gap between the official traditional aims proclaimed at Bodenstown and Milltown cemeteries [where many republican dead are buried] and the realistic, everyday politics practised at Stormont and Leinster House' (the Irish Parliament).[20] The contradictions were apparent in the way Sinn Féin's regular commemorations of IRA members killed in operations designed to kill members of the police and British Army until 1997 were now accompanied by the condemnation of those continuing such actions as 'traitors to Ireland' by Martin McGuinness, the Sinn Féin Deputy First Minister. McGuinness argued that such actions were bereft of any mandate following the support expressed by nationalists for the Good Friday Agreement. Previously, he had criticized the lack of military clout of dissidents, declaring at Sinn Féin's 2007 special conference on policing that: 'We fought the British to a standstill. These people have yet to fight them to a start'.

'Mired by Militarism'? The Real IRA and 32 County Sovereignty Movement

Of the 'dissident' groups which have emerged, the most important has been the RIRA. While vulnerable to splits, it has contained the deadliest capacity. This was evidenced in the RIRA's killing of 29 civilians at Omagh in 1998, four months after the Good Friday Agreement was reached, an action which yielded widespread revulsion and forced the organization to call a temporary ceasefire. Sinn Féin condemned the bombing, arguing that the RIRA were 'not psychopaths', but were nonetheless a group 'mired by militarism who would be defeated due to their inability to recognise that armed struggle was a mere tactic, not a principle, of Irish republicanism'.[21] This mainstream republican analysis criticized the 'dissidents' as groups which elevated the need to perpetuate an armed campaign above the attainment of goals. 'Dissidents' highlighted how Sinn Féin had failed to advance the stated goals of Irish republicanism in their compromises. Most difficult to rebut was the pithy criticism offered by the sister of the first of the ten IRA hunger strikers to die in 1981, Bobby Sands, that her brother 'did not die for cross-border bodies with executive powers', the key all-Ireland features of the Good Friday Agreement.

The Good Friday Agreement was dismissed as entirely inadequate by the RIRA's political associates, the 32 County Sovereignty Movement (32CSM) (initially the 32 County Sovereignty Committee), comprising mostly members expelled from Sinn Féin for opposing the compromises being initiated by the party leadership. The 32CSM denounced the deal:

> [It is morally wrong because it] abandons the basic principle of Irish Republicans, the indefeasible right of the Irish people to sovereignty across the national territory and legitimises British rule and the loyalist veto. It is pragmatically wrong because it will delay rather than hasten Irish re-unification.[22]

According to the 32CSM, the Good Friday Agreement was erroneously portrayed by a range of forces, ranging from the British and Irish governments to Sinn Féin, as the only possible deal, one which could not realistically be opposed. The 32CSM briefly pursued its case for Irish self-determination via the United Nations, a route which predictably proved fruitless. Sinn Féin highlighted the overwhelming support for the Agreement amongst nationalists and contended that no alternative option was available, to the chagrin of the 32CSM, which responded:

> The most persistent charge levelled against Republicans is 'where is your alternative' [to the Good Friday Agreement]? Its monotonous use has transformed it into a comfort blanket for supporters and doubters of the agreement alike ... It is an age-old political ploy designed to justify failure by highlighting the supposed lack of credible alternatives. British withdrawal and the ending of partition can only be realised by a political

strategy, which is firmly rooted in a support base, which holds these two aims as its primary objectives.[23]

In urging a fundamentalist political strategy, 'dissident' republicans relied upon historical 'lessons' to justify continuing armed actions, asserting that 'in every generation the Irish people have rejected and challenged Britain's claim to interfere to Ireland's affairs'.[24] The attempted positioning of the RIRA as the vanguard of this continuing struggle was nonetheless problematic. Its leader in Belfast, Joe O'Connor, was killed by the PIRA in 2000 and the organization struggled to obtain support in the wake of the Omagh atrocity, amid rapid electoral advancement for Sinn Féin, boosted by a strong youth vote. Nonetheless, the RIRA resisted efforts by the Irish government, led by the special advisor to the Taoiseach, Martin Mansergh, to call a permanent ceasefire. Concurrently, the RIRA revived sufficiently to launch a small-scale campaign in London, which included a bombing at the BBC and an attack upon MI6 Headquarters. By August 2001, there were reports of overcrowding on the paramilitary wings of Portlaoise jail in the Irish Republic, which housed forty-four RIRA and three CIRA prisoners, plus ten from the Irish National Liberation Army, which, while opposed to the Good Friday Agreement, decommissioned its weapons and made permanent its ceasefire in 2010.[25] RIRA's local support in Northern Ireland, while very limited, was indicated by, for example, the setting up of patrols in Strabane in 2002.[26] During that year, the RIRA killed a worker at a British Territorial Army base in Londonderry.

By the mid 2000s, RIRA prisoners were serving sentences averaging 10 years. At an average age of 34 years, those prisoners did not fit easily with assumptions concerning the recruitment of vulnerable teenagers (almost half were married) or with perceptions that they were ex-PIRA 'veterans'. The RIRA attempted to intensify its activities as the PIRA wound itself up in 2005. Dissident republicans were responsible for 57 shooting and 48 assault casualties in the first four years after the PIRA departure from the stage.[27] In 2009, the RIRA shot dead two British soldiers outside the Massereene Army base and the CIRA killed a police officer in Craigavon. The period March to August 2009 saw an 85 per cent increase in casualties caused by dissident republican shootings and assaults, up from 34 to 63 compared to the previous six months.[28] Antrim, Belfast, Derry, Craigavon, Lisburn, Larne, Strabane and Limavady were the areas where the vast majority of attacks took place.

The RIRA's 2010 New Year statement was vitriolic concerning the condemnation of its 'gallant volunteers' as 'traitors to Ireland', declaring that 'a former comrade [Martin McGuinness] has come full circle'. Arguing that 'the tactical use of armed struggle can and does bring results', the RIRA threatened more of the same, insisting that 'any young person foolish enough to join the colonial police in the belief that the leadership of the Provisional movement will protect them, or give them cover, is sadly mistaken . . . they [the PSNI] are the first line of defence for the British government'.

Concurrently, the 32CSM's 2010 New Year statement insisted it would 'give leadership to our communities . . . in a disciplined approach the 32CSM will liaise directly with local communities to explore ways of reclaiming their sovereignty and, under these auspices, help them pursue their political and social objectives'. This appeared to be a thinly veiled indication that 'policing' of local communities would be increased by the organization. The previous two years saw an increase in the number of 'punishment attacks' carried out by dissidents upon suspected local criminals, in an attempt to exert community authority and supplant the police service as custodians of communal 'protection'.

Politically, the 32CSM is less committed to the traditionalist 'purism' of Republican Sinn Féin (RSF), being more concerned with supporting a revived armed campaign, than with the issue of abstention from the Irish Parliament in Dublin, an issue which it regards as arcane and irrelevant to its 'struggle'. Many 32CSM members had stayed with Sinn Féin and PIRA after 1986, when those organizations had accepted the Irish Parliament, presiding over 26 of the 32 counties on the island of Ireland. It was compromise over the status of Northern Ireland, not the Irish Republic, and the abandonment of armed struggle, which prompted their departure from Sinn Féin and the focus of the organization is very much upon the 'occupied North', where the need for some tactical flexibility is recognized. The 32CSM's 2009 Easter statement insisted:

> We need to set our case against British occupation in a way that is relevant to our people's needs today. Our aims cannot solely be the product of the past nor can they be a slave to that past. British reasons for remaining in Ireland will change according to modern British interests. Republican strategies opposing these interests must adapt accordingly.

Mired by 'Purism'? Republican Sinn Féin and the Continuity IRA

RSF's formation in 1986 followed the decision of the Sinn Féin and IRA leadership to recognize as legitimate the Irish parliament in Dublin, allowing Sinn Féin to take seats in that institution once sufficiently electorally strong, an ambition fulfilled by 1997. For RSF members, based mainly within the Irish Republic rather than the 'war theatre' of Northern Ireland, this decision constituted 'the biggest betrayal ever'.[29] The exit of the PIRA from the stage and Sinn Féin's subsequent entry into a Northern Ireland Assembly were viewed as inevitable once that party had begun to ride a constitutional political horse in 1986.[30] Abstentionism has been downgraded from principle to tactic within mainstream republicanism, with the solitary exception of the refusal to take seats in the UK Parliament at Westminster, given the requirement to swear an oath of allegiance to the Queen.[31] Although a Continuity Army Council was formed soon after the emergence of RSF, its existence was concealed, the embryonic CIRA anxious to avoid confrontation with other republicans. As an armed wing surfaced, the CIRA claimed: 'The Provisionals [PIRA] are not too happy about our existence, but we don't want any friction with them. When we were reorganised in 1986 there were threats made against us'.[32]

Labelled a terrorist organization in the United States and banned there since 2004, on the grounds that it is an 'alias' for the CIRA, RSF protests that it 'has no military wing, nor are we the political wing of any other organisation'.[33] Yet the Continuity Army Council was constituted at the time of RSF's formation and RSF's newspaper carries coverage of CIRA actions. Although it has a Belfast office, RSF's strength in Northern Ireland is limited. While the organization claimed that 'more than 250 delegates and visitors' attended its 1997 Ard Fheis, including 'one-third from the Occupied 6 Counties' the figures are exaggerated.[34] The 2004 equivalent attracted fewer than 60 attendees despite claims of a 'packed' event.[35] Despite the US prohibition, RSF has succeeded in organizing some small branches there, organized as the National Irish Freedom Committee USA (Cumann na Saoirse Náisiúnta).

Offering an undiluted brand of traditionalist republicanism, the demands of RSF and the CIRA are clear and identical to those once offered by Sinn Féin and the PIRA: a British declaration of intent to withdraw from Northern Ireland within the lifetime of a Westminster parliament, to be followed by an amnesty for 'political prisoners' and the establishment of all-Ireland assembly which would draw up a constitution to be put to the people. This constitution would be based upon the federal principles espoused in Éire Nua, RSF's political programme (Republican Sinn Féin 2008). This fundamentalist republicanism brooks no compromise; RSF implores republicans to 'End British rule: don't update it' arguing:[36]

> There is no middle ground on the question of accepting British police, British laws and British courts in Ireland. Those who sign up [to] the institutions of the British state in Ireland must do so in the knowledge that they will be forced by their English masters to confront that section of the Irish people who will never accept British rule.[37]

Gradual routes to Irish unity are ruled out as delusional, with the supposed transitional features of all-island bodies established under the Good Friday Agreement scorned. Thus RSF quotes approvingly Mansergh's argument 'there is no evidence let alone inevitability, from international experience, that limited cross-Border cooperation necessarily leads to political unification'.[38]

In common with the 32CSM and RIRA, RSF expends much of its energy criticizing the perceived 'sell-out' of Sinn Féin, contending that this has made the task of Irish reunification much more problematic. RSF argues that 'a new reinforced Stormont will be much more difficult to remove than the old corrupt regime which was brought down by the people's struggle in 1972' and that the Good Friday Agreement was 'the updating and strengthening of English rule here through a New Stormont'.[39] The hostility and sense of betrayal is heightened by the willingness of former comrades to support action against those republicans prepared to continue an armed campaign. RSF thus claims that the position of Sinn Féin on CIRA prisoners is 'similar to that of Fianna Fáil ministers of the 1940s who had themselves been political prisoners in the 1920s'.[40] While this again exaggerates (ministers in the 1940s supported executions of erstwhile comrades) the comparison is a sensitive issue within Irish republican circles.

Dissident Heterogeneity and Divisions

While sharing a determination to achieve a united, independent, socialist Irish Republic, 'dissident' republicanism has been characterized more by fluidity of membership, heterogeneity and division than by solidity, homogeneity and unity. The common bond extends only to universal criticism of Sinn Féin's 'sell-out' and duplicity, dissidents of all shades agreeing that 'the political process has created a class of professional liars and unfortunately it contains many Republicans'.[41]

Beyond this, inter- and intra-dissident disputes have been evident, with different groups emerging; splits and rivalries evident within those groups and infiltration by the British and Irish security services are regular features.[42] For republican prisoners, there are two separate support groups, according to whether they are RIRA or CIRA members. Within the RIRA, there was a major split in 2002. It involved the departure of those RIRA prisoners serving the longest jail sentences (for conspiracy to cause explosions in London) who claimed that the RIRA was now controlled by 'a junta whose financial motivations far outweighed their political commitment to our struggle'; lambasted the leadership's 'inability to develop or articulate a medium-to-long term political strategy' and highlighted its 'neglect of, and failure to maintain contact with, IRA prisoners in English and Irish prisons'.[43]

Moreover, this section of the RIRA appeared to acknowledge the futility of continued violence, declaring that

> republicans opposed to the Belfast Agreement must accept political reality irrespective of how unpalatable it may be. One does not need to be a political genius to realise that there is no popular support for armed struggle in Ireland at this time. Indeed there is no tangible support for an armed campaign within the broad republican or nationalist community. If republicans continue to ignore these political facts, it will prove politically fatal. Republicans cannot claim on the one hand to fighting on behalf of the people while on the other hand dismissing their expressed wishes'.[44]

One long-term prisoner, Darren Mulholland, part of the 'Forum group' which quit the RIRA in protest at the leadership's actions, argued for 'strength in diversity' contending that what was needed was a common manifesto around the goal of Irish unity and the type of Republic to be created, rather than agreement upon methods. Mulholland conceded that the extent of internal division among republicans was such that 'there is no chance of getting all republicans into one big happy organisation to fight for that goal [of Irish unity]'.[45]

The emergence of the Republican Network for Unity (RNU) in 2007 has attempted to fulfil an 'umbrella' role, offering shelter for a wide variety of republicans disaffected by the compromises yielded in the peace and political processes. RNU provides a broad front for republicans supportive or non-supportive of continuing armed actions. It emerged after 'dissident' republicans fielded a number of candidates in the 2007 Northern Ireland Assembly elections. These candidates fared badly, averaging only 3 per cent of the nationalist vote. This was despite the prominent backing, publicized in, for example, the main nationalist newspaper, the *Irish News*, of 317 former republican prisoners and current activists, under the umbrella label of 'Irish Republican Ex-POWs against the RUC/PSNI and MI5'. Of those prisoners, nearly half (140) were drawn from Derry, more than three times the number (38) of signatories from Belfast and indicative of the respective strengths of 'dissident' republicanism in the two locations. Indeed it was in Derry that a dissident candidate, Peggy O'Hara, mother of the INLA hunger-striker, Patsy O'Hara, polled best of the 'ultras', securing 6.5 per cent of the nationalist vote, while the 32CSM argues that 'all republican banners are welcome because all republican banners are needed' (Easter statement, 2009) and the Republican Network for Unity provides voice for such argument. RSF's insistence that it alone represents the embodiment of republican principles has inhibited efforts to forge unity amongst those groups dismissive of the Good Friday Agreement. The former President of RSF, Ruairí Ó'Brádaigh, made clear at his party's 1999 Ard Fheis (conference) that alliances with other groups were not possible:

> [T]he establishment politicians attempted early in December last to discredit us by linking us in the public mind with groupings such as the 32 County Sovereignty Movement and the IRSP [Irish Republican Socialist Party] and calling such a collection 'dissidents'. Once more and for the record there have been no formal discussions with the groups named and no 'joint strategy' has been considered. There are deep ideological differences . . . Republican Sinn Fein refuses to accept the 26 County partitionist assembly at Leinster House which actively collaborates with British rule in Ireland. As 'we ourselves' we adhered to that position since 1986 when all of today's 'dissidents' would have us go with the tide in the direction which leads inevitably: first to Leinster House, then to the abandonment of the people's struggle, followed by acceptance of Stormont and of British rule here . . .[46]

Successive RSF Ard-Fheisanna reiterated this position, leaving those preferring broader alliances with little choice but to exit the party. Indeed cumann (branches) in Limerick and Cork left RSF in 2010 for this reason.[47] During the same year, an internal attempt to oust the leadership of CIRA by elements wanting more military 'action' was thwarted. Three years earlier, RSF lost members in Tyrone, when it attempted to prevent them supporting a monument to the 'Loughgall Martyrs', PIRA members killed by the SAS in 1987, on the grounds that they had stayed with the Provisional Republican Movement after RSF left in 1986 over the issue of abstention from the Irish parliament. These isolationist positions have angered other republicans, unimpressed by the apparent lack of military capability of CIRA and arguing that RSF's positioning impairs the building of broader republican strength.

Armed Campaigns, Resources and Political Isolation

The options for republican ultras in terms of developing their armed campaign or advancing their political objectives remain highly constrained. Weapons supply lines from, for example, Eastern Europe, have been disrupted, while there have been hundreds of arrests of suspected dissidents. The main target for 'dissident' republicans has been the PSNI. Recruiting equal numbers of Catholics and non-Catholics, the PSNI promised a new culture and ethos in policing, compared to the Unionist, British and Protestant identity which nationalist critics claimed was associated with its predecessor. These changes elicited support for policing from Sinn Féin, a move more sensitive to the republican base (many of whom had been arrested by the old RUC) than support for the Good Friday Agreement. Changes in modus operandi and composition of the police service failed to impress republican ultras, who argued that any British force, even if locally operated, was illegitimate. According to the President of Republican Sinn Féin, Des Dalton:

> The RIC [Royal Irish Constabulary] became the RUC and they ultimately became the PSNI. But while the cap badge may change, the point of these forces remains the same. They are there to uphold British rule, they are an integral part of British state forces ... if you join a force which upholds British rule you are putting yourself in the line of fire.[48]

Republican 'dissident' positions on policing were unaffected by the transfer of devolution and policing justice powers to Northern Ireland in April 2010. Within minutes of the formal transfer, the ultras detonated a bomb outside the headquarters of MI5 in Northern Ireland, which oversees intelligence-based counter-terrorist activity. The bombing was significant in highlighting the view of 'dissidents' that 'political policing' remained in place, overseen by the British-run MI5. This rejection of the idea that policing is now local was heightened by claims that special British Army units remained engaged in counter-terrorism activity, while republicans also insisted that routine British Army operations continued beyond demilitarization and the formal ending of Operation Banner in 2007, the Army's 38-year role in Northern Ireland.

Republican 'dissidents' have attempted to prevent acceptance of the police by the nationalist community, attempting to portray an increasingly civilianized force as still a defender of a Unionist–British state. With the PSNI recruiting on a 50–50 Roman Catholic–non-Catholic basis and enjoying support from many of those who once targeted police officers, 'dissidents' have struggled to ferment residual republican distrust of the police. Orange parades and the ongoing and unsolved aspects of sectarianism in Northern Ireland provide potential resources for ultra groups. A number of Protestant parades are allowed to proceed, under certain conditions, through predominantly nationalist areas, where such parades remain unpopular beyond a dissident core. Dissident groups have been active in fermenting nationalist unrest over such parades and were prominent in serious rioting which affected North Belfast in July 2009 and 2010. The rise of PIRA owed much to communal 'defenderism' and RIRA and CIRA continue to view confrontations over marches as opportunities. The role of former PIRA prisoners in stewarding protests and preventing attacks upon Orange parades or the police and Army escorting such parades has been criticized by dissidents: 'Provos protect British soldiers' was one headline in RSF's outlet.[49]

Republican Sinn Féin's frank internal analysis of its strengths, weaknesses opportunities and threats, conducted in 2004, highlighted a greater number of weaknesses and threats than strengths and opportunities.[50] Those weaknesses included few members, small branches and lack of outreach. Threats, which were acknowledged as 'considerable indeed' included draconian legislation, anti-Republican media, revisionism, acceptance of the Unionist veto, attempted removal of British responsibility for the problem, apathy and indifference and the revulsion generated by the Omagh massacre. Strengths were seen as core values, which provided continuity for the organization, its publications and the solidarity produced by commemoration, although it was significant that retrospective events and an ideology which celebrates the past were held as key features. Opportunities included the instability of the Northern Ireland Assembly, the potential furore of a British royal visit to Ireland, anti-war demos and trade union involvement.

Even allowing for methodological difficulty in quantifying support for 'dissidents', given public reticence in declaring support for armed groups, republican ultras have little backing. The Sinn Féin narrative that dissidents are 'micro-groups' bereft of a mandate is true, albeit a narrative that overlooks the absence of votes for Sinn Féin or PIRA during the most ferocious years of conflict, from 1970 until 1981. The lack of a visible mandate during that era has not retrospectively delegitimized that campaign in the perceptions of Sinn Féin. The other argument of Sinn Féin, that the context has changed, is also true, in that the structural conditions of nationalists have clearly altered. Economic equality and parity of esteem have arrived, but the 'dissident' viewpoint reduces 'context' to who claims sovereignty over the territory and in that respect the only change has been a reverse: the removal of Ireland's constitutional claim to part of the United Kingdom.

The 1998 Good Friday Agreement referendum saw overwhelming nationalist support for the deal in Northern Ireland and the Irish Republic. Yet RSF argued that the small rejectionist vote offered potential, declaring that the 5.6 per cent 'No' vote in the Irish Republic 'compares to the core Republican vote in the 1981 H Block (5% plus) and 1957 (5.3%) general election votes [periods of limited Republican support during an IRA border campaign and hunger strikes respectively] . . . Republican Sinn Féin must now organise and put itself at the head of the 85,748 "No" voters south of the Border as the only political body which stood up and campaigned against the sell-out throughout the island'.[51] In that referendum only 38 per cent of 18- to 24-year-olds and only 44 per cent of under 40-year-olds bothered to vote, but this reflected apathy, not hostility to the removal of the Republic of Ireland's constitutional claim to Northern Ireland.[52] A BBC Northern Ireland Hearts and Minds Poll in autumn 2002 suggested support for 'dissidents' ran at 7 per cent among nationalists (one-seventh of the level recorded for Sinn Féin), but this figure was not attained when tested in the 2007 Assembly election. For 'dissident' groups claiming to act on behalf of the Irish people, there was very little electoral succour. Such organizations have been forced to rely on assertions that no armed campaign, including that of the Easter 1916 rebellion against British rule, ever enjoyed formal electoral backing; the 'mandate' and 'right to resist' is derived from the British 'occupation' of Ireland.

Mainstream republicans, competing successfully in the electoral marketplace of Northern Ireland, are dismissive of what they see as the outdated tactics of 'micro-group' republicans. Thus Sinn Féin's Chair, Declan Kearney (whose police officer cousin had been seriously injured by a 'dissident' bomb two months earlier) denounced 'militarists whose only interest is in seeing the British Army back on the streets' at the party's 2010 Ard Fheis. The lack-of-mandate claim was palpably true, although it overlooked inconvenient historical truths. 'Dissidents' could equally highlight the absence of any electoral mandate for the PIRA's armed campaign from 1970 until 1981 and the limited mandate beyond, Sinn Féin being the minority political choice of nationalists from 1982 to 1994. 'Dissidents' thus contend that political violence in Ireland, from the Easter Rising against British rule in 1916, has never enjoyed a clear mandate. PIRA former prisoners, most of whom have stayed loyal to the Sinn Féin leadership, are divided over whether the new breed of republican ultra prisoners are 'political prisoners'.[53] While often dismissive of dissidents, there is a reluctance to dismiss them as mere criminals. The legacy of the republican struggle against criminalization from 1976 until the Good Friday Agreement has had a marked impact.[54]

The criticism from non-republicans of dissidents ignores the historical antecedents of armed republicanism and the mainly targeted nature of their violence since the revulsion generated by the Omagh bombing. Critics have highlighted the perceived antediluvian nature of those still engaged in violence. Rejection of their paramilitary and political approaches has been accompanied by attempts to portray them as psychopaths. Shaun Woodward, the Secretary of State for Northern Ireland from 2007–10 in the outgoing Labour government, described 'dissidents' as 'criminals who just like shooting people' and contrasted them with the 'clearly political' ambitions of the PIRA.[55] Woodward's predecessor Labour government of the 1970s declined to view the PIRA as 'clearly political', ending the special category status accruing to their prisoners and treating them as common criminals. In common with previous eras, there appeared to be a determination among British and Irish governmental representatives to distinguish between acceptable 'old' IRAs and unacceptable 'new' IRAs.

Conclusion

The reliance upon historical determinism within Irish republicanism, the longevity of the cause and the belief, however implausible, in the inevitability of eventual victory and Irish reunification, all ensured that the emergence of 'spoiler' groups was even more likely in the Northern Irish peace process than in other arenas of conflict management. Irish republican spoiler groups do not see themselves as new entities established to destroy a peace process. Instead, they posit themselves as the custodians of an enduring tradition dating back centuries, acting merely as the latest organizations entrusted to keep the 'struggle' going. In this respect, the criticism from recently constitutional republicans in Sinn Féin (and from others) that armed struggle is an 'end in itself' for dissidents is correct. Republican ultras recognize that their armed campaign cannot in isolation achieve a united Ireland. Although an unlikely prospect, the short-term aim of continued violence is to provoke a security force backlash, expose the British state as 'draconian' and still essentially colonial and thus elicit sympathy for 'oppressed' republicans in their community, allowing the armed campaign to gather momentum.

Beyond the armed campaign lies a fundamentalist political ideology which believes that any political arrangement short of Irish unity is untenable. All dissident groups are united in their belief that the assertion of Irish national sovereignty supersedes Unionist national rights as British citizens. While the dissident groups offer the language of accommodation with Unionists and stress the non-sectarian nature of their political struggle, their armed actions are designed to promote unification regardless of whether Unionist consent is forthcoming. The attempts of the British government and the PSNI to develop an entirely convincing counter-narrative to 'dissident' activity may need refinement. Dismissal of republican ultras as common criminals is similar to the language used unsuccessfully against PIRA from the 1970s until the 1990s. Common criminals tend not to bomb courthouses or MI5 headquarters. A more convincing counter-narrative has commonly been found in the language of the Irish government, which has emphasized the futility of armed actions and the unattainability of avowed goals via the methodologies deployed by 'dissidents'. Until – and if – that more convincing counter-narrative is developed and has impact, it remains unlikely that Northern Ireland's association with political violence will be fully eradicated.

Notes

1. Independent Monitoring Commission, *Twenty-Second Report of the Independent Monitoring Commission*, HC 1085 (London: The Stationery Office, 2009).
2. Police Service of Northern Ireland, *Security Situation Statistics 2009/10*, www.psni.police.uk/index/updates/updates_statistics/updates_security_situation and_public_order_statistics.htm (accessed 16 May 2010).
3. *Hansard*, 12 October 2009.
4. Police Service of Northern Ireland, *Number of Persons Arrested under TACT 41 and Subsequently Charged*, 2010, www.psni.police.uk/persons_arrested_and_charged_cy.pdf, 2010.
5. Powell, J. *Great Hatred, Little Room: Making Peace in Northern Ireland* (London: Bodley Head, 2008).
6. Ruane, J. 'Contemporary Republicanism and the Strategy of Armed Struggle', in Bric, M. and Coakley, J. (eds), *From Political Violence to Negotiated Settlement: The Winding Path to Peace in Twentieth-Century Ireland* (Dublin: University College Dublin, 2004), pp. 115–32.
7. Hayes, B. and McAllister, I. 'Sowing Dragon's Teeth: Public Support for Political Violence and Paramilitarism in Northern Ireland', *Political Studies*, 49 (2001): 901–22; and Bric and Coakley, p. 9.
8. Tonge, J. '"They haven't gone away y'know": Irish republican "dissidents" and "armed struggle"', *Terrorism and Political Violence*, 16, 3 (2004), 671–93.
9. Stedman, S., Rothchild, D. and Cousens, E. *Ending Civil Wars: The Implementation of Peace Agreements* (Boulder, CO: Lynne Reiner, 2002); and Stedman, S. 'Peace Processes and the Challenges of Violence', in Darby, J. and MacGinty, R. (eds), *Contemporary Peacemaking: Conflict, Violence and Peace Processes* (Basingstoke: Palgrave Macmillan, 2002).
10. Laffan, M. *The Resurrection of Ireland: The Sinn Fein Party 1916–1923*, (Cambridge: Cambridge University Press, 1999).
11. *An Phoblacht*, 'Freeman', June 1975: 6.
12. Alonso, R. *The IRA and Armed Struggle* (London: Routledge, 2006); Maillot, A. *New Sinn Fein* (London: Routledge, 2004); McIntyre, A. 'Modern Irish Republicanism: The Product of British State Strategies', *Irish Political Studies*, 10 (1995), pp. 97–121; McIntyre, A. 'Modern Irish

Republicanism and the Belfast Agreement: Chickens Coming Home to Roost or Turkeys Celebrating Christmas?' in Wilford, R. (ed.) *Aspects of the Belfast Agreement* (Oxford: Oxford University Press, 2001); and McIntyre, A. *Good Friday: The Death of Irish Republicanism* (New York: Ausubo Press, 2008).
13. English, R. *Armed Struggle: The History of the IRA* (London: Macmillan, 2003) and Patterson, H. *The Politics of Illusion: A Political History of the IRA* (London: Serif, 1997).
14. McGladdery, G. *The Provisional IRA in England: The Bombing Campaign 1973–1997*, (Dublin: Irish Academic Press, 2004) and Moloney, E. *A Secret History of the IRA* (Harmondsworth: Penguin, 2002).
15. Smith, M. *Fighting for Ireland? The Military Strategy of the Irish Republican Movement* (London: Routledge, 1995).
16. Bean, K. *The New Politics of Sinn Fein* (Liverpool: Liverpool University Press, 2007).
17. Shirlow, P., Tonge, J., McAuley, J. and McGlynn, C. *Abandoning Historical Conflict? Former Political Prisoners and Reconciliation in Northern Ireland* (Manchester: Manchester University Press, 2010).
18. Tony Catney, 'Sinn Fein's Electoral Growth', *Fourthwrite*, 2 Summer 2000: 7.
19. Ibid.
20. Kevin Beane, 'Every picture tells a story', *Fourthwrite*, 1 2000: 9.
21. *An Phoblacht*, 'Omagh', August 1998.
22. *Sovereign Nation*, 'First Edition – Sovereign Nation Launched', August 1998: 1.
23. *Sovereign Nation*, 'Republicanism is the key', January/February 2000: 4.
24. *Sovereign Nation*, 'Real IRA statement', January/February 2000: 1.
25. *Sunday Business Post*, 'Overcrowding fear at Portlaoise', 5 August 2001.
26. *Derry Journal*, 'Real IRA gunmen 'patrol' streets', 25 October 2002.
27. Independent Monitoring Commission, *Twenty-Second Report* (London: The Stationery Office, November 2009).
28. Ibid. p. 30.
29. *Saoirse*, '1986 – biggest betrayal ever', 218, June 2005: 1.
30. White, R. *Ruairí Ó Brádaigh: The Life and Politics of an Irish Revolutionary* (Bloomington, IN: Indiana University Press, 2006).

31. Lynn, B. 'Tactic or Principle? The Evolution of Republican Thinking on Abstentionism in Ireland, 1970–1998', *Irish Political Studies*, 17, 2 (2002): 74–94.
32. *Saoirse*, 'Continuity IRA to target British Crown Forces', 121, May 1997: 2.
33. *Saoirse*, 'Day of action against US ban', 210, October 2004: 3.
34. *Saoirse*, 'Pledge to oppose six and 26-County referendums in May 1998', 128, November/December 1997: 7.
35. *Saoirse*, '100th Ard Fheis of Republican Sinn Fein held in Dublin', 212, December 2004: 7.
36. *Saoirse*, 'End British rule – don't replace it', 128, November–December 1997: 1.
37. *Saoirse*, 'Disband the RUC PSNI', 238, February 2007: 1.
38. *Saoirse*, 'Provo hopes dashed', 162, October 2000: 1.
39. *Saoirse*, 'Gradual freedom a con-trick', 132, April 1998: 9.
40. *Saoirse*, 'Mayo hunger strikers honoured in Ballinan', 167, March 2001: 9.
41. *Fourthwrite*, 'Interview with Brendan Hughes', March/April 2000: 1.
42. For example, Mooney, J. and O'Toole, M. *Black Operations: The Secret War Against the Real IRA* (Ashbourne: Maverick House, 2003).
43. *Forum*, 'Interview with republican prisoners', 8 October 2003, pp. 6–7; *Forum*, 'Interview with republican prisoners', 1 February 2003 pp. 1–5; *Irish Independent*, 'Corruption brings down terror group', 20 October 2002; private correspondence, 13 April 2004.
44. *Forum*, Interview with republican prisoners', 8 October 2003: 7.
45. *Forum*, Darren Mulholland, 'Strength in diversity', 10 December 2003: 5.
46. *Saoirse*, 'We renew our pledge never to surrender to British imperial rule', 152, December 1999: 8.
47. *Saoirse*, 'RSF will not be deflected from its work', May 2010: 8.
48. www.guardian.co.uk/uk/2010/feb/07/catholics-psni-line-fire, 'Catholics who join devolved PSNI "in line of fire" says Republican Sinn Fein'.
49. *Saoirse*, 'Provos protect British soldiers', 208, August 2004: 1.
50. *Saoirse*, 'England has no right to rule our country', 212, November/December 2004: 10.
51. *Saoirse*, 'Nationalist Ireland stampeded into less than Sunningdale', 134, June 1998: 1.

52. *Irish Times*, 'Low turnout of voters', 11 December 1998; *Saoirse*, 'The begrudgers guide to the Stormont Agreement', 144, April 1999.: 8.
53. Shirlow et al., 2010.
54. Ross, F. Stuart (2006) 'Between Party and Movement: Sinn Fein and the Popular Movement against Criminalisation, 1976–1982', *Irish Political Studies*, 21, 3 (2006): 337–54.
55. *BBC Newsnight*, 29 October 2010.

CHAPTER 6

Radicalization and Internet Propaganda by Dissident Republican Groups in Northern Ireland since 2008

JOHN NALTON, GILBERT RAMSEY AND MAX TAYLOR
UNIVERSITY OF ST ANDREWS

Introduction

The Provisional IRA officially ended its armed campaign to reunify Ireland in July 2005. However, several splinter groups reject its policy of negotiating with the British government, and remain committed to removing British influence from Northern Ireland and sabotaging the peace process through violence.

It has become increasingly clear that a number of those splinter groups constitute a 'dissident revival', with fresh new faces engaged in Irish republican violence, especially associated with the Real IRA, and operations have become increasingly professional. A series of Independent Monitoring Commission (IMC) reports (including the most recent IMC report November 2010)[1] have indicated that *'the overall level of dissident activity was markedly higher than we have seen ... since 2003'.*[2] It is quite clear that dissident capabilities have improved over the course of the past two years, and this is a matter of concern, not only for the security status of the Province, but also in terms of effects on the political process. Should these dissidents be able to wage an effective campaign of violence, this may cause tensions within the power-sharing executive parties as well as between Sinn Féin and the British government.

According to the IMC, the Real IRA and Continuity IRA are increasingly working more closely together to increase the threat posed to security forces. While the IMC report of November 2009 observes that there still 'has not been effective strategic collaboration between the main dissident groups,' it does suggest that there is ad hoc tactical cooperation between individuals from different groups and backgrounds. The IMC assesses this to be down to personal and social networks rather than through organizations specifically. The IMC summarizes that *'there are emerging signs that the phenomenon of fluidity is more significant than before'*. The twenty-third IMC report (2010) notes that the dissident groups remain 'highly active and dangerous' and there clearly is evidence of a growing threat.

This chapter will explore the apparent role of the internet in contributing to the growth and increasing interconnectedness of Dissident Republican (DR) groups. It aims to do this by providing a descriptive account of Dissident Republican propaganda being disseminated via sites such as YouTube, and an examination of the development of the main Republican web forums, identifying key sites of interest.

It will be argued that these groups, and their sympathizers, are taking advantage of the internet as a fast and relatively unregulated medium to convey their message to multiple audiences. Indeed, in addition to cultivating support, Dissident Republican groups seem to be using the internet to actively attract potential recruits, particularly young people. It seems that postings to many electronic bulletin boards, chat rooms and user nets are designed in such a way as to allure potential recruits, by offering opportunities for people to engage in political discussions, and to seek advice and support. It is also reasonable to assume that cross factional cooperation and development of social networks could be being fuelled by the burgeoning of Republican social forums, bulletin boards and networking sites on the internet.

Dissident Recruitment

Recruitment is an important element of terrorist activity and probably one of the most significant requirements for a terrorist group to survive over time. Groups need new members, both to grow in strength and to replenish losses and defections. Recruitment can be so important that one study of left-wing terrorism in Italy from 1970–83 found that groups conducted increasingly lethal attacks, in part, in order to gain more recruits.[3] If this is indeed the case, we might expect RIRA and other DR groups to expend considerable resources on recruitment.

Functioning as a small terrorist cell, the RIRA originally drew most of its recruits from the ranks of former PIRA fighters.[4] This recruitment allowed the RIRA to begin its activities with an immediate pool of hardened operatives, already skilled at building explosive devices and avoiding British authorities. More recently, other reports suggest that the RIRA attempts to recruit young people without a past record of violent activities, in such areas as South Armagh, Derry and Dublin.[5] The twenty-second IMC report (November 2009) reflects this:

> we comment on the apparent growth of RIRA and CIRA as a result of recruitment ... What really matters is not so much the number of members as the experience and skills of those available to an organisation, whether formally members or not. The majority of new recruits are inexperienced young males. There are, however, now indications that former republican terrorists have as individuals provided services in some instances to dissident republican groups, which even if occasional can significantly add to the threat.[6]

Thus, the RIRA, if it is to be operationally effective, must achieve three things in terms of recruitment. First, it must be able to attract new members prepared to engage in violent action. Ideally, these should be ideologically motivated young people without a previous criminal record. Second, these new members must be networked with existing core members and with experienced former terrorists who, even if not members, are prepared to share expertise with the group. Third, a larger group of passive supporters must be cultivated which is prepared to shield or turn a blind eye to the group's activities. As far as the latter is concerned, the RIRA seems to operate in a relatively constrained and urban environment in Northern Ireland and maintains a limited presence in cities outside Northern Ireland, such as Dublin. As a result of this operating environment, RIRA members rely on active and passive support from local residents to evade British authorities.

The Potential of the Internet for DR Recruitment and Organization

In principle, the internet has two major things to offer DR groups. First, it is a platform for the dissemination of propaganda material. Second, it is a social networking tool that is ideal for building 'virtual communities'.[7] In this sense, it has the potential to assist in solving all three of the major recruitment problems outlined above, helping to draw in new people in both passive and potentially active roles, and to connect these people to each other, and to better established members.

Propaganda is an integral part of terrorist recruitment and it might be assumed that it plays a key role in accounting for why people become terrorists. Many terrorists report that they first joined an organization after witnessing events on television or other media.[8] Maleckova (2005) argues that belief in a political cause is the main reason for involvement in terrorism, rather than factors such as economic deprivation.[9] More specifically, a desire for vengeance has long being recognized as a key motivation for joining a terrorist organization.[10] Such a desire depends necessarily upon the belief that one's self, or a group with which one identifies, has been wronged in the past.

The internet offers a networked form of communication which goes hand in hand with the decentralized structure of terrorist organizations like the DR groups, lowering overheads and bringing down barriers both to entry into the field of propaganda production, and individuals' ability to access this propaganda. Hence, for such organizations, the internet has overcome the limitations of traditional publishing, offering a quick, inexpensive and anonymous way of disseminating ideological material through a powerful medium. While DR groups have previously used hard copy pamphlets for purposes such as claiming responsibility for attacks, internet propaganda has potentially greater impact and greater reach than such material. On the other hand, it also has the potential to reduce dependence on gaining a mass media platform[11] which at least until recently has been seen as a key need for terrorist groups, both encouraging, but also limiting and bounding the kinds of violence they use.

Recognizing the value of visual media, DR groups have accordingly developed their own video production capabilities, enabling them to self-produce propaganda films, a number of which appear on YouTube for example (see below). These films, which may also be disseminated on DVD, allow DR groups to exert a high degree of editorial control over content, carefully targeting the message. Moreover, as we shall see, DR propaganda content is easily accessible on the internet. This would seem to stand in direct contradiction to claims such as those made by Reilly (2008) that Northern Irish terrorists and their sympathizers are unlikely to achieve a greater degree of 'visibility' online than they enjoy in the conventional mass media.[12]

As Payne (2009) identifies, another key trend in modern media that has undoubtedly aided the distribution of the DR messages is the gradual supplanting of mass communications with online social networks.[13] A distributed network is at once a powerful communication medium and a virtual sanctuary for DR militants, enhancing both information flow and influence. It allows for recruitment, ideological development and operational planning. It is also difficult for opponents to map and suppress. Online web forums such as those described below may play an important role in radicalization in republican communities by providing a social environment for group processes known to play a role in involvement in terrorism. Within the group context, it might be argued that individuals gradually adopt the beliefs and faith of the group's more extreme members in a psychological process known as 'risky shift'. Sageman (2004) found that such polarization experienced within the group, combined with an increased sense of group identity and commitment, has helped to radicalize individuals and facilitate their entry into terrorist organizations.[14] Thus, as well as playing a networking role in terms of widening individuals' social circle to include people who may be able to offer operational assistance or share expertise, such online environments may have a media effect of their own in terms of promoting radical beliefs and sense of belonging to a political community.

Crenshaw (1981) explains this mechanism in the terrorist context succinctly: 'a pattern of mutual reassurance, solidarity and comradeship develops, in which the members of the group reinforce each others self-righteousness, image of a hostile world, and sense of mission . . . terrorists are not necessarily people who seek belonging or personal integration through ideological commitment, but once embarked on the path of terrorism, they desperately need the group and the cause.'[15]

Internet Statistics

The internet is becoming a mass media platform for DR groups in Northern Ireland, and the proliferation in a Dissident Republican presence in discussion forums and social networking sites have been fuelled by the rapid development of the Northern Ireland telecommunications infrastructure. This is mirrored in the Republic of Ireland as shown below:

Table 6.1. Republic of Ireland (ROI) internet statistics

Year	Users	Population	% Population
2000	784,000	3,755,300	20.9
2002	1,319,608	3,780,600	34.9
2008	2,060,000	4,156,119	49.6

Sources: ITU (www.itu.int), Nielsen NR (www.Nielsen-netratings.com), CI Almanac (www.c-I-a.com)

A contract to provide 100 per cent broadband coverage in Northern Ireland, which was funded under the EU Building Sustainable Prosperity Programme, was awarded to BT at the end of March 2004. Prior to winning that contract, BT had enabled between 55–60% of exchanges in Northern Ireland. Following the enablement of BT's exchanges, over 200 ISPs and other companies have used the upgraded infrastructure to deliver broadband services to customers in Northern Ireland.

Demand for broadband in Northern Ireland has increased dramatically as exchanges have gone live. In just 12 months, the region moved from being one of the lowest levels of broadband uptake in the UK to become the fastest growing area.

Table 6.2. Northern Ireland households with internet access

Year	Coverage (%)
2006	50*
2007	52
2008	58

* Split as 28% broadband access and 22% non-broadband. Sources: National Statistics Reports, 23 August 2006 and 26 August 2008 (www.statistics.gov.uk)

Dissident Republican Propaganda

Media attention and direct external communications enable groups to promote their ideology, advertise their accomplishments, and otherwise get their message out to various audiences. Historically, terrorist groups have appealed to three primary audiences: their own members, supporters outside the group and adversaries and other observers.[16] RIRA have historically claimed their attacks, either in calls to media outlets or locally distributed leaflets.

RIRA videos are still freely available on open websites such as YouTube:

- 'Real IRA Video'.[17] Interestingly, this video carries an attribution to Óglaigh na hÉireann, and contains a pastiche of clips, some probably not of Irish origin, despite the protestations of Lagan Valley MP Jeffrey Donaldson, who described these YouTube videos as a form of cyber-terrorism:

It's entirely wrong that terrorist organisations can engage in blatant propaganda and cyber terrorism without any apparent sanction. Democratic governments need legislation to limit the capacity of these groups to spread their propaganda. At present, in effect, YouTube are broadcasting hardcore terrorism, unfiltered.

- The YouTube search facility was used to identify the following additional RIRA propaganda videos:

Table 6.3. YouTube RIRA propaganda videos

Video Title	Published Date	Posted by	Run Time	Number of Views
RIRA Propaganda Video	11 March 2009	TiocfaidhArLa1967	1:14	2915
Irish Republican Media – RIRA	3 November 2006	IrishRepublicanMedia	1:27	22832
32 County Sovereignty Movement	2 September 2009	Flemmy1916	8:48	5793
RIRA Colour Party at Derry 32CSM Easter Commemoration 2010	6 April 2010	Flemmy1916	2:09	4807
Oglaigh na h'Eireann Real IRA (RIRA)	1 December 2009	Flemmy1916	5:06	3058
RIRA CIRA	3 February 2007	truerepublican	10:05	19289
RIRA Drugs Cartel	3 March 2010	RIRAdontdodrugs	2:09	1160
RIRA/32CSM	2 February 2010	Flemmy1916	3:25	907
CIRA RIRA we haven't gone away you know!	2 February 2010	Flemmy1916	2:59	1479

In August 2009 YouTube[18] investigated the presence of films praising the DR groups. However, as of August 2010, RIRA and CIRA propaganda videos are still available on the YouTube video-sharing network. The YouTube guidelines clearly say that You Tube '*don't post videos showing... bomb making*'.[19] Some of these videos may well be in breach of the YouTube Company guidelines and furthermore in some circumstances may be in breach of the UK Terrorism Act 2006 if there is evidence of indirect incitement to commit terrorist acts. Many of these video files have been published on file sharing platforms in recent months, and very few are historical in nature.

One such video posted by a group called the 'Free Derry Media' entitled 'The War Goes On' is accompanied by a song denouncing the Provisional IRA. The lyrics include a verse telling the British to 'stick your decommissioning up your ass'. The imagery in the video includes masked gunmen firing a final salute over the coffin of Real IRA activist Joseph O'Connor who was allegedly shot dead by the Provisional IRA in West Belfast 10 years ago. The Free Derry Media (FDM) is an Irish republican broadcasting group with videos from various republican organizations. It is claimed to be run by a handful of young republicans from Derry City.[20]

In an interview with IrishRepublican.net on 18 October 2007, FDM stated their mission thus: 'our chief aim is to motivate youth and to encourage them to embrace republicanism, as well as educate those abroad who are curious.' The FDM are internet based and reliant on media such as YouTube to publish their product. FDM is heavily involved with www.IrishRepublican.net.

The Republican Network for Unity (RNU) was established in 2009 and aims to develop republican networking and partnerships with strategically allied groups including republican political parties or pressure groups, socialist movements and trade unions. Two of their key objectives are to:

- communicate positions effectively to the media and to the public
- facilitate internal communication, networking, organization and coordination within the broader Irish republican family.

A key element to all of this is the use of the internet as a propaganda tool. The RNU website (www.republicannetwork.ie) suggests a pseudo-paramilitary nature to their activities. RNU also has visible internet presence at Bebo, Facebook and Flickr.[21]

Irish Republican Web Forums

With the proliferation of the internet access in the ROI and Northern Ireland as noted above, so the use of Irish republican web forums has risen significantly in the last few years. The key web forums are listed below:

- Irish Republican (www.irishrepublican.net). Current membership: 11,754 (27 April 2010).
- Irish Freedom News (www.irishfreedomnews.com). Current membership: 513 (27 April 2010).
- Irish Republican Socialist Forum (http://rsmforum.proboards.com/index.cgi). Current membership 1667 (27 Apr 2010).
- Up the RA! (www.upthera.free-forums.org). Current membership: 336 (27 April 2010).
- Irish Republican Bulletin Board (IRBB) (http://admin2.7.forumer.com). Current membership: 1,209 (27 Apr 2010).
- Irish Nationalist (www.irish-nationalism.net). Current membership: 1,364 (27 April 2010)
- Ireland's Future (http://irelandsfuture.free-forums.org). Current membership: 1,107 (27 April 2010).

Membership Trends

Web forums generally provide readily visible statistics on their current membership and levels of activity. For this study, membership and activity data for the forums described above were collected over a period of several weeks, to ascertain the most significant sites in terms of membership base and also growth rate. The results are presented in Table 6.4, and visually in Figure 6.1.

Over the course of the period of analysis, by far the largest number of users (11,754 by 27 April 2010) was on the main republican site (www.irishrepublican.net). It also had the largest number of new users (216) over the period. This membership base makes it the most popular site by a factor of ten over the other known republican web forums. This makes it the most interesting site to focus on in the latter part of the study.

Interestingly, however, the largest growth rate in accordance with the

Table 6.4 Republican web forum membership

Web forum	19 Mar 10	23 Mar 10	12 Apr 10	22 Apr 10	27 Apr 10	New Members	% Growth Rate	Most Users Ever Online
Irish Republican	11,538	11,615	11,691	11,728	11,754	216	1.8	745
Irish Freedom News	496	507	512	513	513	17	3.3	34
Irish Republican Socialist Forum	1,634	1,638	1,658	1,663	1,667	33	1.9	142
Up the RA!	285	292	320	329	336	51	15.2	88
IRBB	1,188	1,192	1,205	1,207	1,209	21	1.7	133
Irish-Nationalism	1,337	1,338	1,356	1,361	1,364	27	1.9	339
Irelands Future	1,095	1,096	1,103	1,107	1,107	12	1.1	67

total membership is that related to 'Up the RA!' (www.upthera.free-forums.org) with a current growth rate between 19 March 2010 and 27 April 2010 of 15.2 per cent. Access to this forum requires registration.

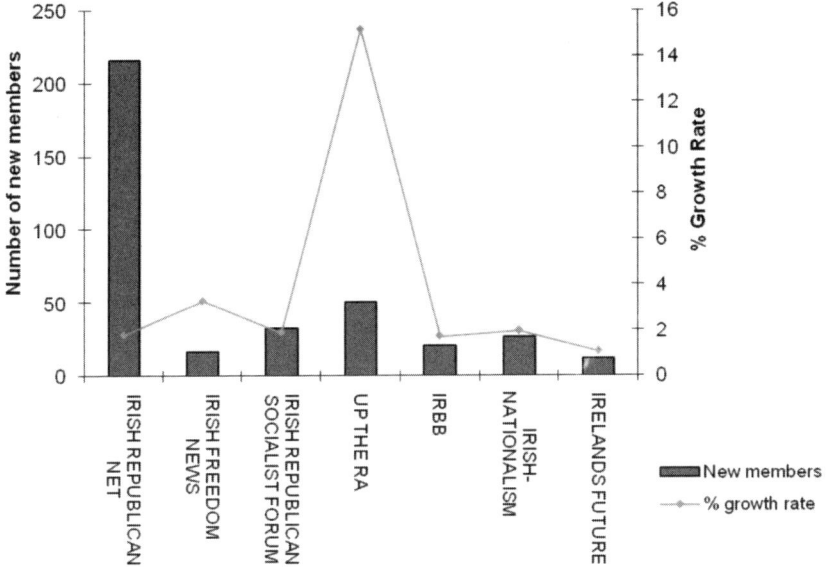

Figure 6.1 Increase in membership of main Irish republican web forums, 19 March 2010–27 April 2010

Web Forum Activity Levels

The numbers of posts on a forum give an indication both of levels of activity and levels of popularity of a site and are presented in Table 6.5 and Figure 6.2.

Both Table 6.5 and Figure 6.2 clearly show the distinctly higher levels of activity on IrishRepublican.net. The numbers of posts on this site are significantly higher than all the other main republican forums mirroring the differing levels of membership across the sites. One would expect that with a much higher membership base we would see more activity online, and this is certainly the case. Unexpectedly, however, as noted earlier, the highest growth rate (15.8 per cent) in levels of posting is ascribed again to the Up the RA! site during the period studied.

Table 6.5 Number of posts on key republican web forums

Web forum	19 Mar 10	23 Mar 10	12 Apr 10	22 Apr 10	27 Apr 10	New Members	% Growth Rate
Irish Republican	585,790	589,395	607,438	617,478	622,841	37,051	5.9
Irish Freedom News	12,622	12,685	12,833	12,861	12,874	252	1.9
Irish Republican Socialist Forum	19,556	19,616	20,076	20,277	20,385	829	4.1
Up the RA!	10,791	11,010	12,120	12,566	12,810	2,019	15.8
IRBB	52,137	52,270	52,798	53,477	53,666	1,529	2.8
Irish-Nationalism	125,024	125,107	125,793	126,227	126,352	1,328	1.0
Irelands Future	1,416	1,416	1,416	1,417	1,417	1	0.1

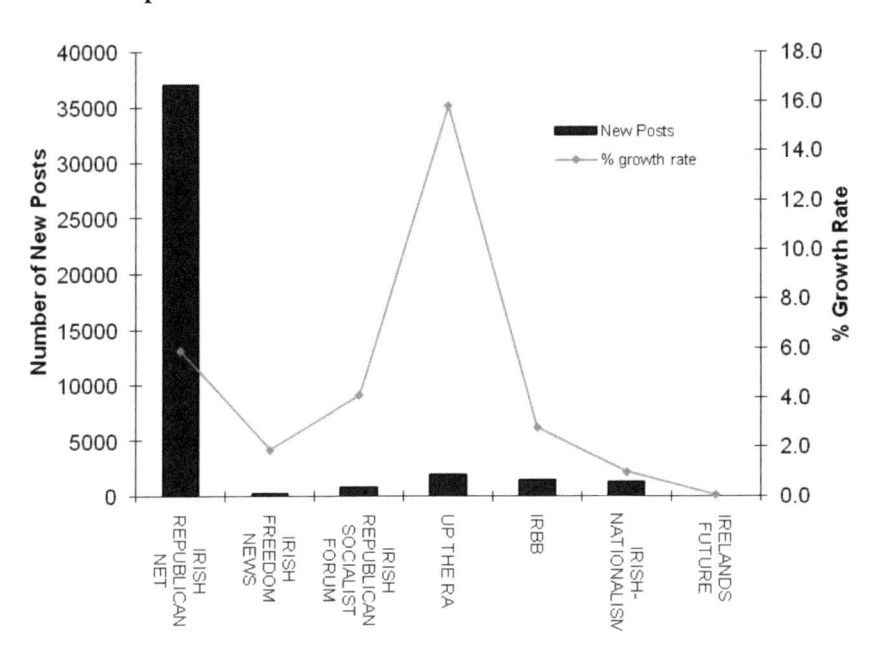

Figure 6.2 Number of new posts on Irish republican web forums, 19 March 2010 – 27 April 2010

Detailed Investigation into Main Republican Web Forum IrishRepublican.net

The data and graphics listed in the previous section clearly identify www.irishrepublican.net as a key dissident republican propaganda site on the internet with a large membership base and high levels of activity by site users. The site was created in May 2007 and within the first two months it had 116 members, which increased to 2000 after nearly a year. With over 11,700 members on the site (as of 27 April 2010) it is the most dominant site by a considerable margin. Figure 6.3 shows the exponential increase in the site's membership base since it was created.

Figure 6.4 illustrates the main themes of discussion on irishrepublican.net, and Figure 6.5 the percentage of posts for key categories (also presented in tabular form below).

132 DISSIDENT IRISH REPUBLICANISM

Figure 6.3   Irishrepublican.net web forum membership since May 2007

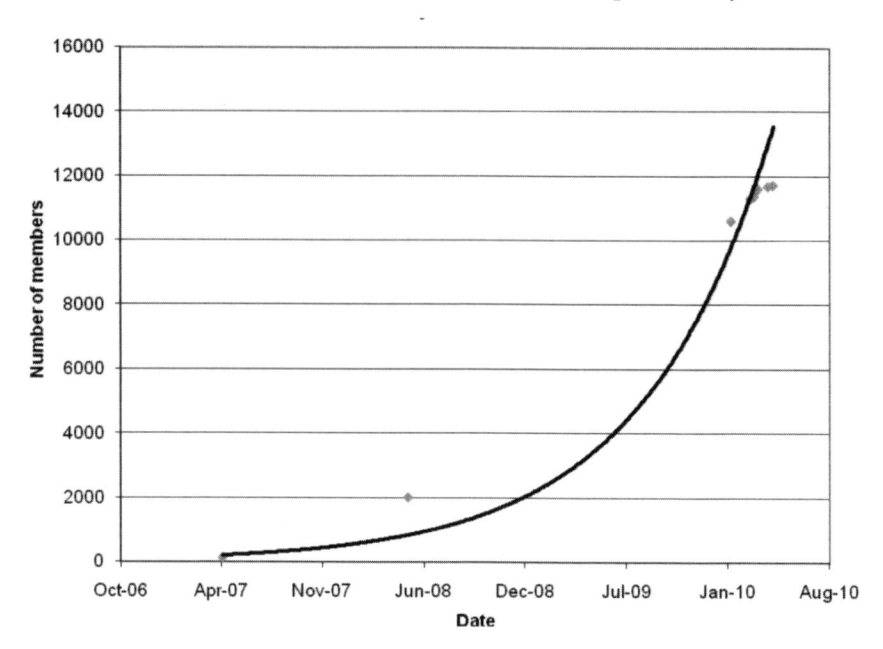

Figure 6.4. Distribution of main thread themes on irishrepublican.net web forum (data captured 22 April 2010)

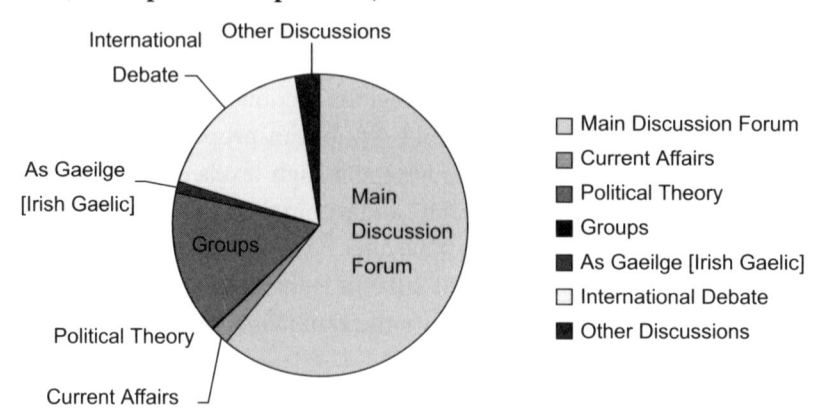

Figure 6.5 Distribution of key themes within irishrepublican.net forum posts (data captured 22 April 2010)

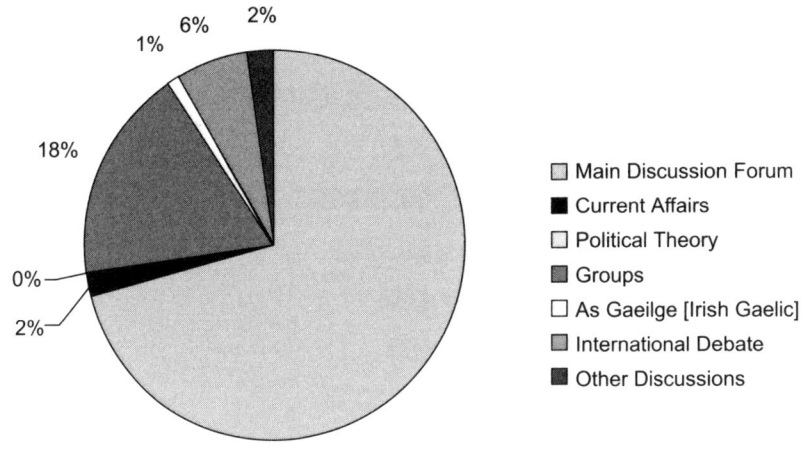

- Main Discussion Forum
- Current Affairs
- Political Theory
- Groups
- As Gaeilge [Irish Gaelic]
- International Debate
- Other Discussions

Table 6.6 Number of views for irishrepublican.net discussion sub-categories

Sub-Category	Views
Rights under Section 44	1,725
IRA's Green Book	3,720
Children of the Volunteers	1,380
Michael McKevitt[23]	1,731
Liam Hannaway[24]	3,288
Why I would not attend the Independent Hunger Commemorations	4,946
MI5 bomb marks terror innovation	1,094
MI5 HQ at Palace Barracks attacked with car bomb	11,364
Full blown armed campaign in 10–15 years' time	1,598

Noted previous threads from the site include a discussion on the UVIED (Under Vehicle Improvised Explosive Device) in January 2010 and the legitimacy of British soldiers as targets in March 2009. The main discussion areas are shown in Figure 6.6.

The content on the main area for members on the site clearly displays DR

Figure 6.6 Irishrepublican.net discussion sub-categories (data captured 22 April 2010)

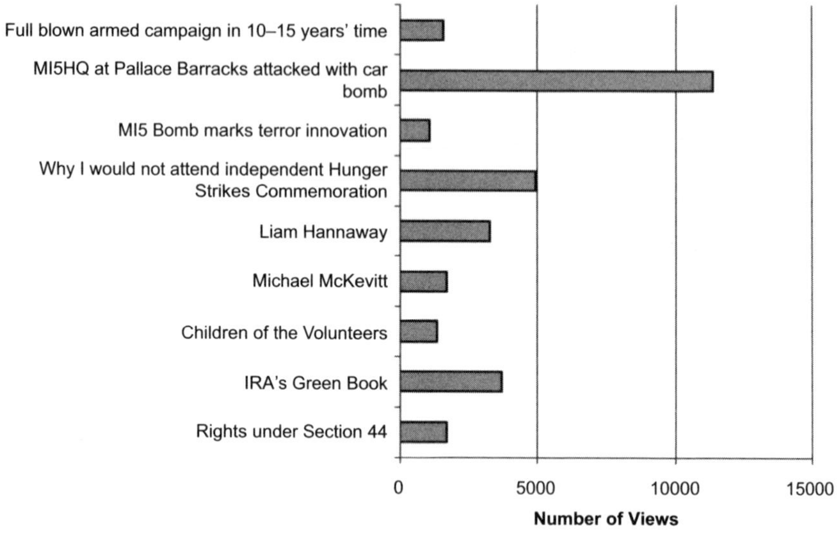

related material. Many of the mainstream websites and forums are allegedly coordinated by political bodies such as the 32CSM and RNU, but in reality they may be fronts for DR groups operating in the Province.

Discussion

As recently as 2008, it was possible for Reilly (2008) to argue, on the basis of the low visibility of republican and loyalist forums and websites in results returned by web search engines, that Northern Irish terrorists and their sympathizers are unlikely to achieve a greater degree of 'visibility' online than they enjoy in the conventional mass media.[25] As this chapter has shown, this is no longer the case. Dissident republican propaganda material is easily available on social networking sites, and dissident republican web communities appear to be growing at a rate that by far outstrips the overall increase in internet uptake in the region – even though, as noted, Northern Ireland already has the fastest growing broadband usage in the UK.

Whether this increase in DR activity on the internet is originally a cause or an effect of the overall upsurge in DR activity in the Northern Ireland and the Republic of Ireland generally is a question beyond the scope of this study. However, since radicalization processes in communities may be understood as constituting vicious circles in which radical sentiment begets violent effect and violent effect begets radical sentiment, it may be beside the point to determine whether the chicken or the egg came first in this case. Either way, the growing presence of DR content and communities on the Web is clearly a matter that warrants further attention, given the plausibility of radicalizing effects resulting both from consumption of propaganda and from social psychological factors (i.e., 'risky shift' as noted earlier) pertaining in online communities devoted to radical politics.

One potentially interesting point which seems to be raised by the data presented regarding the main subjects for discussion on 'IrishRepublican.net' is a potentially more subtle interplay between traditional terrorist strategies of producing spectacular, mass-media friendly attacks and the role of niche online media and communities particularly with local content or relevance. By far the most popular discussion thread on this forum was the car bombing of the MI5 headquarters at Palace Barracks, which presumably means that this event had the effect of attracting comments and log ins from people who were otherwise only occasional posters, or lurkers. This suggests that, rather than being simply a means of bypassing mass media, forums of this sort may represent a way for radical groups to frame coverage of their own attacks, and better retain and preserve waves of positive sentiment produced by such actions.

Further research could usefully be undertaken into the question of whether these active DR groups are developing their own media networks to publish propaganda and generate online social network platforms for recruitment purposes. This is an area that needs further attention but, judging by the professionalism of the material produced currently online, media cells may have evolved already within these groups. If so, this would correspond to the online modus operandi of al-Qaeda affiliate groups, which have developed their own distinct affiliate media production arms.[26]

It is unclear whether the content is the result of relatively stable and organized production teams or of more isolated and/or sporadic efforts, but further work into the relationship between the propagandists and the process of involvement in DR violence would clearly be of great value.

One final point is worth making in conclusion. The growing volume and sophistication of DR material should not necessarily be read as meaning that DR groups have developed a particularly sophisticated ideology. There is still reason to believe that these small micro dissident groups ultimately revolve around certain key personalities and cliques more than any well developed set of ideas, and that their interests have up to now been self-serving rather than driven by political strategies (see, for example, Morrison in this volume). Indeed, the online content surveyed in this chapter is at least as notable for its relatively simplistic, emotive themes as for any more nuanced argumentation (although this is also the case for example with some forms of al-Qaeda related material). Any strategies aimed to counter the effects of this material (e.g. 'counter-narrative' strategies) should therefore take this into account.

It may be worth trying to locate any counter-narrative initiatives focused on this context into our broader understanding of what we mean by preventing problematic and at times probably illegal behaviour on the internet.[27] Brantingham and Faust (1976) identify three kinds of crime prevention initiatives that may be relevant to our understanding of the development of counter-narrative strategies: *Primary prevention*, focused on stopping a crime before it occurs; *Secondary prevention*, directed at individuals thought to be at high risk of committing an offence; and *Tertiary prevention*, focused on known offenders.[28]

Within the context of dissident republicanism, the development of counter-narratives seems to most naturally fall within notions of primary prevention (i.e. stopping crime before it occurs), although there is also clear relevance for those farther along a trajectory towards violence. Typically primary prevention initiatives are divided into social preventative measures, and situational preventative measures. Social preventative measures in the main address the 'inclination' to offend, and are generally conceptualized in terms of educational initiatives or in broad social engineering terms where initiatives tend to be undifferentiated as to target group, and available to all, regardless of risk. Mass publicity initiatives aimed at alerting people in general to the dangers of smoking are examples of this approach. In terms of addressing dissident violence, such initiatives may have a place, but are essentially long term and necessarily lack a focus on the specific potential criminal incident or context. It should be noted that initiatives of this kind are often regarded as inefficient and of limited value in other crime prevention terms; poster campaigns, for example, to alert people to the dangers of drink-driving, have little effect on the incidence of driving under the influence of alcohol. In the context of the very wide availability of the internet, such initiatives can only be expected to have even more limited achievements. Their popularity, however, perhaps relates to a political imperative to be seen to be doing something, rather than an evidenced-based analysis of the problems.

Cornish and Clarke (2003) offer a typology of situational crime reduction techniques identifying five broad categories, each containing strategic sub categories – increase effort, increase risk, reduce rewards, reduce provocation, and remove excuses.[29] These five broad categories individually and together may offer a way of conceptualizing and structuring counter-narrative initiatives (see Freilich and Newman 2009 for an extensive discussion of these ideas);[30] indeed, they may offer a template for the development of a range of targeted initiatives, and the practical implications of this need to be further explored. Some of these strategies are likely to be more effective than others, and all are likely to be grounded in the specific context in which the individual finds him- or herself; quite clearly, one size will not fit all. This argues therefore for a range of initiatives premised on a systematic analysis of the nature and form of radicalization targeted, the kinds of individuals potentially involved, and the characteristics of the medium (i.e. internet protocol, type of involvement) to be used. This study provides a basis on which this further analysis might be developed with respect to problematic internet activity.

However derived, expression of violence that has its origins in internet activity requires transition from on-line to off-line activity to be effective and for the potential for violence to be expressed. As in other areas, where this transition point involves contact with others, it offers probably the most effective principal focus for practical law enforcement attention and intervention, with general educational programmes and other counter-narrative efforts to offer alternative perspectives and opportunities being developed in parallel by other agencies (actual or quasi civil society agencies). In general terms, and also with particular reference to dissident republicanism, we need more empirical information about transition points to identify qualities of vulnerability, but the development of strategies based on the five broad situational crime reduction techniques identified above (i.e. increase effort, increase risk, reduce rewards, reduce provocation, and remove excuses) seem to offer the most conceptually coherent strategies around which to structure intervention. Co-ordination and liaison between agencies will be necessary to ensure maximum impact and effectiveness. Experience in policing e-commerce crimes suggests that partnership arrangements with private agencies are necessary to achieve success (Newman and Clarke 2003).[31]

A tentative way of thinking about the nature of radicalization sites/problematic internet arenas accessed might be to think in terms of four categories:

1. *International – high profile* (for example al-Qaeda brand material appears on known propaganda sites and has high status accorded by for example Osama bin Laden or other well known figures).
2. *International – low profile* (for example, accessed through word of mouth – typically in a cafe after jumma prayer on a Friday afternoon a young Muslim is told about a site or a discussion forum that he should access).
3. *Local – known* (these might include the many extremist sites that operate in a grey area between legal campaigning and tacit support for al-Qaeda or dissident republican groups and the participants in discussions are sometimes well known to each other in the real world too).
4. *Local – unknown* (for example the plethora of clandestine sites which increasingly attract suspicion if users cannot get someone in the real world to vouch for them).[32]

Looking at the kind of areas people access in these terms might give an objective and systematic way of categorizing activity in terms of potential dangerousness, and also in terms of generating appropriate counter-narrative activities. It is important, however, to note the role of offline contact, and the difficulties this can present for access. Evidence from other areas involving similar activities (such as the child pornography world, for example [Jenkins 2009]) suggests that law enforcement activity can focus on the 'easier' areas that, while yielding high-profile arrests, may be of less significance and indeed be largely irrelevant in terms of addressing the substantive problems.[33] A clear sense of the target audience, and the outcomes expected or desired, is obviously important.

This paper offers a basis for the development of systematic initiatives to counter the Web-based influence of dissident groups. However, what we can say in summary is that the dissident republican movement can now be said with some confidence to have entered the information age. While the full significance of this development will take time and a good deal of further work to understand, it is an issue that clearly warrants such attention.

Notes

1. All reports can be found on the Independent Monitoring Commission website at: www.independentmonitoringcommission.org/.
2. *Twenty-First Report of the Independent Monitoring Commission*, 7 May 2009, www.independentmonitoringcommission.org/publications.cfm?id=71.
3. Della Porta, D. 'Left-Wing Terrorism in Italy', in Crenshaw, M. (ed.). *Terrorism in Context* (State College, PA: Pennsylvania State University Press, 1995), pp. 134–7.
4. Cragin, K. and Daly, S. *The Dynamic Terrorist Threat: An Assessment of Group Motivations and Capabilities in a Changing World*, Monograph Report MR-1782-AF (Santa Monica, CA: Rand Corporation Report, 2004).
5. Boyne, S. 'The Real IRA: After Omagh, What Now?' *Jane's Intelligence Review*, 24 August 1998; Cowen, R. 'Real IRA "Ready to Attack"', *Guardian Unlimited*, 21 October 2002.
6. *Twenty-Second Report of the Independent Monitoring Commission*, 4 November 2009, p. 6.
7. Rheingold, H. *The Virtual Community: Homesteading on the Electronic Frontier* (Reading, MA: Addison-Wesley, 2003).
8. O'Callaghan, S. *The Informer* (London: Granta, 1998).
9. Maleckova, J. 'Impoverished Terrorists: Stereotype or Reality?' in Bjorgo, T. (ed.) *Root Causes of Terrorism* (London: Routledge, 2005), pp. 33–43.
10. Schmid, A. and Jongman, A. *Political Terrorism*, 2nd edition (Oxford: North Holland, 1988).
11. Schmid, A. and De Graaf, J. *Violence as Communication: Insurgent Terrorism and the Western News Media* (London: Sage Publications, 1982).
12. Reilly, P. 'Googling Terrorists: Are Northern Irish Terrorists Visible on Internet Search Engines?' *Information, Science and Knowledge Management*, 14, 3 (2008), 151–75.
13. Payne, K. 'Winning the Battle of Ideas: Propaganda, Ideology and Terror', *Studies in Conflict and Terrorism*, 32 (2009), 109–28.
14. Sageman, M. *Understanding Terrorist Networks* (Philadelphia, PA: University of Pennsylvania Press, 2004).

15. Crenshaw, M. 'The Causes of Terrorism', *Comparative Politics*, 13, 4 (July 1981), 393.
16. Hoffman, B. *Inside Terrorism* (New York: Colombia University Press, 1998).
17. www.youtube.com/watch?v=6vH7IOnuVyU&feature=related
18. McDonald, H. 'MP calls on YouTube to remove Real IRA propaganda videos', *The Observer*, 2 August 2009, www.guardian.co.uk/technology/2009/aug/02/youtube-ira-facebook-cyber-terrorism.
19. www.youtube.com/t/community_guidelines
20. 'An Interview with Free Derry Media', Independent Media Centre Ireland, 18 October 2007, www.indymedia.ie/article/84716.
21. www.bebo.com/RepublicanN4, http://www.facebook.com/group.php?gid=271508519579 and www.flickr.com/photos/republicannetworkforunity.
22. The main category on the site is the 'Main Discussion Forum', which has numerous sub-categories.
23. Michael McKevitt originally launched the Real IRA after splitting from PIRA and was sentenced in August 2003 to 20 years in Portlaoise Prison.
24. Liam Hannaway is serving a 10-year sentence in Maghaberry prison for possession of explosives and ammunition. He is believed to be linked to the DR group Saor Uladh.
25. Reilly (2008), pp. 151–75.
26. Kimmage, D. *The al-Qaeda Media Nexus: The Virtual Network behind the Global Message*, Radio Free Europe/Radio Liberty Special Report (Washington, DC: RFE/RL, May 2008), http://www.scribd.com/doc/3792892/AQ-Media-Nexus
27. For a discussion of issues related to counter-narratives, see Akerboom, E. *Countering Violent Extremist Narratives* (Netherlands: National Coordinator for Counterterrorism, January 2010), http://english.nctb.nl/current_topics/reports/.
28. Brantingham, P. and Faust, F. A. 'Conceptual Model of Crime Prevention', *Crime Prevention and Delinquency*, 22, 3 (1976), 284–96.
29. Cornish, D. and Clarke, R. 'Opportunities, Precipitators and Criminal Decisions: A Reply to Wortley's Critique of Situational Crime Prevention', in Smith, M. and Cornish, D. (eds), *Theory for Practice in Situational*

Crime Prevention, Crime Prevention Studies 16 (Monsey, NY: Criminal Justice Press, 2003), pp. 151–96.
30. Freilich, J. D. and Newman, G. R. *Reducing Terrorism through Situational Crime Prevention*, Crime Prevention Studies 25 (Cullompton: Willan Publishing, 2009).
31. Newman, G. R. and Clarke, R. *Superhighway Robbery: Preventing e-Commerce Crime* (Cullompton: Willan Publishing, 2003).
32. Personal communication to M. Taylor by R. Lambert.
33. Jenkins, P. 'Failure to Launch: Why Do Some Social Issues Fail to Detonate Moral Panics?' *British Journal of Criminology*, 49 (2009), 35–47.

CHAPTER 7

'Not Like in the Past': Irish Republican Dissidents and the Ulster Loyalist Response

JAMES W. McAULEY
UNIVERSITY OF HUDDERSFIELD

... people who might have approved of the fact that the Provos were getting a bloody nose ... would also have realised that that wasn't the way to do business indefinitely and it couldn't go on like that ...[1]

Introduction

Although everyday social relations in Northern Ireland are much changed and politics is increasingly afforded a more leading role in societal organization, political violence remains a constant. Despite huge advances made towards ending overt conflict and transforming civil society, such violence is still experienced, albeit at a far less intense level than during the height of the conflict. Thus, part of everyday life for many is still reflected in the more than 3,000 sectarian crimes and incidents reported by the Police Service of Northern Ireland (PSNI) in 2006.[2]

While low-level sectarian conflict remains a reality, there are also occasional peaks in the level of violence. Within loyalism this violence has largely been turned inwards, in a series of murderous and bloody inter-loyalist feuds. Sections of republicanism, however, have engaged in consistently escalating acts of armed violence, driven by what have become known as 'dissident groupings' claiming that they continue to challenge the British presence in Ireland.

Emergence of Republican Dissidents

Since the accord of 1998 militaristic actions undertaken by republican dissidents have grown in frequency and intensity, providing a channel for those identified by Alonso[3] as having rejected the overt politicization of the republican movement by the provisional leadership and instead demanded that primacy be given to maintaining a military campaign. Thus, a grouping calling itself the Continuity IRA (CIRA) declared it had parted company from the Provisional movement as early as 1986, while another faction, the Real IRA found recognition in 1997, and public infamy in 1998 when it planted a no-warning car bomb in Omagh that killed 29 people.

Forced onto the back foot by widespread international condemnation of the Omagh bomb, and the reaction of security forces, the occurrence of dissident violence abated for some years, but resumed in 2000 with an attack on the London headquarters of MI6, followed with a device at the BBC Television Centre in London in 2001 and, in August 2002, the killing of a civilian worker at a Territorial Army base in Londonderry, with a bomb hidden in a lunchbox.[4]

Eventually, after several failed attempts, dissident republicans succeeded in the killing of state security forces. On 7 March 2009 RIRA members disguised as pizza deliverymen killed two British soldiers at an army base near Antrim, the first such deaths in Northern Ireland since 1997. Three days later the CIRA claimed responsibility for the first fatal shooting of a PSNI officer in Northern Ireland since 1998. Since then dissident republicans have been engaged in a continual and escalating campaign of violence, involving 'pipe bombs', large-scale explosive devices, car bombs and shootings.

The Response of Ulster Loyalism

One of the key features of the contemporary period has been the response of loyalism in general, and loyalist paramilitarism in particular, to actions of dissident republicanism. That riposte from loyalism, certainly in military terms, has been muted, indeed all but entirely absent. In previous times much of the dynamic of loyalist paramilitarism was driven by a desire, to use David Ervine's phrase, to 'return the serve' to republicans. Loyalist paramilitaries were engaged in what they regarded as their own brand of 'counter-terrorism'.

Thus, reports that dissident republican paramilitary groups 'remain highly active and dangerous'[5] would undoubtedly have set loyalist paramilitarism into a state of high alert. Certainly, for long periods of recent history it is almost inconceivable that an increase in republican violence would not have been mirrored by loyalist groupings and incidents such as the killing of soldiers or attacks on the Police Service of Northern Ireland (PSNI) would have drawn a direct, and most likely bloody reply from loyalist paramilitaries.

So how can we explain this response (or rather lack of it) from loyalism? There may be a very straightforward answer; that loyalists have bought completely into the political process following the Belfast and St Andrew's Agreements, decommissioning and the subsequent move towards the primacy of politics away from armed conflict. That is, indeed, true for sections of loyalism. To answer the question fully, however, involves widening our gaze to include a series of factors including loyalist perceptions and understandings of republicanism before and at the point of 'settlement', and the subsequent levels and direction of loyalist engagement with the peace process and civil society, particularly through conflict transformation. This has involved active processes of defining and redefining the 'enemy' and the desirability and 'legitimacy' of responses to them.

Following the outbreak of conflict in the early 1970s, loyalism found expression in a number of ways, through a wide variety of organizations. This eventually resulted in two major paramilitary groupings, the Ulster Defence Association (UDA) and the Ulster Volunteer Force (UVF), both of which at the community level began to organize and take coherent shape. Within these, the two main threads of 'militarism' and 'politics' quickly emerged, sometimes they were intertwined, sometimes diversified.[6]

Thus, as Northern Irish society split apart into highly sectarianized geographical, political and social structures, the objectives and tactics of various loyalist paramilitaries groupings sometimes differed and sometimes coalesced. Their activities and organization differed: the UDA, was large, openly organized and federal in its structure with high levels of autonomy at the local level, compared to the smaller UVF, which was underground and organized in cells, most often known as 'units' or 'teams'.

Defining the 'Enemy'

Although the actions of the groupings varied, underpinning loyalist paramilitarism was often some element of a sectarianized definition of 'the Other'. Described in classic terms by Said,[7] the construction of the Other involves processes of inclusion and exclusion, whereby one group is defined as different or inferior in relation to another. In this case of loyalists the place of nationalists (and therefore most Catholics) was reinforced as untrustworthy and excluded from the political organization and dominant culture of 'Ulster'.

But the above offers only one part of our understanding; there were always other overtly stated goals such as 'protecting their community' and 'taking the war to republicanism', often driven by the notion that the state forces were unable (or unwilling) to do so. What this meant on the ground varied considerably at different times and in different phases of the conflict, and the dynamic shifted over time. Shirlow and McEvoy suggest that both loyalists and republicans 'viewed violence as the logical response to the denial of their respective rights'.[8] More broadly, loyalist paramilitarism operated with a remit of what Harris[9] calls its own 'strategic environment' and the spectrum for involvement ranged from open sectarianism, to the protection of localized districts, to what many involved regarded as an engagement in counter-terrorism.

By the mid 1980s, loyalist paramilitarism drew heavily on the notion of a 'pan-nationalist front' that was finding a central place across unionist thinking. This reflected a growing belief that the Irish government, the White House, the Irish American lobby and the republican movement were working in accord to undermine unionism. Moreover, there was a growing belief (again shared across much of unionism) that the British government was no longer willing directly to defend Unionist interests and that they had uncritically taken onboard the political analysis of the pan-nationalists as a central organizational principle of the peace process.[10]

Loyalist paramilitarism interpreted and acted on this in particular ways. By the 1990s the conception of those seen as 'enemy' (and thus a 'legitimate' target) had become very wide indeed, broadening from republican paramilitaries, to members of the republican movement, to those who did (or might) support republicanism, to those who lived in republican areas or even those who read or sold republican literature. For some, especially a section of the

UDA based on the Shankill Road, it was often enough that the target was a Catholic, their actions bringing Belfast to 'the verge of all-out sectarian warfare' by the end of 1991.[11]

Broadly, loyalist paramilitary actions became located in an increasingly loose ideology of breaking support for the PIRA within Catholic districts, instilling widespread fear of attack, thus 'drying up the sea from the fish'[12] and separating republicanism from its community support. Overall, loyalist paramilitaries sought to justify what they did as within a framework of pro-state violence and 'terrorising the terrorists'.

The Politics of Paramilitarism

There were also other dynamics at play. As I have argued fully elsewhere the contested nature of the Northern Irish state, experiences of Protestant working-class life, the social structure of Unionism and the conflict all combined to give loyalism a particular form and direction.[13] Throughout the past 40 years, some of those involved in loyalist paramilitarism have at various points also sought to find forms of political organization to express collective concerns. Again, there was a range of experiences across the main paramilitary groupings.

The UDA and politics

The UDA has had several political outlets for its support within working-class Protestant areas. The New Ulster Political Research Group (NUPRG) emerged in the mid 1970s openly promoting a negotiated Independent Ulster as a solution to the deepening conflict. Details of the proposals were revealed in their policy document, *Beyond the Religious Divide*.[14] By the mid 1980s the UDA had formed a more formal political organization, the Ulster Loyalist Democratic Party (ULDP), which in 1989 became the UDP, winning a local council seat in Londonderry.

Throughout the 1970s and 1980s, the strength and form of political organization, and the desire to find some form of public political expression varied considerably, often determined by broader paramilitary reactions to the conflict, the levels of violence in the wider society (in which, of course the UDA was centrally involved) and loyalist attempts to counter the strategies and tactics of the republican movement. During that time, however, and no matter how contradictory the position often appeared, the UDA continued to promote some notion of a 'shared identity' as the possible basis for conflict resolution.

The political position of the UDA was rethought in light of reactions to the signing of the Anglo-Irish Agreement in 1985 and in particular what was seen as the inability of the established unionist leadership to influence events in their favour.[15] Following widespread involvement on the streets, and growing disillusion with the mainstream unionist response, the UDA again turned directly to the main tenets outlined in *Beyond the Religious Divide* to formulate a new position articulated in *Common Sense*.[16] Among the central proposals of this document was the establishment of a devolved power-sharing government in Northern Ireland. Although it often remained difficult to see how this married with events on the streets, the political direction outlined in *Common Sense* still stood as the determinant of UDA's political agenda and direction.

Politics and the UVF

Those directly associated with the other main loyalist grouping, the UVF have also sought to find conduits for political expression. The earliest was in the 1970s in the shape of the failed Volunteer Political Party (VPP). Although the political thinking of the UVF throughout the 1970s was erratic[17] a more significant grouping was eventually to emerge from within the UVF comprising an identifiable group of members directly politicized and made socially aware by events undergone whilst in gaol.[18] It was this cohort that was eventually to form the nucleus of the leadership of the Progressive Unionist Party (PUP) and Spence can claim with much justification to be midwife to the movement that was later to become known as 'new loyalism'.[19]

A key part of the strategy devised by Spence was to provoke self-questioning and examination of individual and political motives among UVF prisoners.[20] One result was a heightened awareness of political and social issues among some loyalist prisoners, often brought about by the participation in both informal discussions and more formal political debates. Although neither the numbers involved, nor its extent should be over-emphasized (and while recognizing that this took place in the somewhat 'rarefied' atmosphere of prison), Spence and his immediate followers did seek to reconstruct given wisdom within loyalism and some of the relationships between loyalists and republicans.

While UVF prisoners had little time for the Provisional IRA (PIRA), dismissing them as devoid of 'a political agenda',[21] within the gaols Spence developed working relationships with the Official republican movement, whom he saw as 'military men'.[22] There was even a joint protest organized between Official IRA (OIRA) and UVF prisoners to demand political status.[23] Moreover, he actively encouraged those UVF prisoners on prison education classes (such as those run by the Open University) to discuss political ideas with OIRA inmates.

None of this is to say that this new political input marked a step change for the UVF. Many UVF prisoners saw little or no value in the form of democratic socialism promoted by Spence and his colleagues, and even less worth in their willingness to accept Catholics into the Northern Ireland state.[24] For many other UVF members the political debates were simply too much, too soon.[25] Although Spence provided classic charismatic leadership it was not until many years later that the views expressed by the UVF within the prisons found concrete expression in the form of the PUP.

The UDA did not have an equivalent of Gusty Spence in the gaols[26] nor anything resembling his regime of political and educational development. Indeed, the organizational structure of the loyalist paramilitaries inside prison directly reflected the configuration outside of the gaols, meaning that within the UDA leadership was much looser and more autonomous than that of the more hierarchical UVF. One consequence was that in the prisons the UDA was less likely to engage in organized educational activities[27] and the scope for prisoners to organize themselves into discussion groups was limited.[28] The majority of incarcerated UDA regarded themselves as little other than 'prisoners of war'.[29]

Further, there can be little doubt that the main dynamic of loyalist paramilitarism was determined by those 'fighting the war' outside the gaols, rather than those incarcerated. That said, loyalist prisoners played an important role in the development of loyalist political thinking, but the process was never linear and was complicated by factionalism, overlaps in the membership (sometimes ideological, sometimes pragmatic and sometimes personality driven) and changing emphasis among those involved. As one former UVF member[30] explained, there has always been fluidity in the tactics and positions taken by many within the paramilitaries and any analysis that sought to reduce paramilitary dynamics to 'hawks and doves', or good and bad paramilitaries misunderstood the nature of loyalist paramilitarism.

Hence, ideological and more down-to-earth conflicts, military and political differences (and the intertwining of these), internal disputes, personality differences and clashes over control of territory all continued to surround the positioning of loyalist paramilitaries and the political groupings emerging from them. The situation was not made any more transparent because of the tendency of individuals and clusters of paramilitaries to move between these positions in response to wider political circumstances or events on the ground.[31]

Loyalist Perceptions at the Point of Settlement

Thus, when the PIRA called a halt to its armed campaign in late 1994 there were a variety of views on offer within loyalist paramilitary circles, ranging from those voices strongly supporting engagement in the political process, to those who sought to step up the war machine.[32] Some at least, believed that the PIRA decision to call a ceasefire was a sign of republican weakness arguing that the intensity of the loyalist military campaign should be heightened until Irish republicanism was completely defeated or openly surrendered.[33]

For some, what had been achieved had not been brought about by stalemate,[34] rather it marked a military victory for loyalism and that republicans had been forced to sue for peace. Others believed that while they may indeed have reached the point of compromise, loyalism should not move (or be seen to move) until complete and public surrender was declared by the PIRA. Broad sections of the paramilitaries thought the best response was to 'wait and see', believing that the PIRA was unable to hold its position, which it had entered into merely as a tactical ploy. This partly explains in the wake of the PIRA ceasefire announcement why the response from loyalist paramilitaries was much slower in coming than many had expected (or hoped).

As it became apparent that the PIRA ceasefire was likely to hold, and the possibility grew that the armed PIRA campaign was really at an end, a number of major contradictions within loyalist paramilitarism were brought to the surface. Many had long justified loyalist paramilitarism as providing a direct response to republican violence. Some members recognized the central justification of their organization's existence now seemed removed. It took some time, however, for loyalist paramilitarism to work through the variances arising from the PIRA ceasefires, and the struggles that arose structured and framed loyalist paramilitary politics for over a decade following the accord. More immediately, some six weeks after the PIRA ceasefire, and crucially, following acceptance of further government assurances that the Union was secure, loyalists too announced that they would terminate their violent campaign. Three points in this ceasefire announcement are particularly noteworthy in understanding the structure of events that followed. First, the expression of 'abject and true remorse' offered to 'the loved ones of all innocent victims' of the conflict; second, the expression that the Union was safe; finally, the claim that 'the sole responsibility for a return to war' would rest with Irish republicanism and that the loyalist ceasefire would be permanent unless republican groupings resumed violence.[35]

The Politics of the Paramilitaries

The subsequent response of loyalism can be seen as an engagement with the two core questions underpinning the Combined Loyalist Military Command (CLMC) statement; whether the Union was completely secured, and whether the 'war' really had indeed ended. Much of loyalist politics since has been driven by attempts to resolve their position in direct relation to these key factors, and, as we shall see, contemporary loyalist attitudes to dissident republicanism reflect the way in which a consensus was framed across loyalism in answer to these questions. Subsequent difficulties in loyalist political developments reflect the level of disagreement across loyalism concerning the Belfast Agreement, the lack of trust towards the UK government and the intentions of Sinn Féin, and strong feelings from within sections of the loyalist community that they had lost out in the peace process.

The dynamic did begin to shift towards those promoting a political dimension and what became known as 'new loyalism' began to establish a political foothold within unionism. In summary, the main perspectives offered by both the Progressive Unionist Party (PUP) and the Ulster Democratic Party (UDP) suggested a distrust of unionist leadership,[36] a strong belief that loyalists had throughout the conflict been used, both ideologically and logistically, by established unionist politicians.[37]

Commonplace among loyalist paramilitaries were the views that mainstream unionist politicians had often 'sabre rattled', created a broad political atmosphere whereby some saw a paramilitary response as justified, only to 'walk away' from those gaoled for paramilitary activity; and a developing articulation that the effects of social marginalization experienced in many working-class Protestant communities were neither recognized, nor of concern, to the unionist political leadership.[38]

By the late 1980s both the PUP (with strong links to the UVF) and the UDP (as the political voice of the UDA) sought to present themselves as alternatives for unionist votes. Their subsequent directions were determined not just by reactions to broader political issues, but also by the relationship they were able to construct with the paramilitary groups to which each was affiliated. Moreover, all of this was contested, witness the Loyalist Volunteer Force (LVF), led by the late Billy Wright, the formation of which was driven, in part at least, by its opposition to PUP support for the Agreement.

Tensions also quickly surfaced, between the UDA and the UDP. The party had been allocated two seats in the Forum election (under the special arrangements designed to ensure inclusivity). In the election of the first Assembly, however, the UDP failed to win representation (unlike the PUP that had two members elected). From that point the UDP was all but dead in the water; the gap between the party leadership and the mainstream UDA membership increasingly apparent, the value of politics to the UDA undermined and at best postponed. It was clear that the UDA leadership was unable (or unwilling) to mobilize its membership in electoral support for the UDP.

Within UDA ranks the perceptions that British citizenship and the Union had been diluted by the Agreement, were widespread by the mid 1990s. The majority of UDA rank and file membership remained anti-Agreement, and the distance between many UDA members and their supposed political representatives in the UDP was obvious. By the end of the decade the UDA was part of that section of loyalism, which felt increasingly disenfranchised from the peace process, and UDA members were expressing palpable hostility towards the UDP and the political consequences of the Agreement.

This phase culminated in July 2001, when, under the banner of the Ulster Freedom Fighters (UFF), the UDA released a statement making clear the leadership's opposition to the Agreement and the entire peace process.[39] For some time it appeared that the UDA ceasefire was 'teetering on the brink'[40] under pressure from much of its membership who regarded the political path as largely resulting in the marginalization of the UDA and its ability to influence events.

The UDP was dissolved on 28 November 2001, and replaced by the Ulster Political Research Group (UPRG) which was made up from those much more sympathetic to the UDA's then leadership and the dominant anti-Agreement stance of the membership. It was charged with providing political advice rather than seeking a political mandate and the notion of contesting elections was largely abandoned. It was far from coincidental that the period also saw an upsurge in sectarian tensions and violence, mounting attacks on Catholic homes, severe intra-loyalist violence, and growing evidence that sections of the UDA were involved in criminal activities including drugs.

Transforming Conflict

It was to be early 2005 before any coherent political platform emerged from the UPRG amidst claims that the UDA was now fully committed to developing a political role and seeking to implant new political initiatives based on reconciliation across the ranks of the organization.[41] Thus began the meaningful engagement of the UDA with the notion of conflict transformation, understood here broadly as the reframing of conflict and a reworking of social conditions to allow mutual coexistence,[42] in circumstances of much reduced (or no) violence and the participation of the minority political and social grouping in a power-sharing government.[43]

Such notions had held currency within the UVF/ PUP grouping for some time, the actual term 'conflict transformation' first appearing in material produced by PUP in the early 1980s. The route taken by the UVF was, however, different and within that grouping those who were active in the political arena were given a greater level of legitimacy (both internally and externally) much earlier than their equivalent in the UDA. Further, although there were some exceptions, the UVF remained largely supportive of, or at least non-interventionist in, PUP politics.[44]

Decision-making was also easier within the UVF as decisions were taken by fewer people and by a much longer established leadership. The dominant attitude toward the PUP reflected a willingness to allow them to 'get on with it' provided the UVF was assured that the Union was secure. The issue was much more contested within the UDP/ UDA grouping, which was less able to persuade its followers that the Union was 'copper-fastened' or that a deal had not been struck between the UK government and Sinn Féin.

Further, the PUP had also been able to present a much more coherent analysis and far more friendly media face than the UDP/ UPRG. The PUP's approach reflected a more broadly based sociological understanding, located in the broad notion that the Protestant working-class had also suffered disadvantage during the period of Stormont rule.[45] The PUP was also able to convince its supporters that they would be able to engage fully in the politics of the post-settlement period, in a way that the UDA grouping could not with its followers. Further, there was also a belief that working relationships could be developed between the PUP and representatives of Irish republicanism.[46]

In loyalist working-class districts, paramilitaries, former paramilitary prisoners, other community activists, and members of the UDP and PUP were coming together to engage in and develop new post-conflict politics. Within and around the PUP grouping there emerged a discourse that was both self-critical of existing unionist politics and pluralistic in its political outlook.[47]

This sought to distance 'ordinary Protestants' from the traditional unionist political leadership and to promote both intra- and inter-community dialogue. Indeed, PUP perspectives proved important in promoting introspection and in creating an atmosphere where at least political change could be contemplated among key elements of the Protestant working-class, including the transformation of existing sectarian social relations.[48]

But the rate of promotion of 'transformation' was far from constant, differing not just because of differing political positions taken by the main paramilitary groupings (and their representatives), but also because of structural and organizational limitations. Experiences and processes differed both between and across the UDA and UVF groupings and across various sections within them. The internal relationships of the UDA grouping remained complex and the determination of events highly localized.[49] Nonetheless, while in the period following the Agreement the organization continued to engage in violence and criminal activity, this should not mask the political direction that many within the organization were seeking to take.

Loyalism overall was in a state of flux. Certainly there was no unified political response from loyalist paramilitarism and future political direction remained contested. The UDA came to the notion of conflict transformation much more slowly than the UVF, and amidst much internal opposition and resistance. It was only after 2004 that some form of transition to the political sphere could be seen as central to the thinking of the UDA. Even then they remained extremely wary of new threats from republicans in 'peacetime' and openly concerned about what they regarded as an increasing number of 'concessions' to Sinn Féin and processes of destabilization and territorial aggrandisement by republicanism.

Processes of Transformation

As key sections of loyalist paramilitarism (and post-paramilitarism) sought to engage more fully with processes of political change and conflict transformation they were forced to seek to resolve wider issues around their very existence, the decommissioning of weapons, their involvement in crime and criminality, the desire of some to 'police' working-class communities and their wish to influence politics and other relationships within the broad unionist community and between that community and Irish nationalism.

None of this was settled quickly, but one key grouping determining the direction of loyalism at street level was made up from former combatants whose experiences helped reshape their political input often following a reassessment of why they had participated in paramilitarism, and what had been achieved by the conflict.[50] This led some former combatants to develop approaches, based on community engagement and developing community cohesion,[51] that have, with varying levels of success, sought to change social relationships both within and across loyalist communities.

A core aim for many former loyalist combatants, for example, now is to ensure that 'ethno-sectarian segregation between communities is not bolstered by the promotion of oppositional discourses'.[52] The impact of such groupings has increasingly been seen in a range of voluntary political and social activities,[53] most of which take place outside the arena of formal state intervention and organization (in that political arena which is often referred to as civil society).

But the path for some has been a long one. The primacy of non-violent means to achieve the goals for the UDA has been subject to much internal debate and dispute. The position was reached through a series of informal and formal consultations with its membership badged under the 'Loyalism in Transition' initiative. It found political expression through *A New Reality*, published by the UPRG in October 2006 and the consultations were outlined well in a series of pamphlets edited by Michael Hall.[54]

Taken together these sources reveal a UDA membership whose major concern remained the security of the Union. While most reflected that the time was right to move the focus for the organization away from the military towards the political, this did not mean that most conceded that the war was over. Rather, the bulk of the UDA membership saw loyalism as now engaged in a different form of struggle, and while they conceded (albeit sometimes reluctantly), that the PIRA's military campaign might be at a close, they believed they were now entering a different phase and form of conflict.[55]

As Hall records, when UDA members were asked if they thought 'was the war over?' a majority stated that they believed that it was not. However, as Hall explored their views in more depth, he then explains that as discussions among UDA members progressed it became apparent that while most members thought the PIRA's military campaign might be over, most were convinced that their political war certainly was not.[56]

Hall has provided further details on some of the discussions held by the UDA membership through the proceedings of an international workshop on conflict transformation.[57] Although the UDA did concede that 'they too have been part of the problem' the documentation suggests that discussions among rank and file quickly returned to longer standing themes within UDA thinking such as how the unionist political leadership, particularly the DUP, have abandoned 'ordinary Protestants' and broad disaffection with what is perceived as the lack of strong community leadership.[58]

The riposte from the UPRG has seen increasingly articulated concern regarding the social and economic conditions within loyalism, calling for government measures to counter low employment levels and opportunities and the lack of educational success in Protestant working-class areas. They also point to the fear of the diminution of their cultural heritage, through processes whereby Ulster Protestant identity is constantly challenged and the perceived need to 'face down republicans' by defending the 'British culture' of Northern Ireland, which has been undermined by political events.[59]

This culminated in late 2008 with a UDA statement that they would seek to retrain members to engage in peaceful struggle 'on a new battlefield' of cultural politics to be fought out on the terrain of media presentation, education, politics, social and community work and business.[60] Thus, the consensus that emerged was that, while the PIRA may have changed its tactics, their prime goal of a united Ireland remained exactly the same. For a majority of members the UDA remains Ulster's 'last line of defence' to take the 'fight into the political arena'.[61]

Redefining Loyalism

So while the understanding of conflict transformation differed between the UVF and the UDA and while within the latter grouping it was more contested, there has been a growing recognition in the post-conflict period of the need for paramilitaries to deepen local involvement in processes of community development. Sections of the paramilitaries and former combatants remain embedded in the community and display examples of leadership through the negotiation for scarce social, economic and political resources on behalf of working-class communities, rather than direct involvement in violence.[62]

The broad dynamic for much of the above is provided through the concept of conflict transformation, operating both within and between the two communities.[63] Further, it is clear that paramilitaries, former prisoners and their associates have been involved in a range of activities successfully aimed at de-escalating confrontation between communities[64] and positive engagement within their own communities.[65]

While not denying the 'negative social equity that all paramilitaries (to a greater or lesser extent) impose upon their own communities',[66] within identifiable geographical locations many of those who have been involved with the paramilitaries retain social status and some level of authority when involved in community development activities.[67] Violence perpetrated by paramilitaries (both within and without loyalist communities) was always a limiting factor in political expansion and in attempts to have the voices of paramilitary representatives heard. Nonetheless, since the ceasefires some sections of paramilitarism (notably former prisoners) have shown leadership in the transformation from cultures of violence towards other forms of political and social expression.[68]

Sections of paramilitarism, former paramilitarism and the political representatives that have emerged continue to be seen from within to represent those loyalist communities that 'are not reaping the benefits of the new era . . . and feel isolated'.[69] Social and political relationships surrounding former combatants and the wider unionism community are still not fully formed, however; witness the resignations of Dawn Purvis as leader of the PUP, and those of other leading members, following a murder in Belfast by the UVF in June 2010. Explaining her decision, Dawn Purvis claimed that she could 'no longer offer leadership to a political party . . . expected to answer for the indefensible actions of others'.[70]

Within loyalist communities, social connections and networks are complex. In many instances that which others have called bonding capital remains extremely strong,[71] but social and political relations remain confined. In the contemporary period, while some paramilitaries and loyalist former prisoners are active in cross-community processes of conflict resolution and transformation, these remain with a limited impact in structuring the broader response from many loyalist communities. Likewise, within loyalist communities there is an identifiable weakness in any collective community or political actions designed at building levels of bridging capital and still limited opportunities to interact with those of different backgrounds or values.[72]

Loyalism: Reactions to Dissidents

All of the above considerations framed the loyalist response to the dissidents. Some still saw them merely as the 'Provos in disguise', but there has been little or no evidence of any structured military reprisal from loyalist paramilitarism. This was directly illustrated following the outbreak of violence by dissident republican groupings in March 2009, when both of the main loyalist organizations made clear in their responses that they remained committed to the political path and that a military reaction was not an option,[73] aiding the eventual move towards the decommissioning of loyalist paramilitary weaponry some three months later.[74]

Open commitment to non-violence was made by UDA leader, Jackie MacDonald in confirming that 'the UDA has no intentions of doing anything to anybody . . . there is no danger of retaliation'.[75] Indeed, the broad UDA leadership confirmed its belief that it was now the sole job of the police to deal with republican terrorists. The successful intervention of the PSNI and the proper resourcing of their response were seen as central. As Jackie McDonald put it:

> The paramilitaries are trying to move on but we need the PSNI [Police Service of Northern Ireland] to succeed. People still come to the paramilitaries for some sort of justice, now [the UDA is] telling people they must go to the PSNI, but the PSNI are doing nothing about it because they haven't got the resources.[76]

This recognition of the legitimacy of the state in exercising authority in response to republican political violence is of no little consequence. It was after all the perceived inability of the state to respond to such political violence that was seen as the justification for the formation of loyalist paramilitary organizations.

Much of the loyalist response also recognized the actions of the dissidents as a direct attempt to goad them into retaliation. As the prominent UDA 'brigadier' Jackie McDonald put it, 'people on the loyalist side are determined not to fall into any more traps. That's what groups like the Continuity IRA and Real IRA want us to do'.[77] And in an appeal unthinkable for many years he continued, 'there has to be a coming together of loyalism and republicanism to show everybody that there is solidarity here'.[78] Indeed, it is worth considering the public statements of loyalism regarding republican dissidents in some further detail. Take this, from a leading UDA figure:

> Dissident republicans are trying to create a climate where they become the defenders of the people but what I'm saying is that there are genuine nationalists, Catholics and republicans who don't want this anymore than we do.[79]

Two things are noteworthy. First, it reveals a level of analysis not always apparent across loyalism during the conflict, and second, it identifies 'genuine nationalists, Catholics and republicans' and in so doing recognizes different interests and dynamics within the nationalist bloc. This position marks some distance from the notion driving loyalist paramilitarism in the 1980s and 1990s that the interests of all Catholics, nationalists, and republicans were as one. Indeed this new understanding was expressed directly by Jackie McDonald when he said, the 'message has to go out to the loyalist community – and most of them do understand it – that this is not the pan-nationalist front, as it was deemed in the past.'[80] Likewise the UVF have made clear that they do not regard the actions of the dissidents as offering any real challenge to the state, but rather something that may be compartmentalized as an internal dispute within republicanism.

To justify this stance loyalist paramilitaries look to an unusual source. Frankie Gallagher of the UPRG, for example, recently claimed that 'to be fair to Sinn Féin, they have come out and said some very robust stuff and they've condemned the people out of hand, as we all must do'.[81] Indeed several leading loyalists have insisted it was the statement made by Martin McGuinness that the dissidents were traitors to Ireland[82] that was central to easing tensions within the loyalist community, 'because they understand it's not coming from the same old source'.[83]

Conclusion

Much of the political positioning by loyalist paramilitarism and those groups representing them can be understood as a continuing engagement with the two key questions as set out by Gusty Spence in the loyalist ceasefire declaration surrounding the integrity of the Union and the end of the armed republican campaign led by the PIRA. Loyalist understanding of the answers to such questions has framed their response since.

Loyalist paramilitarism, despite reservations, and concerns over concessions to Irish nationalism are, like most unionists, now largely assured that the Union is secure. Within this context the main political thrust of loyalist paramilitary groupings has been inward, to seek to ensure a legitimate position within their immediate communities and to broaden this to the arena of civil society to engage with the state in what can commonly be understood as community development.

The legitimacy of such groups to operate on this terrain has been far from universally accepted, not just because the origins of many of those involved in such development lie within paramilitarism, but also because the negative effects of years of paramilitarism on Protestant communities and an established culture across working-class Protestantism that draws on conservative social values, apathy, mistrust and opposition to anything resembling organized state intervention.

Within both major loyalist paramilitary groupings the growing conviction that the conflict involving mainstream republicanism was at an end has been central to a repositioning of their politics. While a continuing and intensifying dissident republican campaign will always bring internal pressure upon the loyalist leadership, and individuals or small groups may feel themselves forced to react at a local level, the dominant view within loyalist paramilitarism is that the current violent actions of dissidents do not merit more than an official state response, representing as they do little more than what O'Neill calls voices from the 'ghosts of history'.[84]

Notes

1. Colin Robinson, former UVF prisoner, cited in Edwards, A. and Bloomer, S. *A Watching Brief? The Political Strategy of Progressive Loyalism Since 1994* (Belfast: LINC Resource Centre: 2004), p. 8.
2. Special EU Programmes Body, *Operational Programme for Peace III: Annex A Socio-Economic Profile of Northern Ireland and the Border Region of Ireland* (Belfast Office: SEUPB, 2007).
3. Alonso, R. 'The Modernization in Irish Republican Thinking Toward the Utility of Violence', *Studies in Conflict & Terrorism*, 4, 2 (2001), 31–144.
4. Sharrock, D. 'Analysis: who are the dissident republicans?' *The Times*, 8 March 2009.
5. Independent Monitoring Commission, *Twenty-Second Report of the Independent Monitoring Commission* Reports, HC 1085 (London: The Stationery Office, November 2009).
6. McAuley, J. W. '"Not a Game of Cowboys and Indians": Loyalist Paramilitary Groups in the 1990s', in A. O'Day (ed.), *Terrorism's Laboratory: Northern Ireland* (Dartmouth, NH: Dartmouth Press, 1995); McDonald, H. and Cusack, J. *UDA: Inside the Heart of Loyalist Terror* (London: Penguin, 2004).
7. Said, E. *Orientalism*, (Harmondsworth: Penguin, 1978)
8. Shirlow, P. and McEvoy, K. *Beyond the Wire: Former Prisoners and Conflict Transformation in Northern Ireland* (London: Pluto, 2008), pp. 9–10.
9. Harris, L. 'Duck or Rabbit? The Value Systems of Loyalist Paramilitaries', in Busteed, M., Neal, F. and Tonge, J. (eds), *Irish Protestant Identities* (Manchester: Manchester University Press, 2008); and Harris, L. 'Exit, Voice, and Loyalty: Signalling of Loyalist Paramilitaries in Northern

Ireland', in Edwards, A. and Bloomer, S. (eds), *Transforming the Peace Process in Northern Ireland* (Dublin: Irish Academic Press, 2008), pp. 79–98.
10. *Belfast Telegraph*, 11 June 2002.
11. Lister, D. and Jordan, H. *Mad Dog: The Rise and Fall of Johnny Adair and 'C Company'* (Edinburgh: Mainstream, 2004), p. 105.
12. McAuley, 'Not a Game of Cowboys and Indians' (1995).
13. McAuley, J. W. *Ulster's Last Stand? Reconstructing Unionism after the Peace Process* (Dublin: Irish Academic Press, 2010).
14. New Ulster Political Research Group, *Beyond the Religious Divide*, (Belfast: NUPRG, 1979).
15. McAuley, J. W. *The Politics of Identity: A Loyalist Community in Belfast* (Aldershot: Avebury, 1994).
16. Ulster Political Research Group. *Common Sense* (Belfast: UPRG, 1987).
17. Bruce, S. 'Terrorists and Politics: The Case of Northern Ireland's Loyalist Paramilitaries', *Terrorism and Political Violence*, 13, 2 (2001), 27–48.
18. McAuley, J. W. and Hislop, S. '"Many roads forward": politics and ideology within the Progressive Unionist Party', *Études Irlandaises*, 25, 1 (2000), 173–92.
19. McAuley, *Ulster's Last Stand?* (2010).
20. Garland, R. *Gusty Spence* (Belfast: Blackstaff Press, 2001).
21. Ibid.
22. Bruce, S. 'Terrorists and Politics: The Case of Northern Ireland's Loyalist Paramilitaries', *Terrorism and Political Violence*, 13, 2 (2001), 27–48.
23. McAuley, *Ulster's Last Stand?* (2010).
24. Bruce, 'Terrorists and Politics' (2001).
25. Fearon, K. 'The Conflict's Fifth Business: A brief biography of Billy Mitchell', unpublished article, 2002, pp. 1–72.
26. Shirlow, P., Tonge, J., McAuley, J. W. and McGlynn, C. *Abandoning Historical Conflict? Former Paramilitary Prisoners and Political Reconciliation in Northern Ireland* (Manchester: Manchester University Press, 2010).
27. Irwin, T. 'Prison Education in Northern Ireland: Learning from our Paramilitary Past', *The Howard Journal*, 42, 5 (December 2003), 471–84.
28. Shirlow et al., *Abandoning Historical Conflict?* (2010).

29. Crawford, C. *Inside the UDA: Volunteers and Violence* (London: Pluto Press, 2003).
30. Cited by Edwards, A. and Bloomer, S. *A Watching Brief? The Political Strategy of Progressive Loyalism Since 1994* (Belfast: LINC Resource Centre, 2004).
31. McAuley, *Ulster's Last Stand?* (2010).
32. Adair, J. and McKendry, G. *Mad Dog* (London: John Blake, 2007).
33. Lister, D. and Jordan, H. *Mad Dog: The Rise and Fall of Johnny Adair and 'C Company'* (Edinburgh: Mainstream, 2004).
34. McAuley, J. W., McGlynn, C. and Tonge, J. 'Conflict Resolution in Asymmetric and Symmetric Situations: Northern Ireland as a Case Study', *Dynamics of Asymmetric Conflict: An International Interdisciplinary Journal*, 1, 1 (2008), 88–102.
35. Combined Loyalist Military Command (CLMC), 'Ceasefire Statement, 13 October 1994', http://cain.ulst.ac.uk/events/peace/docs/clmc131094.htm (accessed 6 November 2006).
36. McAuley, J. W. '"Flying the One-Winged Bird": Ulster Unionism and the Peace Process', in Shirlow, P. and McGovern, M. (eds), *Who Are 'The People?'* (London: Pluto, 1997), pp. 158–75; McAuley, J. W. 'Surrender? Loyalist Perceptions of Conflict Settlement', in Anderson, J. and Goodman, J. (eds), *(Dis)Agreeing Ireland* (London: Pluto Press, 1998), pp. 193–210; and McAuley, J. W. '"Very British Rebels": Politics and Discourse within contemporary Ulster Unionism', in *Transforming Politics: Power and Resistance*, Bagguley, P. and Hearn, J. (eds), (Basingstoke: Macmillan Press, 1999), pp. 106–25.
37. McAuley, J. W. 'The Ulster Loyalist Political Parties: Towards a New Respectability', *Études Irlandaises, Le Processus de Paix en Irlande du Nord*, special volume, 22, 2 (1997), 117–32; McAuley, J. W. 'Still "No Surrender"? New Loyalism and the Peace Process in Ireland', in Harrington, J. and Mitchell, E. (eds), *Politics and Performance in Contemporary Northern Ireland* (Amherst, MA: University of Massachusetts Press, 1999), pp. 57–81; McAuley, J. W. 'The Emergence of New Loyalism', in Coakley, J. (ed.), *Changing Shades of Orange and Green* (Dublin: University College Dublin Press, 2002), pp. 106–22.
38. McAuley, J.W. 'Divided Loyalists, Divided Loyalties: Conflict and Continuities in Contemporary Unionist Ideology', in Gilligan, C. and

Tonge, J. (eds) *Peace or War?* (Aldershot: Ashgate, 1997), pp. 37–53; and McAuley, J. W. and Hislop, S. 'Many Roads Forward' (2000)

39. Rowan, B. *The Armed Peace: Life and Death after the Ceasefires* (Edinburgh: Mainstream Publishing, 2003).
40. Murray, A. 'UDA truce "teetering on brink"', *Sunday Life*, 18 January 2004.
41. McAuley, *Ulster's Last Stand?* (2010).
42. Jeong, H. W. *Conflict Management and Resolution* (London: Routledge, 2010).
43. Esman, M. J. 'Ethnic Pluralism: Strategies for Conflict Management', in Wimmer, A., Goldstone, R., Horowitz, D., Joras, U. and Schetter, C. (eds), *Facing Ethnic Conflict Towards a New Realism* (Lanham, MD: Rowman and Littlefield, 2004).
44. McAuley, *Ulster's Last Stand?* (2010).
45. Ibid.
46. McAuley, J. W. and Tonge, J. 'Politics and Parties in Northern Ireland: The Convergence of Ideological Extremes', *Etudes Irlandaises*, 27, 1 (2002), 177–98.
47. Shankill Think Tank. *A New Beginning*, Island Pamphlets, 13, (Newtownabbey: Island Publications, 1995).
48. Ervine cited in McAuley, 2002 – see note 37
49. Wood, I. S. *Crimes of Loyalty: A History of the UDA* (Edinburgh: Edinburgh University Press, 2006); and Wood, I. 'Loyalist Paramilitaries and the Peace Process', in B. Barton and P. J. Roche (eds), *The Northern Ireland Question: The Peace Process and the Belfast Agreement* (Basingstoke: Palgrave Macmillan, 2009), pp. 181–204.
50. Shirlow et al. (2010).
51. Inter Action Belfast. *The role of Ex-Combatants on Interfaces* (Belfast: Inter-Action Belfast, 2006).
52. Shirlow et al. (2010), p. 171.
53. Cairns, E., Van Til, T. and Williamson, A. *Social Capital, Collectivism – Individualism and Community Background in Northern Ireland*, report to the Office of the First Minister and Deputy First Minister (Coleraine: University of Ulster, 2003).
54. Hall, M. *Loyalism in Transition 1: Learning from Others in Conflict* (Belfast: Island Pamphlets, 2006).

55. Hall, M. (2007) *Loyalism in Transition 2: Learning from Others in Conflict* (Belfast: Island Pamphlets, 2007).
56. Hall (2006), p. 10.
57. Hall (2006), pp. 10–11.
58. Hall (2006).
59. Hall (2007).
60. *News Letter*, 'UDA campaign to defend Britishness', 10 and 11 November 2008.
61. *News Letter*, 'UDA campaign to defend Britishness', 11 November 2008.
62. *Irish News*, 8 March 2006.
63. McEvoy, K. and Shirlow, P. 'Re-imagining DDR: Ex-combatants, Leadership and Moral Agency in Conflict Transformation', *Theoretical Criminology*, 13, 1 (2009), 31–59.
64. Shirlow, P., Graham, B., McEvoy, K., O'hAdhmaill, F. and Purvis, D. *Politically Motivated Former Prisoner Groups: Community Activism and Conflict Transformation* (Belfast: Report to the Northern Ireland Community Relations Council, 2005).
65. Mitchell, C. 'The Limits of Legitimacy: Former Loyalist Combatants and Peace-building in Northern Ireland', *Irish Political Studies*, 23, 1 (2008), 1–19.
66. McAuley (2010); Shirlow et al. (2010).
67. Acheson, N., Cairns, E., Stringer, M. and Williamson, A. *Voluntary Action and Community Relations in Northern Ireland* (Coleraine: University of Ulster, Centre for Coluntary Action Studies, 2007).
68. McAuley (2010); Shirlow et al (2010)
69. *Belfast Telegraph*, 'Stop pussyfooting with UDA, government urged', 20 July 2009.
70. Fealty, M. 'Dawn Purvis Resigns from the PUP . . .', Slugger O'Toole, 3 June 2010. http://sluggerotoole.com/2010/06/03/dawn-purvis-resigns-from-the-pup (accessed 10 June 2010).
71. Cairns et. al (2003).
72. Garland, R. 'Loyalists must take responsibility for themselves', *Irish News*, 10 October 2006.
73. Gordon, D. 'Top loyalist praises McGuinness but warns of "Real UDA clowns"', *Belfast Telegraph*, 12 March 2009; and Rowan, B. 'Loyalist

groups UDA and UVF disarming after decades of terror and 1000 deaths', *Belfast Telegraph*, 18 June 2009.
74. Rowan (2009).
75. Gordon (2009)
76. Fearon, A. 'UDA chief's fears over "dissident" loyalist groups', *South Belfast News*, 18 January 2010.
77. Fearon (2010).
78. Sharrock, D. 'We will not retaliate over latest killings, loyalist paramilitary brigadier promises', *The Times*, 12 March 2009.
79. Ibid
80. Fearon, (2010).
81. Ibid
82. Gordon (2009)
83. Sharrock, D. 'Martin McGuinness's attack on "traitors" outrages past victims of IRA', *The Times*, 13 March 2009.
84. O'Neill, B. 'IRA splinter groups: ghosts from history', *Spiked*, 12 March 2009, www.spiked-online.com/index.php/site/article/6352/ (accessed 6 April 2009).

CHAPTER 8

Conclusion

P. M. CURRIE
UNIVERSITY OF ST ANDREWS

This concluding chapter summarizes key points made by the contributors to this volume in relation to the questions that we had set ourselves to consider. It goes on to reflect on three themes: how to calibrate the threat that dissident republicanism represents; contributors' conviction of the need for a more effective counter-narrative to assist dissidents and potential supporters to reject violence; and the requirement for yet deeper and more detailed understanding of the manifestations of terrorism if they are to be countered successfully.

First, the questions and headline answers.

Who are the dissident republicans and what distinguishes them from the rest of society?

Dissident republicans do not accept the compromises made by PIRA and Sinn Féin which enabled the Good Friday and St Andrews agreements and led to the current political settlement of power sharing and an Executive in Northern Ireland. They are distinguished by extremists who continue to think that some sort of armed struggle in pursuit of a united Ireland is justified. Appendix 2 in Chapter 1 gives a brief overview of the various dissident groups currently thought to be active. Membership of the different groups can, however, be quite fluid and may overlap.

What is the role of dissidents in Irish republicanism? Are current dissidents consistent with republicanism? Are there similarities with earlier dissident outbreaks?

There is a history since 1921 of the republican movement in Ireland splitting over issues that some felt were central to their and their organization's identity. Current dissidents hold that they are true to the traditional republican aspirations of a united Ireland and the methods that will achieve that. Contributors point out the problem of nomenclature that this brings. 'Dissident republicanism' is a misnomer at least for those within these groups who see themselves as the true inheritors of the republican tradition. From their point of view PIRA and Sinn Féin are the dissidents who sold out to the British and traded their ideals for political office.

What is the relationship between dissident activity and the Good Friday Agreement?

The process of which the Good Friday Agreement was a core part is paradoxically central to the violent dissident groupings' identity. CIRA was originally formed in 1986, prompted by PIRA and Sinn Féin's acceptance of the currently constituted Dáil Éireann. CIRA saw this as the start of a process which would make some kind of unacceptable compromise settlement in the North inevitable. RIRA was formed in 1997, the calendar year before the Good Friday Agreement, when the process of compromise was further advanced. The specific prompt came from PIRA's confirmation that its ceasefire would continue.

Contributors have explained how the Good Friday/Belfast and St Andrews agreements did not in fact signal the end of Irish history or of violent republicanism. The assumption that the successes of the peace process would mean that violence would disappear proved overly optimistic. It also ignored the history of splits in the republican movement and the research that suggests that the creation of rejectionist groups is an almost inevitable accompaniment to conflict resolution. And in the Irish context the existence of spoiler groups would seem particularly to have been expected given what has been described above by Jon Tonge as the 'startling' catalogue of change and compromise on the part of mainstream republicans. This catalogue includes moving from:

- rejection of the Dáil as an instance of collusion in a partitioned Ireland to its acceptance
- insistence that the withdrawal of the British from Northern Ireland was a non-negotiable demand to declaring a ceasefire and decommissioning weapons without any undertaking of a British withdrawal
- rejecting the unionist veto to support for the Good Friday Agreement which recognized that Northern Ireland would remain part of the UK for as long as a majority chooses
- refusing to accept Northern Ireland as a legitimate political entity to sharing power with protestant unionists in the Northern Ireland Executive
- PIRA's killing large numbers of the Royal Ulster Constabulary to avowed support for its successor, the PSNI.

Do they have a strategy or political objectives?

There is one overall and enduring objective: a united Ireland without British involvement. In no group is there to date a clearly articulated strategy that explains how this will be achieved, other than through violence and the overthrow of 'British Rule' in Northern Ireland (and by extension, of course, collaborationist rule in the Republic of Ireland). The extreme end of the dissident republican spectrum continues to regard armed struggle as a legitimate way of achieving this. For these groups, no political compromise is acceptable and the British must withdraw from Ireland. The logic that lies behind this for the dissident groups is essentially that of the Provisional IRA before them, and of Irish republican narratives more generally.[1] It is assumed that the establishment of an all Ireland Republic will result in peace and harmony – an almost millenarian expectation; until this happens, however, British intransigence through resisting the establishment of the all-Ireland Republic necessitates revolutionary violence against them. On this view, peace in the absence of a settlement of 'the national question' would result in sidelining or even abandoning the unification imperative. PIRA and the other mainstream republican groups have by accepting peace moved attention away from this imperative, a compromise (or sell out) too far for the dissidents. Thus, the mantle of legitimacy to the republican tradition can be claimed by dissident groups as being true to Irish republicanism's historical and ideological agendas.

Why are they still committed to physical violence?

The answer to this at an individual level is probably both complex and idiosyncratic. In collective terms, however, extreme dissident republicans are committed to violence because as they see the world they think it works and they interpret history to support this view. They believe that there is no other way in the long term to convince the British to cease their involvement in the island of Ireland. In the shorter term, as explained in Jon Tonge's chapter, they hope that their violence will provoke overreaction by the British authorities, thereby eliciting sympathy for 'oppressed' republicans and thereby add momentum and support to their armed struggle.

How and why does someone become a dissident republican?

There is not one answer to the question of how and why someone becomes a dissident republican. Contributors make clear the heterogeneous nature of dissident membership. First, it is important to note that not all dissident republicans are given to violence. The other main variant relates to timing. The dissident groupings were formed by individuals who had fundamental disagreements with the ways in which the leadership of mainstream republicanism were engaging in the political process. Such dissenting individuals have had a powerful influence subsequently on others, mostly younger males, who have been attracted to them for what they purport to represent. Contributors have remarked on the age of active dissident leaders as being greater than would normally be seen in terrorist groups. Their perceived experience as republicans is an important source of influence over younger recruits and sympathizers who will have no first-hand knowledge of the troubles and will be susceptible to glorified narratives of militant republican achievement.

The sense of the continuity and purity of dissidents' commitment to the true republican tradition provides a degree of allure to its adherents that should not be underestimated. They see themselves as part of a lineage that has kept the faith. They project mainstream republicans as the traitors who have forsworn the aspiration of a united Ireland and have a tainted record in the process of doing so. They point to PIRA and Sinn Féin's leaderships 'cheating' PIRA members by conducting peace negotiations behind their backs. Stories of widespread penetration of PIRA by the police and British intelligence add to this negative image, as does the perceived betrayal of, for example, PIRA East Tyrone Brigade at Loughgall. And more recently dissidents would point to PIRA and Sinn Féin's collusion with PSNI in controlling the youth of the Ardoyne[2] and with the DUP in managing Orange Marches. To be called dissidents by such republicans is regarded as a badge of honour.

Additionally, PIRA and Sinn Féin's acceptance of the legitimacy of PSNI has allowed dissidents to start to take over the role of 'policing' in areas where they have influence. PIRA and Sinn Féin's rejection of violence has also provided the dissidents space to take over the commemoration and celebration of republican paramilitary achievements of the past (an issue of huge symbolic significance). Both roles add to the dissidents' appeal to disaffected youths in areas where parity of esteem will have no meaningful reality.

However bizarre the allure of the violent republican tradition may appear to many, it is clearly appealing to increasing numbers of mostly male youth in both Northern Ireland and the Republic. Contributors have additionally noted a variety of factors that push such youth in this direction. Among these are: the consequences of living in relatively deprived areas where there is little chance of benefiting from the significant advances in social, cultural, economic and political status that a majority of Catholics have enjoyed; the bitter ethno-sectarian feelings that continue to exist in such areas; and individuals' personal quest for purpose, identity and excitement.

What would it take for them to disengage or move away from violence?

At the level of organizational aims and identity, it seems that extreme dissident republicans would only move away from violence if and when their purpose of a united Ireland is achieved in terms that they accept, i.e. a British withdrawal. In practice, research shows that individuals move away from terrorism for a variety of reasons: changing personal priorities;

disagreements with, or growing dislike of, the group's membership and/or leadership; personal experience of the consequences of violent attack; the disparity between expectations about membership of an extremist group and the reality; competing loyalties for an individual between the group and family; realization that there is a more powerful and accurate account of recent history and what works and what does not work to achieve progress.[3]

So what conclusions can be drawn in terms of the scale and nature of the threat posed by violent dissidents? The evidence at the moment suggests that they are fractured, unstable and small in number. They have sparse, fragmented and highly localized support. Their capacity for armed struggle has been limited by differences, arrests, imprisonment and disruptions, and they face the opposition not only of the security forces but also of mainstream republicanism. Dissidents are unlikely to have forgotten, for example, the killing of Joe O'Connor, a leading member of RIRA in Belfast in 2000, which was widely thought to have been carried out by PIRA. PIRA continues to hold strong allegiance in the urban heartlands of Londonderry and Belfast. And for the vast majority of the Catholic population who have benefited from considerable improvements in conditions and status, the dissidents' political aspirations are unrealistic and irrelevant and their use of violence simply unacceptable.

There is a consensus in this volume and in the IMC reports referenced by all contributors that the threat from dissident terrorism is not and will not be of the same order of that of PIRA in the 1970s and 1980s. Henry Patterson concludes that the dissident threat will not go away and may become like 'the nagging and only occasionally chronic IRA challenge that faced both states [the Republic of Ireland and the UK, including Northern Ireland] between 1923 and the 1950s'. However, given that, Jon Tonge concludes that 'the sporadic violence of dissidents cannot derail the ongoing peace process'.

Nonetheless, none of the authors in this volume is arguing in favour of complacency. The research of the various contributors and in the IMC reports that they have drawn on suggests that support for dissident groupings is growing. There are indications that they have access to individuals familiar with PIRA attack techniques, especially in terms of bomb-making. Dissidents' attack aspirations are also becoming more ambitious and their attack attempts are no longer beset by the failure rate they experienced in their earlier efforts to target security forces, for example, at Shackleton military barracks, an army observation post in South Armagh, and Rosslea police station in 2000.[4] Their public relations and propaganda activities are taking advantage of the rapid development of the communications infrastructure in Ireland with their own video production capabilities and a presence on widely used social networking sites. We can draw on experience from elsewhere to help understand this. As with al Qaeda, we have seen small-scale organic groupings operating in environments without substantial community support while having huge impact through the use of violence and terror tactics. The current downturn in the economy and the associated public spending cuts may add to the potential for recruitment both of new and experienced members, and may also widen facilitatory community support. Furthermore, it is not unreasonable to assume that the continuing restraint of loyalists in the face of the dissidents' provocation will be an important key to ensuring that the dissidents do not achieve their ambition of destabilizing the political settlement.

Against that background, what suggestions emerge that could further help countering violent dissident republicanism? One consistent theme in this conflict as in others is the need for a more effective counter-narrative to point up the criminality, cruelty and hypocrisy of dissident communications and activity, to undermine the appeal of fictionalized accounts of violent attacks and to promote understanding of the significant achievements of the peace process and the injustices and suffering that went before.

But to do this raises more questions: who would have the responsibility and moral authority for such a counter-narrative to be effective, for what audience and to what end? It is likely that a direct government initiative by itself would probably fail to convince. Furthermore, any authority figure with Provisional IRA associations could similarly in the current climate have a negative impact on those drawn to the dissident movement. This is a challenge to a range of media, political, civic and religious organizations. In tackling this challenge it has been suggested that there are lessons to be learnt from other contexts. One contributor to the workshop on which this volume is based suggested that the language used to describe dissidents in the North could afford to become more sophisticated, and that initiatives might benefit from the approach of the government of the Republic of Ireland where the emphasis is on the futility of armed struggle and the unattainability of dissidents' avowed goals through the use of violent methods. Another contributor recommended borrowing from the arguments of non-violent dissidents while focusing on the diversity and fragmentation of the violent dissident groupings. Undoubtedly this is a challenge that authors in this volume have concluded must be met if the dissident threat is to be countered effectively.

These conclusions are not in any way unique to Northern Ireland. For example, this is very much the consensus reached by an expert meeting on 'counter-narratives and the performative power of counter terrorism' organized by the Netherlands' National Coordinator for Counter-Terrorism and Leiden University with the British and Canadian Embassies in the Hague in June 2009. The proceedings of this Expert Meeting were subsequently published and provide a rich seam to quarry for research and insight to what works and does not work in terms of countering extreme narratives in other contexts and could be found relevant to the Irish experience.[5]

The first essential is recognition of the role that successful counter-terrorist policies and operations by governments and their agencies can have as acts of communication to the terrorists. As noted by Alonso (2010) it was effective 'coercive anti-terrorist measures that provided . . . one of the most successful counter narratives against ETA.'[6] The intense pressure that the Spanish state applied to ETA and its supporters prompted serious tactical and strategic questioning among its members and supporters of the effectiveness of violence. And if terrorism is essentially about communication as well as violence it will also be vital to counter the communications dimension. 'Refraining from communicating a certain message or counter-narrative is also a message in itself'[7] which can provide encouragement to the terrorist cause. The 'ludicrous claims' by al-Qaeda of its successes, for example, 'if not countered, will however, find believers among the ignorant and the semi-educated'.[8]

Terrorist leaders themselves can be helpful in this regard. Abu Yahya al-Liby, an al-Qaeda leader and senior strategist, pointed out in a video, 'Dots of the Letter', how the United States could defeat his organization.[9] Abu Yahya al-Liby identified six weaknesses, which could be used by his enemies in their war for hearts and minds. Although these are framed in the context of Islamic terrorism, these 'weaknesses' may have wider applicability. The weaknesses identified 'are:

1. Focus on amplifying cases of ex-jihadists who have renounced armed action;
2. Fabricate stories about jihadist mistakes and exaggerate mistakes when possible;

3. Prompt mainstream Muslim clerics to issue *fatwas* that incriminate the jihadist movement and its actions;
4. Strengthen and back Islamic movements far removed from jihad, particularly those with a democratic approach;
5. Aggressively neutralize or discredit the guiding thinkers of the jihadist movement; and
6. Spin minor disagreements among leaders of jihadist organizations as being major doctrinal or methodological disputes.'[10]

A range of disciplines may be able to help the counter-narrative endeavour. Further suggestions might be to:

- borrow from the experience of crime reduction strategies
- think imaginatively about the nature of how a counter-narrative might be communicated 'recognizing, for example, the role of music in the shaping and development of popular political as well as social culture'[11]
- recognize the need for the full range of media and technologies used by the terrorists in their own communications in order to reach the right audiences[12]
- avoid a single counter-narrative.

Quite clearly a many-layered approach is required. As Harchaoui notes: 'in order to effectively oppose extremism within a democratic discourse, heterogeneous counter-narratives that represent the fundamental nature of politics, namely dissimilarity, should be produced.'[13]

Kessells emphasizes the credibility of the sender employed as a principle quality of effective counter-narratives. As noted earlier, governments are not the best agents to do this; they tend to lack the necessary credibility among the target audience. Other agencies may have more credibility, especially those having roots in or clear links with civil society. Kessels suggests that NGOs or community organizations may be effective in this endeavour. We do know that community groups have important roles in sustaining terrorism, and presumably reciprocal forces can also be mobilized. In the UK the PREVENT strand of the CONTEST strategy has been designed to fulfil this function among others.

However, Kessels does note what governments can do:

- 'Via various carefully chosen partners, promote multiple narratives;
- Facilitate these partners financially, logistically or content-wise;
- Be open and frank about inconsistencies;
- Support dialogue and peaceful discussion; stimulate [in the case of countering al-Qaeda] the Muslim community to take ownership of certain areas of the issue;
- Acknowledge grievances; and
- Appreciate that in a democratic society there will and should always be a pluralism of narratives and discourses.'[14]

Are these achievable objectives and strategies? A related issue is to consider which different sorts of senders would be appropriate for different types of counter-narratives. While governments and officials have a role in the political counter-narrative, moral and social arguments would more effectively come from civil society, community groups, religious leaders, social workers, peers, families and former violent extremists.[15] While we may not now have clear metrics to determine the effectiveness of these strategies, presenting them in this way does offer a systematic basis for further development, as well as providing a context for future evaluation.

The last theme to draw out from the papers presented in this volume is the consensus that a vital ingredient in the successful countering of terrorism is detailed understanding of it. That has been a purpose of this book with respect to the relatively narrow issue of dissident republicanism, but it points more generally to the need for further research to achieve a yet more granular and detailed understanding of the relationship between historical and local context; individuals' motivations for joining and leaving; what prevents them from signing up or walking away; their networks, communications, relationships and use of the internet; how, why and where membership of terrorist groups can be attractive; and how, why and to whom political violence appeals as logical, inevitable and justifiable. This book has adopted a quite explicit multidisciplinary perspective to address these issues, where similar themes have been explored from a variety of discipline perspectives. If the production of this book stimulates directly or indirectly further such research, another of its purposes will have been achieved.

Notes

1. Shanahan, T. *The Provisional Irish Republican Army and the Morality of Terrorism* (Edinburgh: Edinburgh University Press, 2009).
2. See Craig, O. 'Sinn Fein are yesterday's men', *The Telegraph*, 18 July 2010, www.telegraph.co.uk/news/uknews/northernireland/7896588/Sinn-Fein-are-yesterdays-men.html (accessed 13 December 2010).
3. Bjørgo, T. and Horgan, J. *Leaving Terrorism Behind* (London: Routledge, 2009).
4. *http://news.bbc.co.uk/1/hi/northern_ireland/1056797.stm* 'Timeline: Dissident Republican Attacks' (accessed 26 August 2010).
5. Akerboom, E. *Countering Violent Extremist Narratives* (Netherlands: National Coordinator for Counterterrorism, January 2010).
6. Alonso, R. 'Counter-Narratives against ETA's Terrorism in Spain', in *Countering Violent Extremist Narratives*, p. 32.
7. Kessels, E. 'Introduction', in *Countering Violent Extremist Narratives*, p. 8.
8. Schmid, A. 'The Importance of Countering Al-Qaeda's "Single Narrative"', in *Countering Violent Extremist Narratives*, p. 49.
9. Ibid., p. 53.
10. Ibid., pp. 53–4.
11. Taylor, M. and Ramsay, G. 'Violent Radical Content and the Relationship between Ideology and Behaviour: Do Counter-Narratives Matter?' in *Countering Violent Extremist Narratives*, pp. 108–9.
12. Stevens, T. 'New Media and Counter-Narrative Strategies', in *Countering Violent Extremist Narratives*, p. 121.
13. Harchaoui, S. 'Heterogeneous Counter-Narratives and the Role of Social Diplomacy', in *Countering Violent Extremist Narratives*, p. 129.
14. Kessels, pp. 8–9.
15. Ibid., p. 9.

Bibliography

Acheson, N., Cairns, E., Stringer, M. and Williamson, A. *Voluntary Action and Community Relations in Northern Ireland* (Coleraine: University of Ulster, Centre for Voluntary Action Studies, 2007).

Adair, J. and McKendry, G. *Mad Dog* (London: John Blake, 2007).

Akerboom, E. *Countering Violent Extremist Narratives* (Netherlands: National Coordinator for Counterterrorism, January 2010). Available at: http://english.nctb.nl/current_topics/reports.

Alexander, Y and O'Day, D. *Ireland's Terrorist Dilemma* (Dordrecht, Boston and Lancaster: Martinus Nijhoff, 1987).

Alonso, R. 'The Modernization in Irish Republican Thinking Toward the Utility of Violence', *Studies in Conflict & Terrorism*, 4, 2 (2001), 31–144.

—. *The IRA and Armed Struggle* (London: Routledge, 2006).

Atkinson, D. *Civil Renewal: Mending the Hole in the Social Ozone* (Studley: Brewin Books, 2004).

Bean, K. *The New Politics of Sinn Féin* (Liverpool: Liverpool University Press, 2007).

Bew, P. *The Making and the Remaking of the Good Friday Agreement* (Dublin: Liffey Press, 2007).

Bjørgo, T. (ed.). *Root Causes of Terrorism* (London: Routledge, 2005).

Bjørgo, T. and Horgan, J. *Leaving Terrorism Behind* (London: Routledge, 2009).

'Bobby Sands MP (1954–1981)', h2g2, 3 September 2009. Available at: www.bbc.co.uk/dna/h2g2/A51822849 (accessed 26 January 2010).

Border, T., Darby, J. and McEvoy-Levy, S. *Peace Building after Peace Accords: The Challenges of Violence, Truth and Youth* (Notre Dame, IN: University of Notre Dame Press, 2006).

Bowyer Bell, J. *The Dynamics of Armed Struggle* (London: Frank Cass, 1998).

—. *The IRA 1968–2000: Analysis of a Secret Army* (London: Frank Cass, 2000).

Boyne, S. 'The Real IRA: After Omagh, What Now?' *Jane's Intelligence Review*, 24 August 1998.

Brantingham, P. and Faust, F. A. 'Conceptual Model of Crime Prevention', *Crime Prevention and Delinquency*, 22, 3 (1976), 284–96.

Bric, M. and Coakley, J. (eds). *From Political Violence to Negotiated Settlement: The Winding Path to Peace in Twentieth-Century Ireland* (Dublin: University College Dublin, 2004).

Bruce, S. 'Terrorists and Politics: The Case of Northern Ireland's Loyalist Paramilitaries', *Terrorism and Political Violence*, 13, 2 (2001), 27–48.

Burk, K. 'The Hundred Years' War 1337–1453', lecture, Gresham College, London, 9 February 2005. Available at: www.gresham.ac.uk/printtranscript.asp?EventId=299.

Busteed, M., Neal, F. and Tonge, J. (eds). *Irish Protestant Identities* (Manchester: Manchester University Press, 2008).

Cairns, E., Van Til, T. and Williamson, A. *Social Capital, Collectivism – Individualism and Community Background in Northern Ireland*, report to the Office of the First Minister and Deputy First Minister (Coleraine: University of Ulster, 2003).

Coakley, J. (ed.). *Changing Shades of Orange and Green* (Dublin: University College Dublin Press, 2002).

Cornish, D. and Clarke, R. 'Opportunities, Precipitators and Criminal Decisions: a reply to Wortley's critique of situational crime prevention', in Smith, M. and Cornish, D. (eds), *Theory for Practice in Situational Crime Prevention*, Crime Prevention Studies 16 (Monsey, NY: Criminal Justice Press, 2003).

Cota-McKinley, A. Woody, W. and Ward Bell, P. 'Vengeance: Effects of Gender, Age and Religious Background', *Aggressive Behaviour*, 27 (2001), 343–50.

Cowen, R. 'Real IRA "Ready to Attack"', *Guardian Unlimited*, 21 October 2002.

Cragin, K. and Daly, S. *The Dynamic Terrorist Threat: An Assessment of Group Motivations and Capabilities in a Changing World*, Monograph Report MR-1782-AF (Santa Monica, CA: Rand Corporation, 2004).

Craig, O. 'Sinn Fein are yesterday's men', *The Telegraph*, 18 July 2010. Available at: www.telegraph.co.uk/news/uknews/northernireland/7896588/Sinn-Fein-are-yesterdays-men.html (accessed 13 December 2010).

Crawford, C. *Inside the UDA: Volunteers and Violence* (London: Pluto Press, 2003).
Crenshaw, M. 'The Causes of Terrorism', *Comparative Politics*, 13, 4 (July 1981), 379–99.
—. 'An Organisational Approach to the Analysis of Political Terrorism', *Orbis*, 29, 3 (1985), 465–89.
—. 'Theories of Terrorism: Instrumental and Organisational Approaches', in Rapoport, D. C. (ed.) *Inside Terrorist Organizations* (London: Frank Cass, 2001).
Crenshaw, M. (ed.). *Terrorism in Context* (State College, PA: Pennsylvania State University Press, 1995).
Daddow, O. and Gaskarth, J. (eds). *British Foreign Policy* (Basingstoke: Palgrave Macmillan, in press).
Darby, J. and MacGinty, R. (eds). *Contemporary Peacemaking: Conflict, Violence and Peace Processes* (Basingstoke: Macmillan, 2003).
Della Porta, D. 'Left-Wing Terrorism in Italy', in Crenshaw, M. (ed.) *Terrorism in Context* (State College, PA: Pennsylvania State University Press, 1995).
Dillon, M. *The Enemy Within: The IRA's War Against the British* (London: Transworld Publishers, 1994).
Dingley, J. 'The Bombing on Omagh, 15 August 1998: The Bombers, their Tactics, Strategy and Purpose behind the Incident', *Studies in Conflict and Terrorism*, 24, 1 (2001), 451–65.
Dudley Edwards, R. *Aftermath: The Omagh Bomb and the Families' Pursuit of Justice* (London: Harvill Secker, 2009).
Edwards, A. and Bloomer, S. *A Watching Brief? The Political Strategy of Progressive Loyalism since 1994* (Belfast: LINC Resource Centre, 2004).
—. *Transforming the Peace Process in Northern Ireland: From Terrorism to Democratic Politics* (Dublin: Irish Academic Press, 2008).
English, R. *Armed Struggle: The History of the IRA* (London: Macmillan, 2003).
'Éirígí oppose RIR parade 2/3', 14 December 2008, video clip. Available at: www.youtube.com/watch?v=L7gT1bnB-ZQ (accessed 26 January 2010).
'Éirígí's Rab Jackson addresses Belfast supporters', 13 March 2009, video clip. Available at: www.youtube.com/watch?v=qU5RdCSmUlg (accessed 26 January 2010).

Esman, M. J. 'Ethnic Pluralism: Strategies for Conflict Management', in Wimmer, A., Goldstone, R., Horowitz, D., Joras, U. and Schetter, C. (eds), *Facing Ethnic Conflict Towards a New Realism* (Lanham, MD: Rowman and Littlefield, 2004).

Fair, C. 'Who are Pakistan's Militants and their Families?' *Terrorism and Political Violence*, 20, 1 (2008), 49–65.

'Family blames IRA for murder', *News Letter*, 22 October 2007.

Farrington, D. 'Developmental and Life-Course Criminology: Key Theoretical and Empirical Issues – the 2002 Sutherland Award Address', *Criminology*, 41 (2003), 221–55.

Fealty, M. 'Dawn Purvis Resigns from the PUP . . .', Slugger O'Toole, 3 June 2010. http://sluggerotoole.com/2010/06/03/dawn-purvis-resigns-from-the-pup (accessed 10 June 2010).

'Fearghal Ó hAnluain remembered in Monaghan', *Saoirse*, February 2009, p. 7.

Fearon, A. 'UDA chief's fears over "dissident" loyalist groups', *South Belfast News*, 18 January 2010.

Fearon, K. 'The Conflict's Fifth Business: A Brief Biography of Billy Mitchell', unpublished article, 2002. Available at: www.linc-ncm.org/No.2.PDF.

Feeney, B. *Sinn Féin: A Hundred Turbulent Years* (Dublin: O'Brien Press, 2002).

'Fírinne Protest Against Section 44', éirígí, 22 January 2010. Available at: www.eirigi.org/latest/latest220110.html (accessed 26 January 2010).

Florez-Morris, M. 'Joining Guerrilla Groups in Colombia: Individual Motivations and Processes for Entering a Violent Organization', *Studies in Conflict and Terrorism*, 30, 7 (2007), 615–34.

Frampton, M. 'After Truce and Treaty: The Return of Militant Republicanism', paper delivered at a seminar organized by the US Institute of Peace, London, November 2009.

—. *The Long March: The Political Strategy of Sinn Fein, 1981–2007* (London: Palgrave Macmillan, 2009).

Freilich, J. and Newman, G. *Reducing Terrorism through Situational Crime Prevention*, Crime Prevention Studies 25 (Cullompton: Willan Publishing, 2009).

'Fury as IRA leader joins the Policing Board', *News Letter*, 27 March 2008. Available at: www.newsletter.co.uk/news/Fury-over-IRA-leader-joining.3920741.jp (accessed 13 December 2010).

Garland, R. *Gusty Spence* (Belfast: Blackstaff Press, 2001).
Garland, R. 'Loyalists must take responsibility for themselves', *Irish News*, 10 October 2006.
Gibney, J. 'Conference: Spirit of McElwaine evident among delegates', *An Phoblacht*, 15 June 2006.
Greer, T., Berman, M., Varan, V., Bobrycki, L. and Watson, S. 'We are a Religious People; We are a Vengeful People', *Journal for the Scientific Study of Religion*, 44 (2005), 45–57.
Guelke, A. 'Political Violence and Paramilitaries', in Mitchell, P. and Wilford, R. (eds), *Politics in Northern Ireland* (Oxford: Westview Press, 1999), pp. 29–53.
Hall, M. *The Death of the 'Peace Process'? A Survey of Community Perceptions* (Belfast: Island Pamphlets, 1997).
—. *Loyalism in Transition 1: Learning from Others in Conflict* (Belfast: Island Pamphlets, 2006).
—. *Loyalism in Transition 2: Learning from Others in Conflict* (Belfast: Island Pamphlets, 2007).
Harris, L. 'Duck or Rabbit? The Value Systems of Loyalist Paramilitaries', in Busteed, M., Neal, F. and Tonge, J. (eds), *Irish Protestant Identities* (Manchester: Manchester University Press, 2008).
—. 'Exit, Voice, and Loyalty: Signalling of Loyalist Paramilitaries in Northern Ireland', in Edwards, A. and Bloomer, S. (eds), *Transforming the Peace Process in Northern Ireland* (Dublin: Irish Academic Press, 2008).
Hayes, B. and McAllister, I. 'Sowing Dragon's Teeth: Public Support for Political Violence and Paramilitarism in Northern Ireland', *Political Studies*, 49 (2001), 901–22.
Hirschman, A. O. *Exit, Voice and Loyalty: Responses to Decline in Firms, Organisations and States* (Cambridge, MA: Harvard University Press, 1970).
Hoffmann, B. *Inside Terrorism* (New York: Columbia University Press, 1998).
Horgan, J. *The Psychology of Terrorism* (London: Routledge, 2005).
—. 'Disengaging from Terrorism', *Jane's Intelligence Review*, 18, 12 (2006), 34–7.
—. *Walking Away From Terrorism: Accounts of Disengagement from Radical and Extremist Movements* (London: Routledge, 2009).

Horgan, J. and Taylor, M. 'The Provisional Irish Republican Army: Command and Functional Structure', *Terrorism and Political Violence*, 2, 1 (1997), 1–32.

'I Fought the War but the War is Over says Lynch', interview with Sean Lynch, *Impartial Reporter*, 3 April 2009. Available at: www.impartialreporter.com/articles/1/37667 (accessed 13 December 2010).

Independent Monitoring Commission. *Twentieth Report of the Independent Monitoring Commission*, HC 1112 (London: The Stationery Office, November 2008). Available at: www.independentmonitoringcommission.org/publications.cfm?id=70.

—. *Twenty-First Report of the Independent Monitoring Commission*, HC 496 (London: The Stationery Office, May 2009). Available at: www.independentmonitoringcommission.org/publications.cfm?id=71.

—. *Twenty-Second Report of the Independent Monitoring Commission*, HC 1085 (London: The Stationery Office, November 2009). Available at: www.independentmonitoringcommission.org/ publications.cfm?id=72.

Inter-Action Belfast. *The Role of Ex-Combatants on Interfaces* (Belfast: Inter-Action Belfast, 2006).

'An Interview with Free Derry Media', Independent Media Centre Ireland, 18 October 2007. Available at: www.indymedia.ie/article/84716 (accessed 13 December 2010).

'IRA Easter Statement', *The Sovereign Nation*, May–June 2009.

Irvin, C. L. *Militant Nationalism: Between Movement and Party in Ireland and in the Basque Country* (Minneapolis, MN: University of Minnesota Press, 1999).

Irwin, T. 'Prison Education in Northern Ireland: Learning from our Paramilitary Past', *The Howard Journal*, 42, 5 (December 2003), 471–84.

Jackson, A. *Ireland: 1798–1998* (Oxford: Blackwell, 1999).

Jenkins, P. 'Failure to Launch: Why Do Some Social Issues Fail to Detonate Moral Panics?' *British Journal of Criminology*, 49 (2009), 35–47.

Jeong, H. W. *Conflict Management and Resolution* (London: Routledge, 2010).

Kaufmann, E. *The Orange Order: a Contemporary Northern Irish History* (Oxford: Oxford University Press, 2007).

Kimmage, D. *The al-Qaeda Media Nexus: The Virtual Network behind the Global Message*, Radio Free Europe/Radio Liberty Special Report (Washington, DC: RFE/RL, May 2008), http://www.scribd.com/doc/3792892/AQ-Media-Nexus

Laffan, M. *The Resurrection of Ireland: The Sinn Fein Party 1916–1923* (Cambridge: Cambridge University Press, 1999).

Lister, D. and Jordan, H. *Mad Dog: The Rise and Fall of Johnny Adair and 'C Company'* (Edinburgh: Mainstream, 2004).

Lockwood, L. 'Aspects of the "L'Homme Armé" Tradition', *Proceedings of the Royal Musical Society* 100, 1 (1973), 97–122.

Lynn, B. 'Tactic or Principle? The Evolution of Republican Thinking on Abstentionism in Ireland, 1970–1998', *Irish Political Studies*, 17, 2 (2002), 74–94.

Mac Domhnaill, Brian. 'Remembering McElwaine', *An Phoblacht*, 25 May 2006.

Magouirk, J., Atran, S., and Sageman, M. 'Connecting Terrorist Networks', *Studies in Conflict and Terrorism*, 31 (2008), 1–16.

Maillot, A. *New Sinn Fein* (London: Routledge, 2004).

Maleckova, J. 'Impoverished Terrorists: Stereotype or Reality?' in T. Bjorgo (ed.), *Root Causes of Terrorism* (London: Routledge, 2005).

'Man on Real IRA charge subject to murder probe', *Irish Independent*, 19 June 2004.

McAuley, J. W. *The Politics of Identity: A Loyalist Community in Belfast* (Aldershot: Avebury, 1994).

—. '"Not a Game of Cowboys and Indians": Loyalist Paramilitary Groups in the 1990s', in A. O'Day (ed.), *Terrorism's Laboratory: Northern Ireland* (Dartmouth, NH: Dartmouth Press, 1995).

—. 'Divided Loyalists, Divided Loyalties: Conflict and Continuities in Contemporary Unionist Ideology', in Gilligan, C. and Tonge, J. (eds), *Peace or War?* (Aldershot: Ashgate, 1997), pp. 37–53.

—. '"Flying the One-Winged Bird": Ulster Unionism and the Peace Process', in Shirlow, P. and McGovern, M. (eds), *Who Are 'The People?'* (London: Pluto, 1997), pp. 158–75.

—. 'The Ulster Loyalist Political Parties: Towards a New Respectability', *Études Irlandaises, Le Processus de Paix en Irlande du Nord*, special volume, 22, 2 (1997), 117–32.

—. 'Surrender? Loyalist Perceptions of Conflict Settlement', in Anderson, J. and Goodman, J. (eds), *(Dis)Agreeing Ireland* (London: Pluto Press, 1998), pp. 193–210.

—. 'Still "No Surrender"? New Loyalism and the Peace Process in Ireland', in Harrington, J. and Mitchell, E. (eds), *Politics and Performance in Contemporary Northern Ireland* (Amherst, MA: University of Massachusetts Press, 1999), pp. 57–81.

—. '"Very British Rebels": Politics and Discourse within Contemporary Ulster Unionism', in *Transforming Politics: Power and Resistance*, Bagguley, P. and Hearn, J. (eds), (Basingstoke: Macmillan Press, 1999) pp. 106–25.

—. 'The Emergence of New Loyalism', in J. Coakley (ed.), *Changing Shades of Orange and Green* (Dublin: University College Dublin Press, 2002), pp. 106–22.

—. *Ulster's Last Stand? Reconstructing Unionism after the Peace Process* (Dublin: Irish Academic Press, 2010).

McAuley, J. W. and Hislop, S. '"Many Roads Forward": politics and ideology within the Progressive Unionist Party', *Études Irlandaises*, 25, 1 (2000),173–92.

McAuley, J. W., McGlynn, C and Tonge, J. 'Conflict Resolution in Asymmetric and Symmetric Situations: Northern Ireland as a Case Study', *Dynamics of Asymmetric Conflict: An International Interdisciplinary Journal*, 1, 1 (2008), 88–102.

McAuley, J. W. and Tonge, J. 'Politics and Parties in Northern Ireland: The Convergence of Ideological Extremes', *Études Irlandaises*, 27, 1 (2002), 177–98.

McDonald, H. 'MP calls on YouTube to remove Real IRA propaganda videos', *The Observer*, 2 August 2009. Available at: www.guardian.co.uk/technology/2009/aug/02/youtube-ira-facebook-cyber-terrorism (accesses 13 December 2010).

McDonald, H. and Cusack, J. *UDA: Inside the Heart of Loyalist Terror* (London: Penguin, 2004).

McEvoy, K. and Shirlow, P. 'Re-imagining DDR: Ex-combatants, Leadership and Moral Agency in Conflict Transformation', *Theoretical Criminology*, 13, 1 (2009), 31–59.

McGladdery, G. *The Provisional IRA in England: The Bombing Campaign 1973–1997* (Dublin: Irish Academic Press, 2006).

McGrattan, C. *Northern Ireland 1968–2008: The Politics of Entrenchment* (London: Palgrave Macmillan, 2010).

McIntyre, A. 'Modern Irish Republicanism: The Product of British State Strategies', *Irish Political Studies*, 10 (1995), 97–121.

—. 'Modern Irish Republicanism and the Belfast Agreement: chickens coming home to roost or turkeys celebrating Christmas?' in Wilford, R.

(ed.) *Aspects of the Belfast Agreement* (Oxford: Oxford University Press, 2001).

—. 'Hammering Dissent', *The Blanket*, 5 January 2003. Available at: http://indiamond6.ulib.iupui.edu:81/hammering.html.

—. *Good Friday: The Death of Irish Republicanism* (New York: Ausubo Press, 2008).

—. 'Republicanism: Alive or Dying?' *The Pensive Quill*, 1 January 2008.

—. 'Be Honest Mr Adams: You no longer have a strategy for a United Ireland', *Parliamentary Brief*, April 2009.

—. *The Pensive Quill*, blog. Available at: http://thepensivequill/am/.

Merari, A. *Driven to Death: Psychological and Social Aspects of Suicide Terrorism* (New York: Oxford University Press, 2010).

Mitchell, C. 'The Limits of Legitimacy: Former Loyalist Combatants and Peace-building in Northern Ireland', *Irish Political Studies*, 23, 1 (2008), 1–19.

Mitchell, P. and Wilford, R. (eds). *Politics in Northern Ireland* (Oxford: Westview Press, 1999).

Moloney, E. *A Secret History of the IRA* (Harmondsworth: Penguin, 2002).

Mooney, J. and O'Toole, M. *Black Operations: The Secret War against the Real IRA* (Ashbourne: Maverick House, 2003).

Murray, A. 'Intelligence Failings Hand Initiatives to the Dissidents', *Belfast Telegraph*, 24 February 2010.

Murray, G. and Tonge, J. *Sinn Fein and the SDLP: From Alienation to Participation* (London: Hurst, 2004).

New Ulster Political Research Group. *Beyond the Religious Divide* (Belfast: NUPRG, 1979).

Newman, G. R. and Clarke, R. V. *Superhighway Robbery: Preventing e-Commerce Crime* (Cullompton: Willan Publishing, 2003).

O'Callaghan, S. *The Informer* (London: Granta, 1998).

O'Day, A. (ed.). *Terrorism's Laboratory: Northern Ireland* (Dartmouth, NH: Dartmouth Press, 1995).

O'Neill, B. 'IRA Splinter Groups: Ghosts from History', *Spiked*, 12 March 2009. Available at: www.spiked-online.com/index.php/site/article/6352/ (accessed 6 April 2009).

Oots, K. L. *A Political Organisational Approach to Transnational Terrorism* (Westport, CT: Green Wood Press, 1986).

—. 'Organisational Perspectives on the Formation and Disintegration of Terrorist Groups', *Terrorism*, 12 (1989), 139–52.

Organised Crime Task Force, *Annual Report* (Belfast: HMSO, 2005).

O'Ruairc, L. 'Speaking Truth to Power', *The Sovereign Nation*, May–June 2009.

Patterson, H. *The Politics of Illusion: A Political History of the IRA* (London: Serif, 1997).

—. *Ireland since 1939: The Persistence of Conflict* (London: Penguin, 2007).

—. 'Sectarianism Revisited: The Provisional IRA Campaign in a Border Region of Northern Ireland', *Terrorism and Political Violence*, 22, 3 (July 2010), 337–56.

Payne, K. 'Winning the Battle of Ideas: Propaganda, Ideology and Terror', *Studies in Conflict and Terrorism*, 32 (2009), 109–28.

Police Service of Northern Ireland. *Number of Persons Arrested under TACT 41 and Subsequently Charged*, 2010. Available at: www.psni.police.uk/persons_arrested_and_charged_cy.pdf.

—. *Security Situation Statistics 2009/10, 2010/11*. Available at: www.psni.police.uk/index/updates/updates_statistics/updates_security_situation_and_ public_order_statistics.htm.

Powell, J. *Great Hatred, Little Room: Making Peace in Northern Ireland* (London: Bodley Head, 2008).

Rapoport, D. C. (ed.). *Inside Terrorist Organizations* (London: Frank Cass, 2001).

Reilly, P. 'Googling Terrorists: Are Northern Irish Terrorists Visible on Internet Search Engines?' *Information, Science and Knowledge Management*, 14, 3 (2008), 151–75.

Reinares, F. 'Who are the Terrorists? Analyzing Changes in Sociological Profile among Members of ETA', *Studies in Conflict and Terrorism*, 27 (2004), 465–88.

Republican Network for Unity. 'Armed Struggle: a RNU position for debate', RNU Response Document. www.republicannework.ie/readArticle.aspx?ID=23 (accessed 26 January 2010).

Republican Sinn Fein, *Towards a Peaceful Ireland* (Dublin: Republican Sinn Fein, 2008).

'Republican Unity Meeting, Derry', 13 May 2007, www.youtube.com/watch?v=9b69csAZWSA (accessed 26 January 2010).

Rheingold, H. *The Virtual Community: Homesteading on the Electronic Frontier* (Reading, MA: Addison-Wesley, 2003).
'Rioting Returns', *Lurgan Mail*, 28 August 2008.
Ross, F. Stuart. 'Between Party and Movement: Sinn Fein and the Popular Movement against Criminalisation, 1976–1982', *Irish Political Studies*, 21, 3 (2006), 337–54.
Rowan, B. *The Armed Peace: Life and Death after the Ceasefires* (Edinburgh: Mainstream Publishing, 2003).
—. 'Loyalist groups UDA and UVF disarming after decades of terror and 1000 deaths', *Belfast Telegraph*, 18 June 2009.
Ruane, J. 'Contemporary Republicanism and the Strategy of Armed Struggle', in Bric, M. and Coakley, J. (eds), *From Political Violence to Negotiated Settlement: The Winding Path to Peace in Twentieth-Century Ireland* (Dublin: University College Dublin, 2004).
Sageman, M. *Understanding Terrorist Networks* (Philadelphia, PA: University of Pennsylvania Press, 2004).
—. *Leaderless Jihad* (Philadelphia, PA: University of Pennsylvania Press, 2009).
Said, E. *Orientalism* (Harmondsworth: Penguin, 1978).
Sani, F. and Reicher, S. 'When Consensus Fails: An Analysis of the Schism within the Italian Communist Party (1991)', *European Journal of Social Psychology* 28, 4 (1998), 623–45.
—. 'Identity, Argument and Schism: Two Longitudinal Studies of the Split in the Church of England over the Ordination of Women to the Priesthood', *Group Processes and Intergroup Relations*, 2, 3 (1999), 279–300.
Schmid, A. and De Graaf, J. *Violence as Communication: Insurgent Terrorism and the Western News Media* (London: Sage, 1982).
Schmid, A. and Jongman, A. *Political Terrorism*, 2nd edition (Oxford: North Holland, 1988).
Shanahan, T. *The Provisional Irish Republican Army and the Morality of Terrorism* (Edinburgh: Edinburgh University Press, 2009).
Shankill Think Tank. *A New Beginning*, Island Pamphlets 13 (Newtownabbey: Island Publications, 1995).
Sharrock, D. 'Analysis: who are the dissident republicans?' *The Times*, 8 March 2009.
Shirlow, P. and McEvoy, K. *Beyond the Wire: Former Prisoners and Conflict Transformation in Northern Ireland* (London: Pluto, 2008).

Shirlow, P., Graham, B., McEvoy, K., O'hAdhmaill, F. and Purvis, D. *Politically Motivated Former Prisoner Groups: Community Activism and Conflict Transformation* (Belfast: Report to the Northern Ireland Community Relations Council, 2005).

Shirlow, P., Tonge, J., McAuley, J. and McGlynn, C. *Abandoning Historical Conflict? Former Political Prisoners and Reconciliation in Northern Ireland* (Manchester: Manchester University Press, 2010).

Silke, A. 'Explaining the Psychological Processes of Jihadi Radicalisation', *European Journal of Criminology*, 5, 1 (2008), 99–123.

Smith, M. *Fighting for Ireland? The Military Strategy of the Irish Republican Movement* (London: Routledge, 1995).

Southern, N. 'Territoriality, Alienation and Loyalist Decommissioning: The Case of the Shankill in Protestant West Belfast', *Terrorism and Political Violence*, 20, 1 (2008), 66–86.

Special EU Programmes Body. *Operational Programme for Peace III: Annex A – Socio-Economic Profile of Northern Ireland and the Border Region of Ireland* (Belfast Office: SEUPB, 2007).

Stedman, S. 'Peace Processes and the Challenges of Violence', in Darby, J. and MacGinty, R. (eds), *Contemporary Peacemaking: Conflict, Violence and Peace Processes* (Basingstoke: Palgrave Macmillan, 2003).

Stedman, S., Rothchild, D. and Cousens, E. *Ending Civil Wars: the Implementation of Peace Agreements* (Boulder, CO: Lynne Reiner, 2002).

Stenerson, A. 'The Internet: A Virtual Training Camp', *Terrorism and Political Violence*, 20 (2008), 215–33.

Stryker, S. Owens, T. J. and White, R. W. (eds). *Self Identity and Social Movements* (Minneapolis, MN: University of Minnesota Press, 2000).

Stuckless, N. and Goranson, R. 'The Vengeance Scale: Development of a Measure of Attitudes toward Revenge', *Journal of Social Behaviour and Personality*, 7 (1992), 25–42.

Taylor, M. 'New Labour, Defence and the "War on Terror"', in Daddow, O. and Gaskarth, J. (eds), *British Foreign Policy* (Basingstoke: Palgrave Macmillan, in press).

Tonge, J. '"They haven't gone away y'know": Irish republican "dissidents" and "armed struggle"', *Terrorism and Political Violence*, 16, 3 (2004), 671–93.

Ulster Political Research Group. *Common Sense* (Belfast: UPRG, 1987).

'Unwanted media harassment of former Fermanagh Republican POW',

32CSM Fermanagh, 27 July 2009. Available at: http://32csmfermanagh.blogspot.com/2009/07/unwanted-media-harrasment-of-former.html (accessed 13 December 2010).

Weimann, G. 'Virtual Training Camps: Terrorists Use of the Internet', in Forest, J. (ed.), *Teaching Terror: Strategic and Tactical Learning in the Terrorist World* (Lanham, MD: Rowan and Littlefield, 2006).

White, R. W. 'Issues in the Study of Political Violence: Understanding the Motives of Participants in Small Group Political Violence', *Terrorism and Political Violence*, 12, 1 (2000), 95–108.

—. *Ruairí Ó Brádaigh: The Life and Politics of an Irish Revolutionary* (Bloomington, IN: Indiana University Press, 2006).

White, R. W. and Fraser, M. R. 'Personal and Collective Identities and Long-Term Social Movement Activism: Republican Sinn Fein', in Stryker, S. Owens, T. J. and White, R. W. (eds), *Self, Identity, and Social Movements* (Minneapolis, MN: University of Minnesota Press, 2000).

Wilford, R. (ed.). *Aspects of the Belfast Agreement* (Oxford: Oxford University Press, 2001).

Wood, I. 'Loyalist Paramilitaries and the Peace Process', in Barton, B. and Roche, P. (eds), *The Northern Ireland Question: The Peace Process and the Belfast Agreement* (Basingstoke: Palgrave Macmillan, 2009), pp. 181–204.

Wood, I. S. *Crimes of Loyalty: A History of the UDA* (Edinburgh: Edinburgh University Press, 2006).

Index

9/11 3–4, 6
32 County Sovereign Movement 13, 20, 22–3, 36, 48, 58, 61, 77–8, 83, 87, 103–5, 107, 109

Adams, Gerry, 15, 28, 65, 67, 70, 72, 79, 80, 82–5
Afghanistan 53
Ahern, Bertie 11
Alonso, R., reference to various works in text 144, 174
Al-Qaeda 4, 5, 43, 135–6, 138, 167–8, 173–4
Ard Fheis 28, 77, 80, 106, 109, 113
Ard Fheiseanna 27

Bean, Kevin, *The New Politics of Sinn Féin* 73, 101
Behan, Brendan 2
Belfast 2, 25, 66, 81, 86–8, 90
    Andersonstown 86
    Ardoyne 14, 78, 88
    Ballymurphy 74, 86, 88
    Bodenstown 78
    Crumlin Road
    Divis Street 30, 31
    Falls Road 25, 30, 32
    Leeson Street 30, 31
    Lower Ormeau Road 75
Belfast Agreement *see* Good Friday Agreement
Blair, Tony 11, 70
Blanket 70, 74–5
Brantingham, P. edited with Faust, F. A. *Conceptual Model of Crime Prevention* 136

Bric, M. edited with Coakley, J. *From Political Violence to Negotiated Settlement: The Winding Path to Peace in Twentieth-Century Ireland* 98

Cahill, J. 28
Campbell, Liam 72
Carroll, Stephen, murder of 14, 32, 81
Catney, T. 77–8, 101–2
Citizens Defence Group 27
Clare, county 34
Clarke, R. edited with Cornish, D. *Opportunities, Precipitators and Criminal Decisions: A Reply to Wortley's Critique of Situational Crime Prevention* 137
Collins, Michael 65
Columbian militants 52
Coakley, J. edited with Bric, M. *From Political Violence to Negotiated Settlement: The Winding Path to Peace in Twentieth-Century Ireland* 98
Concerned Republicans 77–8
Connolly House 80
Connolly, James, Irish socialist republican martyr 80, 87
CONTEST, UK's counter-terrorist strategy 175
Continuity Irish Republican Army (CIRA) 2, 5, 13, 15, 17, 19–22, 28, 31–5, 37, 39, 47–54, 56–9, 60, 68, 71–2, 84, 89, 97–9, 104, 106–8, 110–11, 119, 121, 126
Cork, St Finbarr's Cemetery 4, 10
Cornish, D. edited with Clarke, R. *Opportunities, Precipitators and Criminal*

Decisions: A Reply to Wortley's Critique of Situational Crime Prevention 137
Crenshaw, M. *The Causes of Terrorism* 123

Dáil Éireann 20–1, 66–7, 79, 99, 167, 169
Democratic Unionist Party (DUP) 76–7, 100, 113
Derry (Londonderry) 26–7, 58, 77–8, 86–7, 90, 126
  Bogside 25
  Foyle 77
Devolution 2, 8, 89, 111
Dissident Republicans
  age of membership 8, 19, 32–3, 37, 52–7, 61, 104, 170
  attacks, geographic distribution 59
    in Antrim, Belfast, 104
    BBC Television Centre 72, 144
    Craigavon, Derry 104
    DIY stores 72–3
    Dungannon 73
    Ealing 10, 11, 16, 7
    Forkhill, 88
    Hammersmith Bridge 72
    Jonesborough 88
    Massareene Army base 104, 144
    MI6 HQ 72, 144
    Newry 84, 90
    Newtonbutler 86–7
    Omagh 15, 60, 102, 104, 113, 144
    Orange Halls 72
    Palace Barracks 133, 135
    Police 73, 81, 85, 144
    Rosslea 86, 172
    Shackleton Barracks 15, 172
  commemoration of republican traditions 67, 70, 82–3, 112, 125, 171
  counter-narratives 8, 114, 136, 138, 174–6
  employment 9, 53–6
  geographic distribution of members 29–32, 50–1, 53, 56–9, 85–8, 90

  heterogeneity of membership 18–19, 37, 1–7, 10
  nomenclature 5, 13–15, 65–6, 97–9, 165–6
  propaganda 7–8, 46, 120–35, 124–6, 131, 134–5, 173
  recruitment 26, 32–4, 50–4, 77, 104, 120–3, 135, 173
  rioting 78, 81, 88–9, 111
  use of internet 121–38, 173, 176
Donaldson, Denis 70
Donaldson Jeffrey, Lagan Valley MP 125
Downes, Brenda, widow of Sean, victim of a plastic bullet 80
Dublin 58, 71, 79, 80
Duffy, Colin, Lurgan republican 80

Easter Rising 16, 78, 100, 106, 113
Éira Nua 39, 107
Éirigi 61, 80, 83–4
English, R. *Armed Struggle The History of the IRA* 71, 100
Ervine, David 144
ETA 44, 52, 174

Faust, F. A. edited with Brantingham, P. *Conceptual Model of Crime Prevention* 136
Fermanagh 13, 67, 70, 81–3, 87
Fianna Éireann 58, 62
Fianna Fáil 66, 69, 80, 107
Firinne 82
Florez-Morris, M. *Joining Guerrilla Groups in Colombia: Individual Motivations and Processes for Entering a Violent Organization* 52
Ford, David, Northern Ireland Justice Minister 89
Forum Group 108
Fourthwrite 70
Fox, Bernard 84
Free Derry Media 126

Freilich, D with Newman, G. R. *Reducing Terrorism through Situational Crime Prevention* 137

Gallagher, Frankie, Ulster Political Research Group 160
Garvaghy Road 75, 80–1
Global Terrorism Database 46
Global Transnational Terrorism project 43
Gorman, Tommy 74

Hall, M. *Loyalism in Transition* 156
Hannaway, Liam, dissident republican prisoner 146
Harchaoui, S. *Heterogeneous Counter-Narratives and the Role of Social Diplomacy* 175
Harris, L. *Duck or Rabbit? The Value Systems of Loyalist Paramilitaries* 146
Hayes, B. and McAllister, I. *Sowing Dragon's Teeth* 98
Hunger, film by Steve McQueen 84

Independent Monitoring Commission (IMC) 32–3, 72–3, 84, 119–20
Iraq 53
Irish Civil War 85
Irish Freedom Committee 48, 58, 61
Irish National Liberation Army 5, 13, 33–6, 47–50, 51–4, 57–9
Irish Republican Army *see* Provisional Irish Republican Army
Irish Republican Liberation Army 13, 15
Irish Republican Liberation Movement 31
Irish Republican Socialist Party 13, 48, 58

Kearney, Declan 79
Kelly, Gerry 11–12, 66, 77, 83
Kennelly 35
Kerry, Co. 85
Kessells, E. *Countering Violent Extremist Narratives* 175

Leinster House 20, 34, 67, 102, 109
Libya 23, 100
Limerick 31, 33–4, 85
Loughall, death of leading members of PIRA's East Tyrone brigade 69, 110, 167
Loyalists 86, 145–6, 149, 151, 160, 173
    response to ceasefires 150–61
    response to Dissident Republicanism 144–5, 158–61
Loyalist Volunteer Force 152
Lurgan 80, 85
Lynch, Sean 83–4

MacCionnaith, Brendan spokesman for Garvaghy Road residents' group 80
Mackey, Francie 32CSM 20, 77
MacManus, Seán interview with 28
Magouirk, J. et al. *Connecting Terrorist Networks* 44, 50
Maguire, Tom 28
Maleckova, J. *Impoverished Terrorists: Stereotype or Reality?* 122
Mansergh, Martin 104, 107
Maskey, Alex 11
Maze Prison 82
Mcalister, I. and Hayes, B. *Sowing Dragon's Teeth* 98
McCartney, Robert murder of 76, 79
McCrory, Alex, former hunger striker 80, 83
McDonald, Jackie, UDA leader 158–9
McDonald, Mary Lou 80
McElwaine, Seamus 81, 82
McEvoy, K. *Beyond the Wire: Former Prisoners and Conflict Transformation in Northern Ireland* 146
McFarlane, Brendan 82
McGirl, J. J. 28
McGladdery, G. *The Provisional IRA in England: The Bombing Campaign 1973–1997* 100
McGrane, Seamus 87
McGuinness, Martin 26, 67–8, 79, 82–3, 105, 160

McIntyre, Andrew 68, 70-1, 74-5, 84, 88
McKearney, Pádraig 81
McKearney, Tommy 71, 84-5
McKevitt, Kevin 87
McKevitt, Michael 13, 72, 133
McPhillips, Tony 77
MI5 78, 83, 89, 109, 111, 114, 133
Micro groups 65, 113
Mitchell Principles, 23, 40
Moloney, Ed, *A Secret History of the IRA* 69, 71, 100
Monaghan 79, 81-2
Mullholland, Darren, part of Forum group 108
Murphy, Conor, MP. MLA and Stormont Minister 88
Murphy, Kevin Barry 87
Murphy, Sean 11
Murray, G. and Tonge, J. *Sinn Fein and the SDLP: From Alienation to Participation* 65

Netherlands National Coordinator for Counter Terrorism 174
Newman, G. R. with Freilich, J. D. *Reducing Terrorism through Situational Crime Prevention* 137
Northern Bank robbery 76, 79
Northern Ireland Assembly 2, 77, 99
Northern Ireland Office 89
North-South Ministerial Council 100

Ó Bradaigh, Ruari 21, 28, 39, 66, 109
Ó Conaill, Dáithí 21, 28, 66
O'Connor, Brendan 87
O'Connor, Gareth, murder of 88
O'Connor, Joe, murder of 66, 74, 104, 172
O'Donovan Rossa, Jeremiah 67
Official Irish Republican Army (OIRA) 10, 13, 16, 23, 25, 27, 30, 33-4, 74, 149
Official Sinn Féin 66
Óglaigh na hÉireann 4-5, 10, 13, 15, 17, 37, 58, 62, 125

O'Hanlon, Fearghal 67
O'Hara, Patsy, INLA hunger striker 109
O'Hara, Peggy, mother of Patsy 109
Oklahoma City National Memorial Institute for the Prevention of Terrorism 46
O'Neill, B. 161
Operation Banner, deployment of British Army to Northern Ireland 111
Operation Motorman, removal of 'no go' areas from Belfast and Derry 87
Orangees *see* Orange Men
Orange Men 75-6, 86
Orange parades 78, 88, 110
O'Rawe, Richard, PRO for hunger strikers 83
O'Toole, Fintan 12

Pakistani militants 52
Patterson, H. *The Politics of Illusion: A Political History of the IRA* 100
Pearse, Patrick 81
Police Service of Northern Ireland (PSNI) 17, 32, 68, 76, 78, 85, 87-9, 98, 100, 110, 169
Policing Board 83, 90
Policing Partnership 81-4
Portadown, 75
Portlaoise 31, 104
Price, Dolores 36, 66
Price, Marion 66, 72, 78
Progressive Unionist Party (PUP) 148, 151-4
Provisional Irish Republican Army (PIRA) 2, 5, 10, 12-13, 21, 25-8, 33-6, 50, 52, 66-79, 81-9, 98-101, 105-6, 110-12, 119, 121, 126, 156, 160, 167, 169, 171, 173
  Engineering Department 23
  Executive 23
  General Army Convention 27
  General Headquarters 69
  Provisional Army Council 11, 83
Purvis, Dawn, former head of the PUP 158

Quinn, Paul, murder of 75, 88

Rapoport, David, series editor's preface in Bowyer Bell, R. *The IRA 1968–2000: Analysis of a Secret Army* 18
Real Irish Republican Army (RIRA) 13–15, 17, 19, 20–2, 37, 47, 49–52, 54–9, 60, 67–8, 71–3, 84, 89, 97, 102, 104–6, 107, 110–11, 119, 121, 126
Reinares, F, *Who are the Terrorists? Analyzing Changes in Sociological Profile among Members of ETA* 44, 58
Republican Network for Unity 78–9, 83–4, 107–9, 126
Republican Sinn Féin 14, 20–2, 28, 31–2, 35–6, 39, 48–52, 54–5, 57–9, 61, 66–7, 70, 77, 85, 89, 105–7, 109–12
Republican Socialist Movement 34
risky shift 123, 135
Rothstein, R. quoted in Southern, N. *Territoriality, Alienation and Loyalist Decommissioning* 88
Royal Irish Regiment 80
Royal Ulster Constabulary 67–8, 76, 78, 87, 100, 110, 169
Ruane, J. *Contemporary Republicanism and the Strategy of Armed Struggle* 98

Sageman, M. *Understanding Terror Networks* and *Leaderless Jihad* 44, 55, 123
Said, Edward *Orientalism* 146
Saoirse 48, 67, 89
Saor Uladh 13, 15
Scapatticci, F. 70
Shannon, Brendan 74–5
Shirlow, P. and McEvoy, K. *Beyond the Wire: Former Prisoners and Conflict Transformation in Northern Ireland* 146
Sinn Féin 11, 16–17, 21, 28, 66–9, 73–80, 88–9, 98–103, 112, 114, 119, 155–6, 167, 171

Social Democratic and Labour Party (SDLP) 69
Special Air Service (SAS) 81, 110
'Stickies' *see* Official Irish Republican Army
Stormont 21, 34, 67, 73, 75, 99, 102, 107, 109, 154

Thatcher, Margaret 83
Tonge, J. and Murray, G. *Sinn Fein and the SDLP: From Alienation to Participation* 65
Treason Felony Act 67
Trimble, David 11, 16, 76
Tyrone 58, 69, 71, 81, 84, 87, 167

Ulster Defence Association (UDA) 2, 145, 147, 151, 153, 155–60
  and politics 147–8
  Beyond the Religious Divide 148
  Common Sense 148
Ulster Democratic Party (UDP) 151–4
Ulster Freedom Fighters (UFF) 152
Ulster Political Research Group 153–6
Ulster Unionist Party (UUP) 11, 70
Ulster Volunteer Force (UCF) 2, 145, 152, 157–60
  Loyalism in Transition initiative 155–6
  politics 148–50
  prisoners 149
Ultra groups 99, 114
Unionist veto 110, 169
United Nations 103

Violent Dissident Republican Project 43
Volunteer Political Party 148

Weston Park 12, 16
White House 76
Woodward, Shaun, former Secretary of State for Northern Ireland 113
Wright, Billy 152